Meliz's Kitchen

Meliz's Kitchen

Simple Turkish-Cypriot Comfort Food and Fresh Family Feasts

By Meliz Berg

EBURY
PRESS

Contents

Introduction

Terazi (Zygi/Ζύγι) is the name of the Cypriot village where both of my parents were born. Despite never having been to their village, I feel like I have visited a million times, triggered by the countless memories and stories my parents have shared with us over the years.

My mum's parents, Fatma Nene and Ahmet Dede, were well-respected in the community for their philanthropic nature. As well as being the village 'financier' and bookkeeper, my grandfather with the help of my uncle, Ömer Dayı, was also a fisherman. He would catch fish to sell, but with ten additional mouths at home to feed (nine children, and my grandmother) his daily task was no mean feat. My paternal grandfather, Ali Dede, worked in the British Merchant Navy in Cyprus and in the early 1960s, when my dad was a toddler, he decided to move the family to the UK and they settled in Stoke Newington, North London. North London, to this day, remains a popular settlement for the London Cypriot diaspora.

After 1974, Mum's (and Dad's extended) family were all relocated from Terazi to *Mağusa* (Famagusta), from what is now known as the Southern to the Northern side of Cyprus, and when my paternal grandfather would drive the thousands of miles from London to Cyprus to visit his family, my mum and dad and their families and friends from the village would socialise as they did when they were youngsters. As time passed, Dad wrote Mum a love letter, proposed, and in 1981 she moved to London to marry him and for them to start a new life together. My mum lived in Cyprus until she was 18 years old, so her memories of Cypriot village life are intense and vivid, and many of them revolve around food. Through watching my mum cook and visiting my family in Cyprus every year,

my love affair with our beautiful cuisine and the incessant urge to document the recipes in a book one day has now become a reality.

Although I was born in London, I have a very rooted connection to my Turkish-Cypriot heritage. My mum is a wonderful cook but her family recipes have never been written down, and everything has been passed from generation to generation through observation, participation and oral tradition. I watched my mum and my aunt, Meyrem Teyze, cook these dishes when I was growing up and a huge part of my journey has been developing the recipes I watched them making, using some

of them as the foundation to creating new ones, adapting methods and ingredients to suit my own lifestyle while maintaining the flavours and ingredients that make them so quintessentially Cypriot. The recipes in this book resonate deeply with me: they transport me straight back to my deep-rooted family connection with *Kıbrıs* (Cyprus), and some of them I have not dared play around with at all, especially those that my mum learnt from my maternal great-grandmother, Meyrem Nene.

My aunts cook exactly as their mum and grandmother did, and following in his father's and brother's footsteps, my uncle, Selçuk Dayı, has a fishing boat moored at Girne harbour. We all look forward to receiving the WhatsApp messages and social media posts where he shares with us his catch of the day. He would love taking us out on his fishing boat when we were children; we would thrive on such an adventure, and last summer when we were in Cyprus he took my son fishing on the rocks for the first time. It was pure magic, both for us to watch and for my son to experience. My son and uncle caught 14 small fish, which we took back to my uncle's house by the sea and deep-fried on an outdoor gas stove on the veranda. These are the kind of childhood memories that I hold on to and my children can now also enjoy – it makes my heart do a crazy little dance every time I think of it.

As a youngster, fish played a big part on our family dinner table in London and one of my strongest memories is of traipsing up and down Walthamstow Market with my dad, buying our weekly fresh fruit, vegetables and herbs and visiting the one and only fish stall that was on the East London high street at the time. My dad would buy whatever fish was in season and closest in flavour and texture to the ones my grandfather would have caught in his fishing boat. At various times of the year, we would leave the market having purchased red mullet, snapper, baby squid and octopus, and a brown paper packet full of cooked prawns (shells on, because peeling them was part of the fun) to eat on the way back to the car. When we got home, Mum would clean and prepare the fish, then shallow-fry or cook them over hot coals on the *mangal* (barbecue), serving them with Cyprus potato chips and salad in exactly the same way her mother would have done. Sometimes our extended family would join us, in the same way the villagers would flock to my grandparents' house when they had caught wind that my Fatma Nene was making her famous *Balık Çorbası* (Fatma Nene's Fish Soup, page 146).

In fact, our weekends would always be busy with frequent family gatherings and picnics and weekend barbecues at cousins' houses where each family would take it in turns to host. *Kuzu Şiş* (Lamb Kebabs, pages 200–1), *Şeftali Kebap* (Lamb Caul Fat Sausages, pages 208–9) and *Şehriyeli Pilav* (Vermicelli Rice, page 102) would feature weekly, as would many salads and *meze* dishes, such as *Cacık* (Yoghurt, Mint & Cucumber Dip, page 52), *Bakla Salatası* (Broad Bean Salad, page 57) and *Yumurtalı Patates Salatası* (Egg & Potato Salad, page 64).

My dad played football for various London Turkish community football teams and football was a huge part of his life; I would go and watch him every weekend and when he played in North London, we would often swing by Yaşar Halim supermarket on Green Lanes in Harringay. We would buy meat for the *mangal*, stock up on Cypriot breads, such as *Kıbrıs Çöreği* (Cypriot Seeded Bread, pages 224–6) and *Tahınlı* (Tahini Pastries, pages 231–2), olives, salad vegetables and herbs, and we would always order a huge Yaşar Halim cream cake for special family occasions. The grocery and patisserie is still there; it's an institution.

As I write these words, I know that there was definitely a time in my life when I perhaps didn't fully appreciate the experiences I had growing up in a Turkish-Cypriot household. During my time at secondary school I tried to 'Westernise' myself and hide this culturally colourful life of mine in order to fit in, often feeling a little lost and embarrassed of who I was, never really knowing where I belonged. Eventually, food played the biggest part in breaking down those emotional barriers for me. When I reached my late teenage years – and the more I cooked with my mum – there was a sudden urge to invite my friends over to eat 'our' food. Aged 18 years old, after we had left sixth form, three of my closest girlfriends and I chose to holiday in Cyprus. While our peers travelled to international party hotspots, the four of us sunbathed on the beaches I played on as a child, caught cabs to Meyrem Teyze's house where she would cook us dinner, and went out to sea for the day with my uncle Selçuk Dayı on his fishing boat. I was very proud of where I came from and I wanted to celebrate it. Even when I was at university, my friends would come over to my house and my mum would always put on the most wonderful Cypriot spread. My friend Atar still talks about Mum's *Bulgur Köftesi* (Meat-filled Bulgur Wheat Cones, pages 133–5) and asks if we can make them every time we get together.

Most of these recipes come straight from my family's traditional repertoire, and I hope that you will sense the love and history behind them. That's not to say my way and my family's way is the only way to cook them. What I find so fascinating about Cypriot cuisine is how the recipes in this book will be familiar to many but will be cooked in such a variety of ways – they will taste slightly different from region to region, village to village or even family to family – and how one tiny island can hoard such a plethora of recipes. My mum and dad's attitude to food has certainly been shaped by this charmingly frugal village-approach to cooking, where there is no wastage, leftovers are standard practice and every mouthful is not only gratefully enjoyed, but also fully appreciated.

When it comes to the preparation and cooking of the dishes, there are a variety of methods and ingredients that can slightly change the flavour and texture

of a dish from one household to the next. Generally speaking, in Turkish-Cypriot cuisine, we mostly spice meat dishes with earthy cumin, while the same recipes cooked by our Greek-Cypriot neighbours are enhanced with the sweetness of cinnamon (which all Cypriots use abundantly in sweets, pastries, and even tea too). However, the cross-pollination of ingredients and influences is inevitable; the use of cinnamon is essential to sweetly spicing my *Hellimli Domatesli Magarına* (One-pot Halloumi & Tomato Pasta, page 113) and *Tavuklu Patates Kebabı* (Chicken, Potato & Tomato Roast, page 160) recipes, and sometimes I even combine both cumin and cinnamon together, like in my *Patates Köftesi* (Cypriot Potato & Mince Fried Meatballs, page 136).

The same can be said for cuts of meat; Turkish-Cypriots mostly cook with lamb and chicken, and occasionally veal (or beef in the UK), whereas some of these meats will be substituted for pork in Greek-Cypriot kitchens (often with the gutsy addition of wine, which would have traditionally been forbidden for Muslim Turkish-Cypriots to consume). Inevitably, some of the dishes in this book have been influenced by our Turkish neighbours, such as the *Ispanak Yemeği* (Spinach, Mince & Rice, page 105) and *Köfteli Nohut Yemeği* (Meatball & Chickpea Stew, page 85), while the Arab and Levantine influence seen in dishes such as *Molohiya* (Jute Mallow & Lamb Stew, page 76) is indisputable. What is key, however, is that Cyprus has its own abundant compendium of dishes that are specifically unique to the island and its produce. Rarely is a pasta dish eaten without *hellim* (halloumi cheese) or *nor* (anari cheese), and *hellim* and mint as a combination are a staple in every Cypriot household – served with *karpuz* (watermelon) in the summer, or in some kind of savoury cake or bread, like *Bulla Ekmek* (Halloumi, Olive & Herb Loaf, pages 227–9).

I am now a mum and have two wonderful children of my own who love to eat and cook together, and in the same way I was introduced to the kitchen at such a young age, they are now learning from me and my mum. As soon as I had children, preserving Cypriot (food) traditions felt more important than ever and so I started a food blog. The power of social media has enabled me to reach an amazing audience, and I have loved every minute of creating and sharing recipes with them. Naturally, some of the recipes in this book are extensions of the recipes I have shared online, but with special traditional additions that I

have been saving up to share with you in print one day. I have grown up cooking these recipes with my mum and now my children love to help me bake fresh bread and *Kafes Peksemet* (Gate-shaped Breadsticks, pages 251–2) and some of their favourite dishes to eat are stews such as *Kıymalı Taze Fasulye Yahni* (Green Bean & Minced Beef Stew, page 90) that they can dip their freshly baked Cypriot seeded bread into. They adore anything cooked on the *mangal* and fresh fish and soups, especially *Mercimek Çorbası* (Red Lentil Soup, page 150).

I wrote this book with busy family kitchens in mind, to celebrate and share the food that influenced me as a child and has inspired my cooking style, developing the recipes in the most empathetic, considerate and accessible way as possible. But I also wrote this book to preserve the essence of our cuisine and culture; the communal experience of cooking together, sharing food with others and creating memories that are evoked every time these beautiful dishes are prepared.

The majority of people in Cyprus are not rich, but the integration of so many other peoples has steeped one tiny island in a wealth of cultural richness; the combination of Mediterranean and (Middle) Eastern flavours pinpoints Cyprus as that tiny centre between East and West. Our cuisine is simple but has been influenced by so many of our neighbours, far and wide, who over thousands of years have travelled through and to the island, bringing with them a wealth of spices, cooking methods and flavours that set Cypriot food apart as unique.

I hope that when reading through the Breakfast chapter (pages 18–43) you will appreciate the love I have for a simple yet fulfilling Cypriot Breakfast Platter (pages 24–5), and relive holiday memories with me as you cook, even if quickly whipping up some pancakes. I have included what I consider to be only a handful of Cypriot *meze* and salads in the Dishes & Salads to Share chapter (pages 44–69), but they are the recipes that remind me the most of dining outside in Cypriot restaurants and buzzy family parties. Most of the dishes in this chapter can be quickly thrown together and keep well in the fridge for a few days.

With a busy family life of my own, there is always a need for simple, tasty midweek meals and I wrote the Quick Cooking for Busy Weeknights chapter (pages 94–121) with this in mind. However, when you do have more time and energy to spare, you'll find traditional dishes for lazy Sundays and plenty of recipes for nourishing stews and one-tray meals in the Easy One-pots & Slow-cooking chapter (pages 70–93), Traditional Stove-top Dishes chapter (pages 122–51) and Hearty Dishes from the Oven chapter (pages 152–91).

For true Cypriot authenticity, light up your *mangal* (or your grill), invite your family and friends over and cook any of the recipes from the Barbecue chapter (pages 192–219). Freshly baked breads are an essential to serve alongside kebabs. My Homemade Breads, Doughs and Pastries chapter (page 220–253) is packed with traditional Cypriot recipes, so you can dip breadsticks into your *meze* or load up your pitta breads with kebab meat to your heart's content. Or why not freeze and reheat for a nourishing breakfast another day. For the weekends when you want to evoke the aromas and flavours of a Cypriot summer, then I urge you to bake any of the cakes, pastries and sweet treats from the Sweets chapter (pages 254–79) to enjoy and linger over with a cup of Turkish coffee or tea outside in the sunshine.

Whether you have an interest in the dishes because of a favourite restaurant, or a special summer holiday in Cyprus, or whether your connection runs a little deeper than that and the food evokes feelings similar to the personal ones that I have shared, I hope that cooking these recipes will help capture those memories for you. Cyprus has a special place in my heart, and so does every single recipe in this book. I am so proud to finally share my Turkish-Cypriot comfort food and fresh family feasts with you all.

Meliz x

Key Ingredients & Suppliers

I cannot tell you how many times over the years I have been asked what *pul biber* or *tatlı biber salçası* (Turkish sweet red pepper paste) are. However, as people have become more familiar with the ingredients I use in my recipes and the typically (Turkish) Cypriot flavour combinations they produce, they have also realised that with access to the internet, and more conveniently, an international grocery nearby, these ingredients can be very easily sourced. In fact, these shops have always been around – Yaşar Halim supermarket (in Harringay, North London) has been proudly serving the London diaspora community with their most-loved ingredients for over 40 years.

Here is a list of my most-used store cupboard ingredients, and I have included my favourite brands where relevant.

Bay Leaves

Fresh is always best when it comes to bay leaves, so if you have a bay tree or bush in your garden then it's going to come in very handy. Fresh leaves can also be frozen for up to 3 months and retain so much more of their flavour and aroma than dried leaves.

Cinnamon

Cypriots love a bit of cinnamon; in tea, ragùs, pasta dishes, with honey, roasted with chicken and lamb, in cakes, breads and syrups. We use it in abundance, so stock up with both ground cinnamon and cinnamon sticks.

Cumin

The earthy counterpart to cinnamon, I use cumin to flavour grilled meat dishes and to add some umami to sautéed vegetables and stews.

Dry Black Olives

I rarely cook with pitted olives, and instead prefer to buy whole dry black olives that I pit myself before using. I find that the olives retain their texture and moisture much more this way and I favour the *Marmarabirlik* (*Kuru Sele Zeytin*) brand.

Extra Virgin Olive Oil

Cypriots pride themselves on producing the best olive oil in the world (I'm sure many neighbouring nations would place their own at the top too). The extra virgin olive oil produced using olives grown in Cypriot soil has such an intense colour and richness that gives every salad or dish it is dressed with the most exquisite depth of flavour. Therefore, even if you cannot source Cypriot extra virgin olive oil, please do use an excellent quality extra virgin olive oil to dress the salads and *meze* recipes in this book.

Yufka
Filo Pastry

Filo pastry comes in so many varieties; large and slightly thicker circular sheets are often used to make savoury börek, smaller triangular sheets for making *Sigara Böreği* (Cigar-shaped Pastries page 66), and thinner sheets to make baklava and sweet pastries. For the recipes in this book, other than the triangular shaped *yufka* (filo), you will need to source some really good-quality *baklavalık yufka* (baklava filo), where the sheets are larger and softer and less likely to flake and fall apart. My favourite brands are Au Blé d'or and JR Feuilles de Filo.

Nane
Mint

Mint is used in abundance in Cypriot cuisine. We use fresh and dried mint in salads, in *köfte* (meatballs) and add it to baked treats such as *Pilavuna* (Cheese & Sultana Pastries pages 233–5) and *Bulla Ekmek* (Halloumi, Olive & Herb Loaf pages 227–9). I always ensure that I have plenty of dried mint in my store cupboard to add to salads dressings.

Olive Oil

Many of the recipes in this book begin with, 'add three tablespoons of olive oil to a pan' and it is nearly always my oil of choice for cooking with. I even fry chips in olive oil (which is absolutely fine, as they are fried at such a low heat that the oil doesn't even reach smoking point).

Kırmızı Toz Biber
Paprika (red powdered pepper)

I have used paprika in this book, as it is more readily available, but growing up, my mum used Turkish *kırmızı toz biber* (red powdered pepper). Again, if you can source the latter, then please do. If not, regular paprika is fine.

Nar Ekşisi
Pomegranate Molasses

We use this in marinades and salad dressings, and the sweet and tart syrup is used copiously in Turkish cuisine. Much like the extra virgin olive oil, please do make sure that you buy the best molasses you can afford (my favourite brands are Odysea and Secret Gardens) for the quality that comes from purely natural ingredients and a concentrated depth of flavour.

Pul Biber
Turkish Red Pepper Flakes

Turkish *pul biber* chilli flakes are oilier, warmer and sweeter than the standard chilli flakes you'll find in your local supermarket, with slightly salty, lemony and smoky back notes. I use it to sprinkle over dishes, to season recipes and in marinades, sauces and dressings. If you are struggling to find Turkish *pul biber*, then you can also use Aleppo pepper flakes too, which are essentially the same. Do note, however, that I use the regular sized flakes instead of the *ipek* (smaller, silkier) flakes, but both will suffice.

Tatlı Biber Salçası
Turkish Sweet Red Pepper Paste

There are two varieties of *biber salçası* (red pepper paste) – *tatlı* (sweet and mild) and *acı* (hot). I always use the sweet variety in my recipes as I find that the hot paste can take away from the other flavours. Once opened, store the *salça* in the fridge. My favourite brand is Öncü.

Kekik
Wild Oregano

There is an age-old debate over whether *kekik* is actually oregano or thyme in Turkish, and the truth is Turkish *kekik* is neither, but more likened to wild oregano. If you can source *kekik* from your local Turkish or international supermarket, then please do use that. Alternatively, wild oregano from the supermarket (or even regular dried oregano) is fine to use.

Breakfast

Kahvaltı

Cypriot breakfasts are both beautifully simple, and simply beautiful. While rushing to get ready for school in the mornings, my mum would always place a hot, freshly toasted *Kıbrıs pidesi* (Cypriot pitta bread) wrapped in kitchen paper in my hands; the inside of the *pide* pocket would be dripping with melted butter and loaded with thickly cut slices of uncooked *hellim* (halloumi) and tomato. This breakfast would be my fuel to start the morning, alongside a hot cup of black tea infused with cinnamon bark, cloves and aniseed. Those sweet Cypriot smells still evoke memories of the speedy midweek breakfasts of my childhood, as much as the slightly more extravagant spreads that we would all share as family on Sunday mornings.

Sunday morning breakfasts at home really were an event; my younger sister, Yeliz, and brother, Taylan, would set the table, while my dad would hand-slice a loaf he had picked up from the Turkish grocers the day before, half of which we had already eaten for Saturday's lunch or dinner. He would toast the bread under the grill with halved slices of *pastırma* (a Cypriot cured and spiced beef sausage), *hellim* and a large handful of *zeytin* (black olives – slight digression here, but if you've never had *izgara zeytin* (grilled black olives), either under the grill or on the barbecue, then you simply must try them). Mum would be cutting up cubes of Cheddar (or *kaşar peyniri* – a smooth, firm, pale yellow cheese made of cow's milk, similar to Gouda or Edam – if Dad had picked some up from the shop), slicing up thin, crook cucumbers she had already peeled vertical strips off, and cutting wedges of tomatoes and green peppers. I would be peeling the shells off the hard-boiled eggs and pouring cups of spiced tea from the teapot. In the summer, there would always be half a huge *karpuz* (watermelon) on the table, too. The only difference with eating this kind of breakfast in *Kıbrıs* (Cyprus) is that the warm sun beats down on you as you grill the bread and olives on the outdoor *mangal* (barbecue), alongside hot *pide* filled with *helva* (a sweet and slightly crumbly spread made from *tahın* (tahini), hot syrup and nuts) that melts under the heat of the coals, while listening to the chorus of *cırcır böceği* (cicadas) in the distance.

Aside from long and lazy Sunday mornings, quick midweek Cypriot-style breakfasts are also easily achievable and mostly dependent on having a select few ingredients in your fridge, as well as some pre-made baked goods such as *Tahınlı* (Tahini Pastries, pages 231–2), *Kıbrıs Çöreği* (Cypriot Seeded Bread, pages 224–6) and *Pilavuna* (Cheese & Sultana Pastries, pages 233–5) efficiently stocked in the freezer. The beauty of Cypriot breakfasts is that they aren't just suited to the breakfast table, and the variety of simple ingredients are naturally befitting to various times of the day, from quick on-the-go snacks to table-laden brunch and 'brinner' spreads.

I want to show how the recipes in this chapter can bring together all the individual elements of the (Turkish) Cypriot breakfast table, the nostalgic recipes I grew up with, as well as introducing you to some other favourite Turkish breakfast treats that we often eat when in Cyprus, and at home. And there's not a bowl of cereal in sight.

(Turkish) Cypriot Breakfast Platter

This is less of a recipe and more of a guide to assembling the key elements to a beautiful (Turkish) Cypriot breakfast plate. The main components are *hellim* (halloumi), *pastırma* (Turkish-Cypriot cured and spiced beef sausage), tomatoes, cucumber, *siyah zeytin* (dry black olives) and *çakistez* (cracked green olives), eggs, *gabira* (grilled or toasted bread) and *kokulu çay* (scented tea). For something a little more elaborate in the form of a full table spread or platter, you can also add some of the additional components I have mentioned at the end of this list.

Hellim
Halloumi Cheese

Pat the slices completely dry, then fry in a little olive oil until crispy and golden brown on both sides. If the *mangal* (barbecue) is to hand, then grill the *hellim* instead, and eat your breakfast outside.

Pastırma
Turkish–Cypriot Cured and Spiced Beef Sausage

Barbecuing *pastırma* brings out its true authenticity and flavour. Alternatively, cook the sausage under the grill, or fry it without adding any oil to the pan (as it will release its own fatty juices as soon as it gets hot).

Domates
Tomatoes

The best time to source beautiful, ripe tomatoes is of course when they are in season during late spring and early autumn. Serve them thickly sliced or chopped into large chunks. Out of season, fresh, ripe tomatoes can still be sourced and perked up with a drizzle of excellent extra virgin olive oil and a pinch of dried oregano and sea salt flakes.

Salatalık
Cucumber

The most authentic cucumbers to use are crooks or the small, thin baby variety found in Turkish, Greek and Middle Eastern grocers. Peel a couple of strips of the skin off, then thickly slice and season as you would the tomatoes.

Çakistez ve Siyah Zeytin
Olives

The most authentic Cypriot olives to use are *çakistez* (cracked green olives) and dry cured *siyah zeytin* (black olives). However, if you are unable to source either, then make a batch of my *Kekikli Zeytin* (Marinated Olives, page 58).

Yumurta
Eggs

Traditionally, eggs are simply hard-boiled and served in halves or quarters. You can season them with a sprinkling of sea salt flakes or spruce them up with some *kekik* (wild oregano), coarse black pepper, *pul biber* and sumac.

Ekmek
Bread

Freshly baked village loaves or *Kıbrıs Çöreği* (Cypriot Seeded Bread, pages 224–6) are always served with a Cypriot breakfast. After a few days, when the bread has turned a little stale, it is sliced and grilled or toasted (when the bread is then referred to as *gabira*), which makes it perfect for dunking into a cup of sweet *Kokulu Çay* (Spiced Cypriot Tea, page 42).

Karpuz
Watermelon

Best when in season, from early to late summer, I always source my watermelons from international supermarkets who import the best Cypriot and Turkish varieties. People are always nervous about buying watermelons because of the unpredictability of not being able to see how red and luscious the flesh may be. International supermarkets often portion off large watermelons into quarters or halves and cover them with plastic film, so the quality of the flesh inside is clearly visible.

Tahın ve Harnup Pekmezi
Tahini & Carob Molasses

The Cypriot answer to chocolate hazelnut spread, swirl together creamy tahini and sweet carob molasses to dip your freshly baked bread into.

Fresh Fruit & Vegetables

There is usually a selection of fresh fruit and vegetables available, other than the tomato, cucumber and watermelon that is traditionally eaten on a typical Cypriot breakfast plate. Freshly picked *Yeni Dünya* (loquats), *Verigo* and *Sultanina üzüm* (native Cypriot grapes) and *kavun* (honeydew melon) will be offered alongside fresh bunches of *semizotu* (purslane), sweet and fresh red and green peppers and *gabbar turşusu* (pickled caperberry leaves).

Reçeli & Bal
Jam & Honey

Vişne Reçeli (Sour Cherry Jam, page 26), fig jam and fresh honeycomb are served alongside *kaymak* (similar to clotted cream) and cream cheese to eat with fresh bread.

Vişne Reçeli

Sour Cherry Jam

The flavour of sour cherries takes me straight back to memories of flying to Cyprus as a child, where part of the excitement was knowing that I would be served small cartons of *vişne suyu* (sour cherry juice) on the aeroplane. Aside from the juice, the beautiful, sticky, sweet yet tart jam that is made when the cherries are in season every year, usually in July and August, would be the next thing I would savour with my fresh *simit* (a thin and crispy ring-shaped, sesame-seed covered Turkish bread) at the hotel breakfast table. It was my cousin Jeyda who first introduced me to the heavenly combination of sour cherry jam and cream cheese and I can now rarely bake a fresh loaf without slathering pieces of it in this deliciously creamy and sweetly tart duo.

Makes enough for 2 × 325-g (11½-oz) jars

400 g (14 oz) pitted sour cherries
325 g (11½ oz) caster sugar
½ tsp citric acid or 1 tsp lemon juice

Place a saucer in the freezer.

Put the cherries in a large pan, add the sugar and give everything a gentle shake. Place the pan over a medium heat.

Once the sugar starts to dissolve and the fruit begins to release its juices, slowly start stirring. Bring to a gentle boil. The mixture should be bubbling fairly enthusiastically, but do not allow it to spill over – turn the heat down when necessary, but keep stirring every couple of minutes for a total of 30 minutes.

Remove the saucer from the freezer and carefully place a tablespoon of the jammy syrup on to it, tilting the saucer away from you, over the pan. If the syrup drips straight back into the pan, then the jam is not ready. If the juices drip slowly, they have suitably thickened and your jam is almost ready. At this stage, add the citric acid or lemon juice to the pan and stir. Turn down the heat for 5 minutes, then remove the pan from the heat.

Give the mixture a final stir and carefully ladle the jam into the sterilised jars. Tightly close the lids and turn the jars upside down for 4 hours until fully cooled, before turning them the right way up.

Store in a cool, dark place (not the fridge as this will set the jam). Once opened, eat within 6 weeks.

Note

This recipe requires cooled, sterilised jars to decant the hot cooked jam into. Preheat the oven to 170°C/150°C fan/325°F/gas mark 3 and wash your jam jars with hot, soapy water. Once the oven is hot, place the jars on to a baking sheet (right side up) and put in the oven on the middle shelf for 20 minutes. While the jars are sterilising in the oven, place a small pan of fresh water over a high heat, and once it starts to boil, carefully drop the jar lids into the very hot water. Keep simmering the lids for 5 minutes, then transfer them with a large, slotted spoon directly to a clean, heatproof plate. Carefully remove the tray from the oven and allow the jars to cool.

Pastırmalı Yumurtalı Pide

Halloumi, Eggs & Cypriot Spiced Cured Beef Sausage Breakfast Flatbreads

Pastırma is a cured Turkish-Cypriot sausage, which is made using a mix of minced beef and spices, namely paprika and cumin. It has a warm kick to it, and its own unique flavour and texture, unlike any other sausage. It's often simply grilled and served as one of the elements of a Cypriot breakfast. My dad's favourite way to eat *pastırma* is to grill it and pack it into hot, freshly baked bread, so that the soft bread soaks up all the juices. *Pastırma* can also be fried, without any oil (as the sausage releases enough of its own oils while it cooks) and served with scrambled eggs. This particular recipe is a combination of lots of delicious elements in one – eggs, *hellim* (halloumi) and sausage all baked in bread.

Makes 4

For the dough
1 tsp caster sugar
100 ml (3½ fl oz) boiling water
175 ml (6 fl oz) cold water
50 g (1¾ oz) natural yoghurt
2 tbsp olive oil
500 g (1 lb 2 oz) plain flour
1 tsp baking powder
1 tsp salt

For the filling
2 Cypriot sausages (*pastırma*)
150 g (5½ oz) halloumi cheese, diced
6 large eggs
50 g (1¾ oz) halloumi cheese, finely grated
1 tbsp dried mint

Preheat the oven to 220°C/200°C fan/425°F/gas mark 7.

Line two large baking sheets with greaseproof paper and brush with a little olive oil.

To make the dough, put the sugar in a heatproof bowl. Pour over the boiling water and stir until the sugar has dissolved. Add the cold water, yoghurt and olive oil and stir well.

Sift the flour and baking powder into a large bowl and stir through the salt. Make a well in the centre, pour in the water mixture and bring everything together, kneading with clean hands until a dough is formed. Cover the bowl with a clean tea towel and leave to one side for 30 minutes.

Meanwhile, prepare the filling. Halve one of the *pastırma* lengthways, putting one half to the side and roughly chopping the other half. In a bowl, mix together the diced *hellim* with the chopped *pastırma*.

In a bowl, whisk together five of the eggs (reserving one egg for later), then stir through the grated *hellim* and dried mint. Add the diced halloumi and chopped *pastırma* mixture and combine.

Divide the dough into four equal pieces, and roll each piece out to a 5 mm (¼ inch) thickness in an oval shape. Place on to the prepared baking sheets.

Add two large tablespoons of the *pastırma* and *hellim* filling along the centre of each of the dough ovals. Fold up the long sides of the dough so that the shape resembles that of a boat, pinching the shorter ends tightly to form a point. Ensure the sides are folded over enough to encase the remaining filling mixture when it is poured in. Gently and evenly pour the remaining filling mixture equally between the four 'boats'.

Slice the remaining *pastırma* half into 1-cm (½-inch) rounds and distribute them across the top of each 'boat', gently pushing them down into the mixture a little.

Whisk the remaining egg in a bowl and brush the exposed dough with the egg wash.

Bake in the preheated oven for 20–25 minutes until the crusts are golden brown in colour and the filling is bubbling.

Ispanaklı Yumurta

Spinach & Eggs

This is a Turkish-inspired breakfast dish that I was first introduced to as a child while staying at a hotel during one of our many family holidays to Cyprus. My version of the recipe predominantly comprises slowly cooked onions, tomatoes, spinach and eggs, topped with an indulgent drizzling of melted butter and spices. A simple slice of fresh bread, and a small handful of olives on the side ensure a deliciously hearty start to the day, and all in under 30 minutes.

Serves 4 as a side dish, or 2 as a main

4 large, ripe plum tomatoes
3 tbsp olive oil
1 large onion, halved and finely sliced
2 garlic cloves, crushed
¼ tsp ground cumin
¼ tsp smoked paprika
½ tsp salt
½ tsp coarse black pepper
2 tbsp Turkish sweet red pepper paste (*tatlı biber salçası*)
400 g (14 oz) fresh spinach, roughly chopped
100–200 ml (3½–7 fl oz) water
4 large eggs
30 g (1 oz) unsalted butter
½ tsp sumac
½ tsp *pul biber*
1 tsp finely chopped fresh parsley
Sea salt flakes and pepper to taste

Place the tomatoes into a large, heatproof bowl and carefully pour in enough boiling hot water so that they are fully submerged. After a minute or so, with a large spoon, remove the tomatoes, allow them to cool slightly, then peel and discard the skins. Roughly chop the tomato flesh into quarters, and place in a bowl, reserving all of the juices.

Heat the oil in a large frying pan over a medium heat. Once the oil is hot, add the onion slices and soften and brown them for 8–10 minutes so that the edges crisp up a little. Add the garlic, and soften in the oil for a minute, then add the cumin, smoked paprika, salt and pepper and stir well. Add the sweet red pepper paste and the tomatoes and all their juices to the pan, turn down the heat and cook until the tomatoes have softened. You can use the back of the spoon to gently break down the tomatoes a little.

Add the spinach leaves straight to the pan, then the 100 ml (3½ fl oz) water and cook for a few minutes until the leaves have completely wilted down. If the spinach needs loosening, add another 100 ml (3½ fl oz) water, stir through and bring to a simmer. Reduce the heat and make four little spaces in the pan by spreading out some of the cooked spinach. Crack an egg straight into each of the four spaces and cover the pan with a large lid for 2 minutes so that the steam aids the thorough cooking of the eggs.

While the eggs are cooking, melt the butter in a small pan until it goes frothy, then take the pan off the heat. Check the eggs, and if the whites are cooked, but the yolks still have a good amount of jiggle in them (this is a recipe for dippy, runny yolks), then they're ready. If the whites need a little longer, put the lid on for another minute or so, but be careful not to overcook the yolks.

Add the sumac and *pul biber* to the melted butter, carefully swish the spices through, then drizzle over the eggs, trying to get as much on the yolks as possible. Season to taste with a pinch of sea salt flakes, cracked black pepper and parsley.

Peynirli Hellimlli Tost

Cheese & Halloumi Toastie

I'm sure we all know how to assemble a cheese toastie, right? It seemed a bit pointless putting a standard toastie recipe in here, so instead, I created a slightly more indulgent sandwich that took Cypriot-style *peynir* (cheese) and *hellim* (halloumi) toasties up a notch, bringing together salty, crispy, squidgy, oozy, stretchy, sweet, crunchy, seeded, buttery textures into one.

Makes 2 toasties

50 g (1¾ oz) unsalted butter, softened
2 tsp clear honey
½ tsp ground cinnamon
¼ tsp dried mint
2 large, middle segments of *Kıbrıs Çöreği* (Cypriot seeded bread) or 4 thickly cut slices of a seeded loaf
125 g (4½ oz) halloumi cheese, sliced into 4 pieces
1 tbsp olive oil
100 g (3½ oz) *kaşar peyniri* or Gouda, sliced into 4 pieces

Mix the softened butter, honey, cinnamon and dried mint in a small bowl until fully combined. If using the two segments of *Kıbrıs Çöreği*, slice each one straight through the middle so that you end up with four thinner slices of bread.

Lay out the four slices of bread and spread one side of each with the cinnamon butter. Pat the *hellim* slices completely dry with kitchen paper. Brush each slice of *hellim* with a little olive oil on both sides.

Add the tablespoon of olive oil to a large non-stick frying pan over a medium heat, and once hot, fry the *hellim* for a couple of minutes on each side until crispy and golden brown. Remove from the frying pan to a plate lined with kitchen paper to drain any excess oil. Carefully wipe the pan clean with kitchen paper.

Take two of the buttered bread slices and put two slices of *hellim* on each piece. Add two slices of *Kaşar Peyniri* or Gouda to each. Place the remaining two bread slices, buttered sides on the inside and facing the cheese, on top, then butter the outside of the bread too, reserving some of the butter for later.

Place the frying pan back over a medium heat and once hot, add the toasties, buttered side down, into the pan, gently pushing on them with your hands or a large fish slice for 3–4 minutes. When the underside of the toasties start to turn a lovely crispy, dark golden-brown colour, and the cheese slowly starts to melt, spread the remaining butter on the top slices of the toasties. Carefully flip the toasties over to brown the other sides for another 3–4 minutes. Slice and serve hot while the cheese is still oozing.

Menemen

Spiced Scrambled Eggs

This is another beautiful eggy treat that is never far from a *serpme kahvaltı*
(breakfast spread); I first fell in love with it when eating breakfast at one of the
many Turkish restaurants that busily adorn the infamous Green Lanes in Harringay.
The dish starts with a base of onions and peppers which are slowly sautéed in olive
oil, followed by fresh tomatoes, tomato and red pepper pastes, herbs and spices.
Finally, the eggs are whisked in right at the last minute, so that the *menemen* retains
its loose and creamy texture, perfect to dip bread into. I've played around with some
of the spices and have added some fried *hellim* (halloumi cheese) in there too.

Serves 4

6 large eggs
4 large ripe tomatoes
3 tbsp olive oil
125 g (4½ oz) halloumi cheese,
    cubed
1 large onion, finely chopped
30 g (1 oz) unsalted butter
2 large *sivri biber* (Turkish green
    peppers) or 150 g (5½ oz)
    padron peppers, chopped into
    1-cm (½-inch) rounds
1 tbsp Turkish sweet red pepper
    paste (*tatlı biber salçası*)
¼ tsp ground cumin
½ tsp paprika
½ tsp *pul biber*
¼ tsp dried wild oregano
¼ tsp sea salt flakes
½ tsp coarse black pepper
Juice of ¼ lemon
10 g (¼ oz) fresh flat leaf parsley,
    finely chopped

Crack the eggs into a large bowl and leave to one side. Do not whisk
them.

Cut the tomatoes in half, and grate them, flesh side down, into a large
shallow dish, discarding the skins and hard cores. Leave to one side.

Heat one tablespoon of olive oil in a large frying pan over a medium
heat, and once hot, add the *hellim* cubes to the pan and fry them on
all sides until golden and crispy. Remove to a plate lined with kitchen
paper to drain off the excess oil.

Add the remaining two tablespoons of olive oil to the same pan, still
over a medium heat. Add the onion and turn the heat right down so
that it softens but doesn't burn at the edges. Cook it for 12–15 minutes
until completely soft and translucent.

Stir the butter through the warm, softened onions over a low heat
until it has melted, then add the peppers and soften for a further
4–5 minutes. Add the sweet red pepper paste, spices and dried
oregano, salt and pepper and stir to combine, then add the tomatoes,
and bring the mixture to a simmer for a couple of minutes.

Pour the eggs straight from the bowl, into the pan and then break
them up and swirl them through with a wooden spoon. Allow the eggs
to just cook through, then remove the pan from the heat, and squeeze
over the lemon juice. Top with the fried *hellim* cubes and garnish with
parsley to serve. A side of fresh bread is a delicious addition for dipping.

Tepside Kıbrıs Kahvaltısı

One-tray Cypriot Breakfast

This was an idea that came to me a few years ago and a recipe that I knew had to be included in my cookbook, if I ever got the opportunity to write one. It's simple, yet brings together so many of the individual elements and ingredients of a Cypriot breakfast into one single traybake. I love how the roasted oregano potatoes soak up the juices from the tomatoes and *pastırma* (Turkish-Cypriot cured and spiced beef sausage), the texture of the dry black olives when baked, and the fresh acidity from a squeeze of lemon juice at the end; but I think perhaps my favourite part of this dish is dipping the crispy, yet juicy *hellim* (halloumi) into the runny yolks of the eggs. Simply delectable.

Serves 4

3 tbsp olive oil
400 g (14 oz) Cyprus or Maris Piper potatoes, peeled and cut into 2-cm (¾-inch) cubes
1½ tsp dried oregano
2 Cypriot (*pastırma*) or Turkish (*sucuk*) sausages
4 large plum tomatoes
125 g (4½ oz) halloumi cheese, cut into 6 thick slices
4 large eggs
50 g (1¾ oz) dry black olives
¼ tsp *pul biber*
Juice of ½ lemon
1 tbsp fresh flat leaf parsley, finely chopped
Salt and pepper to taste

Preheat the oven to 190°C/170°C fan/325°F/gas mark 3.

Brush a non-stick baking tray with one tablespoon of olive oil and put in the oven to heat up.

Pat the cubed potatoes completely dry with kitchen paper, then place in a large bowl and add one tablespoon of olive oil and half a teaspoon of the dried oregano.

Slice the sausages in half lengthways. Halve the tomatoes lengthways, and gently brush both the cut-sides and skins with half a tablespoon of olive oil and half a teaspoon of dried oregano.

Pat the *hellim* slices completely dry with kitchen paper. Brush them with the remaining half tablespoon of olive oil.

Carefully remove the hot baking tray from the oven, evenly spread the potatoes and tomatoes on to the tray, the tomatoes skin-side down, and place back into the middle of the oven for 12–15 minutes until the vegetables start to change colour a little.

Remove the baking tray from the oven, turn the potatoes over, then add the sausages (cut-side down) and *hellim* and cook for a further 5–6 minutes until the sausages start to sizzle and release some of their oils.

Remove the baking tray from the oven and make four spaces, cracking the eggs into them. Scatter over the olives and place back in the oven for a further 8–10 minutes, until the whites of the eggs are cooked through, but the yolks are still runny. Once cooked, season the eggs, potatoes and tomatoes with a sprinkling of salt and the entire dish with a generous pinch of cracked black pepper, half a teaspoon of dried oregano, the *pul biber* and lemon juice. Garnish with the parsley.

Tahini, Carob & Cinnamon Honey Pancakes

If you have never tried the heavenly combination of *tahın* and *harnup pekmezi* (tahini and carob molasses), which is essentially a Cypriot's answer to chocolate spread, then you simply must. My mum would tell us stories of how, when she was younger, she would dangerously climb the carob trees to pick the pods, then eat them as if they were chocolate bars.

Excellent, light, creamy, nutty tahini is key for this recipe, the very slight bitterness of which is complemented by the slightly saccharine carob and the sweetly spiced cinnamon honey, resulting in a heavenly trio of goodies to pour all over the soft, crispy-edged pancakes.

Makes 6–8 pancakes (depending on the size of your frying pan)

For the pancakes
1 large egg
250 ml (9 fl oz) milk
150 g (5½ oz) plain flour
Pinch of salt
1 tsp icing sugar
25 g (1 oz) unsalted butter

For the cinnamon honey
2 tbsp clear honey
¼ tsp ground cinnamon

To serve
50 ml (2 fl oz) tahini
1 tbsp carob molasses

To make the pancake batter, whisk together the egg and milk in a large bowl or measuring jug until light and frothy. Sift in the flour and whisk until smooth. Stir in the salt and icing sugar.

To make the cinnamon honey, in a separate small bowl, mix together the honey and ground cinnamon.

Heat a small knob of the butter in a frying pan over a medium heat. Once the butter has melted and started bubbling ever so slightly, stir the pancake mixture well one last time, then pour a small ladleful of it into the pan, swirling it around to evenly distribute the batter. Cook the pancake for a minute or two until bubbles start to appear on the top and there is no runny batter visible, then flip it over to cook the other side for another minute or so. Remove the pancake from the pan to a warm plate. Add another tiny knob of butter to the pan and repeat the process with the remaining pancake batter until you have used it all up.

To serve, mix the carob molasses into the tahini and drizzle it liberally over the pancakes along with the cinnamon honey mixture.

Hellimli Zeytinli Kek

Halloumi & Black Olive Cake

My *Hellimli Zeytinli Kek* has to be one of the most popular recipes on my blog and Instagram pages. My mum always makes her *zeytinli* (olive cake) separate to her *hellimli* (halloumi cake), but the combination of both the dry black olives and halloumi together, with the freshness of the coriander and the sweetness of the onions and dried mint is basically the best kind of double whammy, so I've merged my mum's recipes into one epic cake. Is it a breakfast dish? Sure, why not, because when people ask me what to serve it with, my response is simply 'a cup of tea'. Since so many breakfast times in our house have been spent with a slice of this cake in one hand and a cup of *Kokulu Çay* (Spiced Cypriot Tea, page 42) in the other, its deliciousness seemed perfectly fitting for this chapter.

Serves 8–10

3 tbsp olive oil, plus extra
  for oiling
1 small brown onion, finely
  chopped
3 large eggs
250 ml (9 fl oz) milk
200 ml (7 fl oz) olive oil
400 g (14 oz) self-raising flour
1 level tsp baking powder
1 tsp salt
1½ tsp sugar
165 g (6¾ oz) pitted black olives
200 g (7 oz) halloumi cheese
  cut into 2½-cm (1-inch) cubes
4 tbsp fresh finely chopped
  coriander
2 tbsp dried mint
1 heaped tsp sesame seeds
1 heaped tsp nigella seeds
25 g (1 oz) halloumi cheese,
  finely grated

Preheat the oven to 200°C/180°C fan/400°F/gas mark 6.

Line a 23-cm (9-inch) springform cake tin with greaseproof paper and brush the paper with a little olive oil.

Place a large frying pan over a medium heat and add three tablespoons of olive oil. Once the oil is hot, add the onion to the pan, and immediately turn down the heat. Soften the onion for 12–15 minutes until beautifully translucent and lightly caramelised. Remove the pan from the heat and transfer the onion to a plate to cool down.

In a large bowl, whisk the eggs, then add the milk and oil and stir well. Sift in half of the flour and the baking powder, then add the salt and sugar and whisk everything together, before sifting in the rest of the flour and whisking until there are no visible lumps in the mixture. With a wooden spoon or spatula, gently fold in the caramelised onion, olives, *hellim* cubes, coriander and dried mint until combined.

Pour the mixture into the cake tin, sprinkle over half of the sesame and nigella seeds, then the finely grated *hellim*, and finally, the rest of the seeds.

Bake on the bottom shelf of the oven for 40–50 minutes. After 40 minutes, insert a cocktail stick into the middle of the cake. If it comes out clean, it's ready. If not, give it another few minutes.

Leave to cool slightly in the tin, then carefully remove the ring and base and allow to cool fully on a wire rack for an hour before serving in slices with a cup of *Kokulu Çay* (Spiced Cypriot Tea, page 42).

Kokulu Çay

Spiced Cypriot Tea

Kokulu çay (or *tütülü çay* to some) can be served with or without milk, or sugar, but the three spices used to are used to flavour the tea, which are aniseed, cinnamon and cloves, are also the same three spices that are used to flavour many sweet and savoury Cypriot dishes, pastries and breads. The infusion of *kokulu çay* is inevitably embedded with Eastern influences, but the chosen combination of spices is somewhat typically Cypriot in its essence; aniseed, in particular, is regularly used in ground form in baked goods, but also as a seed topper for various breads and pastries. Although *kokulu* çay is a natural staple on the Cypriot breakfast table, you can drink it throughout the day; it is just as perfect in the evenings with something sweet as it is in the mornings with a slice of *gabira* (toasted bread) dipped into it, in the same way that you would happily dunk a biscuit.

Serves 4–8

4 English Breakfast teabags
¼ cinnamon stick, broken up
  into small pieces
¼ tsp aniseed
6 cloves
1 litre (1¾ pints) freshly boiled
  water
Milk and sugar, to serve
  (optional)

Place the teabags, cinnamon, aniseed and cloves in a large teapot and fill with the freshly boiled water, give everything a gentle stir and pop the lid on, then cover the pot with a thick tea towel or cosy and let it infuse for a couple of minutes.

Give the tea another stir, then pour into teacups through a tea strainer. If serving without milk, only half fill the cup and top up with more freshly boiled water to dilute. If serving with milk, fill the cup with only the tea from the pot (do not water it down), then pour in your desired amount of milk. Serve with sugar, if preferred.

(See image on page 22).

Sütlaç

Milky Rice

This recipe is a giver of pure, joyful comfort in every spoonful. There aren't many memories I have of being extremely small and not liking particular foods, but as a child, I really couldn't tolerate drinking milk, which was completely defied by my ability to happily eat bowlfuls of my mum's cosy and satisfying *Sütlaç*. I have kept this recipe really simple, in the same way my mum made it for us as children.

Serves 4

200 g (7 oz) short-grain pudding
   rice
1.2 litres (2 pints) whole milk
45 g (1½ oz) granulated sugar
1 tsp rose water
1 cinnamon stick
½ tsp ground cinnamon

Wash the rice in a sieve until the water runs clear and allow to fully drain.

Add the rice, milk, sugar, rose water and cinnamon stick to a large saucepan and stir well.

Place the pan over a medium heat, and bring to a simmer, stirring constantly. Do not let the milk boil. Keep your eye on it, and turn the heat down to keep it at a constant very gentle simmer.

Cook for around 20 minutes until the rice is creamy and tender, but not stodgy or overcooked. Serve the Milky Rice in wide-rimmed bowls with a generous sprinkling of ground cinnamon.

Dishes & Salads to Share

Meze & Salata

This chapter is dedicated to my late Izzet Dayı, my mum's young-at-heart, forever-dancing, darbuka-playing (drum-playing) brother. Uncle Izzy was the King of the *meze* table and he lived for parties and celebrations and would spend hours preparing a full-*meze* spread ready to greet his friends and family with. He loved the simplicity of a *Kuru Fasulye Salatası* (Cannellini Bean Salad, page 62) and *Pancar Salatası* (Beetroot Salad, page 50) and I can't make either of those dishes now without listening to his favourite songs and reliving the fondest memories of him when I'm in the kitchen. For me, music is as much of a trigger for nostalgia and sentiment as these recipes are, and every family occasion I can think of has a soundtrack to accompany the food; gatherings always start with a good *meze* spread, where eating, drinking and dancing become inextricably linked.

Live Turkish music is a fundamental part of (Turkish) Cypriot celebrations, and the tables are always set with baskets of fresh *Kıbrıs Çöreği* (Cypriot Seeded Bread, pages 224–6) and small plates of cold *meze*, such as *Cacık* (Yoghurt, Mint & Cucumber Dip, page 52), *Hummus* (Chickpea & Tahini Dip, page 53) and *Bakla Salatası* (Broad Bean Salad, page 57). Guests arrive and enjoy snacking in between the impromptu communal dancing, and cold *meze* is followed by dishes of hot *meze*, such as the *Sigara Böreği* (Filo Cigar Pastries, page 66). A generous *meze* table is my absolute favourite way to eat. My own wedding was a real melting pot of cultures (my husband is Jewish), with belly dancers and chair dances and we served all the Cypriot *meze* classics on the menu to begin the meal.

Some of my fondest memories as a child were spent getting dressed up and ready with my mum and two of my aunts, Meyrem Teyze and Aysan Teyze for a wedding or *balo* (dinner and dance) – my sister and I wearing matching dresses that my mum had made for us that day. I absolutely adore my aunties, and my sister and I have a very special relationship with them. They would paint our nails and we would secretly drink Turkish coffee with them while we got ready, in preparation for tackling the *meze* table with our cousins as soon as we arrived, and to give us the energy to dance into the night. When it all got a bit too much, one by one, each of us kids would drop off like flies and fall asleep on chairs pushed together under the table, covered with our parents' coats and jackets to keep us warm before we were carried into our cars to make the journey home.

As well as being a staple for formal events, *meze* is perfect for informal gatherings too. I can recall so many times where we would arrive, mob-handed with our extended family to various picnic locations, carrying tartan zipper bags loaded with makeshift storage boxes fashioned out of recycled ice-cream tubs. The tubs would be filled with *meze* – salads, meatballs and stuffed vine leaves. Whole boiled potatoes and eggs, still warm, would be transported and peeled with plastic-handled knives once we arrived, then dressed with loads of olive oil, fresh coriander, mint, lemon and salt to make *Yumurtalı Patates Salatası* (Egg & Potato Salad, page 64). Similarly, the Christmas dinners of my childhood would have never evoked the same memories for me without my Emine Hala's *Golyandro Salata* (coriander salad, of which you can find my version, which includes tomatoes – *Salata* (Salad) on page 54) and my mum's *Hummus* (page 53). Wherever we would go, we would take a piece of Cyprus with us, and although not every Cypriot *meze* dish is included in this chapter (as that would require a whole book of its own), various *meze*-style dishes can be found throughout the other chapters in the book and are made to be shared.

I now make these *meze* dishes when entertaining my own friends and family, just as my parents and elders did when we were younger, and there is a good variety of accompaniments here to suit any summer barbecue or family dinner. Whether you are hosting a crowd for a large gathering, or just having a couple of friends over in the garden, the dips and salads in this chapter can all be prepared in advance and then brought out to wow your guests with as soon as they arrive.

Pancar Salatası

Beetroot Salad

I adore the sweetness of cooked beetroot, especially when contrasted with the tart, sharp tones of vinegar and garlic, and this is always a regular at family picnics or barbecues. *Pancar Salatası* pairs beautifully with *Yumurtalı Patates Salatası* (Egg & Potato Salad, page 64) or *Kuru Fasulye Salatası* (Cannellini Bean Salad, page 62) in this chapter, but also works with seafood and smoked fish (such as freshwater prawns, mackerel or kippers).

Serves 6–8

500 g (1 lb 2 oz) cooked beetroot
2 large garlic cloves, thinly sliced
25 g (1 oz) fresh coriander, finely chopped
½ tsp dried mint
40 ml (1½ fl oz) extra virgin olive oil
4 tbsp red wine vinegar
¾ tsp sea salt flakes

To garnish
¼ tsp sea salt flakes
30 ml (1 fl oz) extra virgin olive oil
A few fresh coriander leaves, finely chopped

Halve and quarter the beetroot. If the beetroot is particularly large, cut the quarters in half again.

Place the beetroot into a large, deep dish with the rest of the ingredients, except for the salt.

Stir well and chill in the fridge for a couple of hours before serving, if possible.

Sprinkle in the three-quarter teaspoon of sea salt flakes and give everything a good stir again before serving. To serve, season with the quarter teaspoon of sea salt flakes, 30 ml (1 fl oz) extra virgin oil and fresh coriander leaves to garnish.

Cacık

Yoghurt, Mint & Cucumber Dip

I'm going to say something that may be really controversial; I prefer a well-made *cacık* to hummus or any other dip. Just. But it's true. Because when well-made, *cacık* is a pass-me-the-bowl-with-just-a-spoon kind of dip, and with a warm piece of *Kıbrıs Pidesi* (Cypriot pitta bread) it's pure treasure. By 'well-made', I mean the perfect ratio of thick, luscious yoghurt, to finely grated and strained cucumber, garlic and dried mint. Even if I am using thick strained natural yoghurt, I will still strain it myself before making *cacık*. I urge you to do the same in order to create the thickest, creamiest *cacık* possible.

Serves 6

300 g (10½ oz) natural strained or thick set yoghurt
1 tsp lemon juice
1½ tsp extra virgin olive oil, plus extra to serve
1 tbsp dried mint, plus extra to serve
200 g (7 oz) cucumber
1 large garlic clove, finely grated
½ tsp salt

If straining the yoghurt, line a sieve with a muslin cloth (or two thick pieces of kitchen paper) and place the sieve over a bowl. Put the yoghurt in the cloth, cover the sieve loosely with another piece of kitchen paper and leave to strain, in the fridge, for around four hours.

When your yoghurt is ready, in a medium-sized bowl, add the lemon juice, olive oil and dried mint, stirring thoroughly so that the dried herbs soften a little.

Finely grate the cucumber into a bowl, then place all the grated flesh and skin into a sieve and squeeze out as much of the juice as possible. Leave the cucumber to rest in the sieve while you prepare the rest of the ingredients, as it will release even more liquid by the time you are ready to use it.

Add the garlic, yoghurt and salt to the lemon juice, olive oil and dried mint mixture and stir to combine. Give the cucumber one final squeeze to get rid of any remaining juices and add to the mixture. Stir everything together one last time, then place in the fridge for one hour to allow the flavours to amalgamate. Serve with a drizzle of extra virgin olive oil and a sprinkling of dried mint.

(See image on page 51.)

Hummus

Chickpea & Tahini Dip

My mum would make huge batches of hummus for every family gathering, and there are a few tips to take it from mediocre to fabulous, such as using a generous amount of excellent-quality, creamy tahini and lots of tangy lemon and garlic. If using your own boiled chickpeas, ensure that they have fully cooled down before using them to make the *hummus* (see Note below on how to prepare dried chickpeas). My recipe outlines the quantities of chickpeas required depending on whether you use dried, jarred or canned chickpeas. A warm loaf of *Kıbrıs Çöreği* (Cypriot Seeded Bread pages 224–6) is essential when eating *hummus*, and baskets of the freshly baked bread will always adorn the closely-packed tables at family weddings and events.

Serves 6–8

2 × 400 g (14 oz) cans of good-quality chickpeas or 1 × 660 g (1 lb 3 oz) jar good-quality chickpeas
1 tsp finely grated garlic
6 tbsp tahini
1 tbsp olive oil
¾ tsp salt
4 tbsp fresh lemon juice

To garnish
paprika
sumac
ground cumin
extra virgin olive oil
fresh flat leaf parsley

Drain the chickpeas, reserving the aquafaba (chickpea water) before adding the chickpeas to a food processor (set aside a few chickpeas for garnish). Add three tablespoons of the aquafaba from the can, jar or cooled boiling juices.

Add the remaining ingredients to the food processor and blitz together. If the texture is too thick, add a little more of the aquafaba. Blend again, taste and add a little more salt or lemon if desired. The mixture should be lovely and smooth.

Garnish with the reserved chickpeas, a pinch each of paprika, sumac and cumin, a drizzle of extra virgin olive oil and some finely chopped flat leaf parsley.

(See image on page 51.)

Note

If you would like to make this from dried chickpeas, then use 300 g (10½ oz) to make approximately 500 g (1 lb 2 oz) cooked chickpeas. Follow the pack instructions but do ensure you add one tablespoon or bicarbonate of soda to the water the chickpeas are cooked in (to help soften the skins).

Salata

Salad

When we were younger, no dinner table setting was ever complete without a huge bowl of salad. Mum would use whatever fresh vegetables my dad had picked up from the market that week, wash them and then lay them out on clean tea towels to fully dry before she was ready to make the salad. She still finely chops everything straight into her chosen serving vessel using a brown-plastic handled paring knife in one hand, and then douses the vegetables in extra virgin olive oil, freshly squeezed lemon juice and salt just before serving. To this day, if Mum is preparing a salad and shredding the lettuce, she will always cut out the core to share with me; it's my favourite part, and what we call the *kök* (the root). Whenever there is a freshly made salad on the table, Mum will pass me the bowl at the end of the meal, with a large spoon, so that I can blissfully scoop up the juice that always remains at the bottom of the dish even though she loves this part of the salad as much as I do.

Serves 6–8

150 g (5½ oz) white cabbage, finely shredded

100 g (3½ oz) cos lettuce, finely shredded

50 g (1¾ oz) fresh coriander, finely chopped

2 small Turkish/Middle Eastern cucumbers or 150 g (5½ oz) English cucumber

2 large spring onions, finely sliced

75 g (2¾ oz) pitted dry black olives

1 tbsp dried mint

2 large (150 g/5½ oz), ripe plum tomatoes, roughly chopped

3 tbsp extra virgin olive oil

3 tbsp fresh lemon juice

¾ tsp sea salt flakes

Put the shredded cabbage, lettuce and coriander into a large bowl. Peel 2–3 vertical strips of skin off the cucumber, then cut it in half lengthways, then lengthways again and chop into ½-cm (¼-inch) thick pieces. Add the cucumber to the bowl with the spring onions, olives and dried mint. Add the tomatoes, but keep them slightly separate from the other ingredients. Do not stir.

Pour over the extra virgin olive oil and lemon juice. Sprinkle over the salt, give everything a gentle stir and serve immediately. If you are making the salad in advance, then store in the fridge and dress just before serving to keep it as fresh as possible.

Bakla Salatası

Broad Bean Salad

This is another popular *meyhane* (taverna) or cold *meze*-table dish. In Turkey, fresh dill is mostly used to flavour this dish, but when in Cyprus, this is replaced with dried mint and fresh coriander. Adding some of the dressing to the pan of simmering broad beans really lets those flavours absorb into the pulses. Wait for the beans to cool before serving as part of a full table *meze* spread with all, or any, of the *meze* dishes in this chapter, or alongside the *Izgara Köfte* (Grilled Meat Patties, page 205), *Izgara Tavuk* (Barbecue Chicken Wings & Thighs, pages 206–7) and *Izgara Ahtapot* (Grilled Octopus, pages 216–17).

Serves 6

250 g (9 oz) broad beans
¾ tsp sea salt flakes
2 garlic cloves, finely sliced
5 tbsp extra virgin olive oil
2 tbsp white wine vinegar
2 tbsp fresh lemon juice
1 tsp coriander seeds
1 tbsp fresh coriander leaves
1 tsp dried mint

Boil the broad beans in a pan with half a teaspoon of salt for 2–3 minutes until tender. Drain some of the water from the pan, leaving around 50 ml (2 fl oz) in the pan with the broad beans. Add the garlic to the pan along with one tablespoon each of the olive oil, white wine vinegar and lemon juice. Place the pan back over a medium heat, then keep on a low simmer for a couple of minutes. Pour the broad beans and their juices straight into a serving dish and allow to cool a little until warm.

Crush the coriander seeds, stir them through the broad beans along with the fresh coriander, dried mint and remaining quarter teaspoon of salt. Dress the beans with the remaining four tablespoons of olive oil, white wine vinegar and lemon juice before serving.

Kekikli Zeytin

Marinated Olives

This is another recipe that has been on my blog since it began. Cypriot olives known as *çakistez* are homegrown cracked green olives, that, once soaked and brined, are served with copious amounts of extra virgin olive oil (usually made from the olives of the same tree) lemon, garlic and crushed coriander seeds. However, the process is a little laborious, and requires sourcing fresh green Cypriot olives, so a few years ago I decided to create a simple marinade that included some of the key ingredients of *çakistez* while using more easily sourced good-quality olives and condiments that are readily found in mainstream supermarkets. I make a batch of *Kekikli Zeytin* on a weekly basis and store them in the fridge (for up to a week) to keep the herbs as fresh as possible, but remove from the fridge an hour or so before serving to enable the oil to come up to room temperature as it has the tendency to emulsify a little when chilled. I advise making these olives a day in advance so that the flavours really have a chance to intensify.

**Makes approximately
1 × 370-ml (13-fl-oz) jar**

160 g (5¾ oz) pitted Kalamata olives
160 g (5¾ oz) pitted green queen olives
2 tbsp coriander seeds
4 garlic cloves, bashed
1 tbsp fresh flat leaf parsley, finely chopped
1 tbsp fresh coriander, finely chopped
1 small, unwaxed lemon, quartered and thinly sliced
1 tbsp pomegranate molasses
3 tbsp extra virgin olive oil, plus extra to serve
1 tbsp balsamic vinegar
2 tsp dried oregano
½ tsp *pul biber*

Place the olives into a plastic storage box or large jar. Lightly crush one tablespoon of the coriander seeds in a pestle and mortar until some are slightly broken, then add to the olives with the additional tablespoon of whole coriander seeds and the garlic. Add the parsley, coriander and lemon to the olives with the rest of the remaining ingredients. Give everything a stir, then secure the lid and give it a good shake. Store in the fridge for up to a week, and drizzle over a little extra virgin olive oil before serving.

Fine Bulgur Wheat Salad

Typically eaten in long cos lettuce leaves, *Kısır* is traditionally a Turkish *meze* rather than a Cypriot one. However, it is, and has been, served on every Turkish-Cypriot *meze* table I have ever eaten at, and is one of my favourite dishes to enjoy alongside *Cacık* (Yoghurt, Mint & Cucumber Dip, page 52), *Hummus* (Chickpea & Tahini Dip, page 53) and *Pancar Salatası* (Beetroot Salad, page 50). There should be enough dressing to give the dish a juicy, moreish consistency, so feel free to add a little more extra virgin olive oil and pomegranate molasses just before serving. If you are observing a gluten-free diet, you can swap the bulgur wheat for cooked quinoa, leaving out the step of adding the cold water to the dish.

Serves 6–8

½ vegetable stock cube
200 ml (7 fl oz) boiling water
2 tbsp olive oil
1 small onion, very finely chopped
2 tbsp tomato purée
2 tbsp Turkish sweet red pepper paste (*tatlı biber salçası*)
1 tsp *pul biber*
½ tsp paprika
200 g (7 oz) fine bulgur wheat
250 ml (9 fl oz) cold water
50 g (1¾ oz) fresh parsley leaves, finely chopped
10 g (¼ oz) fresh mint leaves, finely chopped
4 large spring onions, finely sliced
4 small ripe tomatoes, roughly chopped
Sea salt flakes and coarse black pepper to taste

For the dressing
4 tbsp extra virgin olive oil
4 tbsp pomegranate molasses
3 tbsp fresh lemon juice
Grated zest of 1 lemon
1 tsp dried mint

Dissolve the stock cube in the boiling water and leave to one side.

Heat the olive oil in a pan and cook the onion over a medium-low heat for 12–15 minutes, until soft and caramelised.

Add the tomato purée, sweet red pepper paste, *pul biber* and paprika to the pan, then sea salt flakes and coarse black pepper to taste and stir for a minute or two so that the spices and pastes come together and smell fragrant. Pour in the vegetable stock and stir well. When the mixture starts to bubble, turn down the heat and gently simmer for 3–4 minutes until the sauce has reduced a little.

Remove the pan from the heat then stir in the dry bulgur wheat until every grain is fully coated in the mixture. Pour into a deep rectangular dish and even out the mixture a little. Pour the cold water into the dish so that the liquid just covers the bulgur wheat, cover with plastic film (to create steam), then leave to one side until the water has fully evaporated, and the mixture has completely cooled. This could take up to an hour.

Once the bulgur wheat mixture has cooled, add the parsley, mint, spring onions and tomatoes to the dish and give everything a gentle stir. Finally, add the dressing ingredients to the dish – olive oil, pomegranate molasses, lemon juice, lemon zest and dried mint. Stir well and serve.

Kuru Fasulye Salatası

Cannellini Bean Salad

My mum makes this traditional cannellini bean salad regularly, and always pairs it with a dressed tuna salad, raw onion wedges and black olives. I like to serve it with the *Pancar Salatası* (Beetroot Salad, page 50) and hard-boiled eggs. The day after, Mum always turns this into a *Kuru Fasulye Yahni* (Cannellini Bean Stew, page 86) which is why it's such a versatile dish. I jazz up my salad with tomatoes, black olives and dried mint, but it's traditional to simply use extra virgin olive oil, lemon juice, salt and fresh parsley in the dressing. The recipe yields enough beans to use half for the salad, and half the following day to make the *Kuru Fasulye Yahni*. However, if you prefer to only make a large batch of the salad, then double up quantities of the dressing ingredients.

Serves 6–8

500 g (1 lb 2 oz) dried white beans
4 litres (7 pints) cold water, for soaking
3 litres (5¼ pints) cold water, for boiling
4 large carrots (400 g/14 oz), peeled and sliced diagonally into 1-cm (½-inch) pieces
600 g (1 lb 5 oz) white potatoes, peeled and quartered
200 g (7 oz) celery, sliced diagonally into 1-cm (½-inch) pieces)
200 g (7 oz) cherry plum tomatoes, halved
50 g (1¾ oz) dry black olives
1 large onion, finely sliced

For the dressing

75 ml (2½ fl oz) extra virgin olive oil
4 tbsp fresh lemon juice
25 g (1 oz) fresh parsley, finely chopped
1 tsp dried mint
1 tsp sea salt flakes

Soak the beans in four litres of cold water in a large pan for no less than 12 hours. I do this overnight and soak the beans at room temperature with the lid on. Once soaked, drain the water and rinse the beans in fresh cold water. Drain again, fill the pan with three litres of cold water and place over a medium–high heat. Bring the beans to the boil, then reduce the heat to a medium simmer, skimming and discarding any foam that forms on the surface. All beans vary slightly in size and texture, but I cook the beans for at least 1–1¼ hours. After an hour, add the carrots, potatoes and celery to the pan and cook for a further 15 minutes until the vegetables are cooked and tender, and the beans squish easily with a fork without any resistance.

Remove half of the bean salad from the pan, drain well and put in a serving dish (reserve the remaining beans to make the *Kuru Fasulye Yahni* the following day. Allow to cool in their cooking liquid and then place in the fridge overnight). Add the tomatoes, olives and onion to the dish, and dress immediately with the olive oil, lemon juice, parsley, dried mint and sea salt flakes so that the warm beans and vegetables soak up the flavours. If necessary, add more sea salt to taste and serve.

Yumurtalı Patates Salatası

Egg & Potato Salad

Although this a salad that is made for sharing, or as a side to accompany other dishes, I could happily eat it all on my own, on its own. The key to this salad is to dress the cooked ingredients while they are still warm, so that they soak up all the beautiful flavours from the dressing ingredients. It's so comforting to know that the combination of good-quality extra virgin olive oil, lemon juice, fresh coriander, dried mint, spring onions, black olives and warm boiled potatoes and eggs can transport me straight back to *Kıbrıs* (Cyprus).

Serves 6–8

500 g (1 lb 2 oz) Cyprus potatoes (or Désirée, Yukon Gold, Charlotte potatoes)

4 large eggs, at room temperature

2 large spring onions, finely chopped

1 tsp dried mint

50 g (1¾ oz) fresh coriander leaves and stalks, finely chopped

4 tbsp extra virgin olive oil

4 tbsp fresh lemon juice

Handful of dry black olives

¾ tsp sea salt flakes

¼ tsp coarse black pepper

Place the whole potatoes, skins on, into a large pan. Fill the pan with enough cold water to fully cover the potatoes. Place over a high heat, bring the potatoes up to the boil, then reduce to a medium heat. Simmer for 45 minutes–1 hour for larger potatoes (or 25–30 minutes if using smaller varieties). Seven minutes before the cooking time is up, gently place the eggs into the pan, allowing the water to come back up to the boil, and cook the eggs for 7 minutes. The potatoes are cooked when you can pierce them with a knife, without them falling apart.

Remove the pan from the heat, drain the potatoes and eggs and return them to the pan, then cover in cold water to stop them cooking any further. Once cooled, place the potatoes and eggs into a colander to dry.

When the potatoes are cool enough to handle (yet still warm), peel off their skins and roughly chop into chunks. Remove the shell from the hard-boiled eggs and roughly chop as well.

Place the potatoes in a large bowl and add the spring onions, dried mint, coriander and salt and pepper. Dress with the olive oil and lemon juice, and stir everything together so that the warm potatoes are fully coated. Their warmth is key to allowing the flavours to come together. Add the black olives and eggs, giving everything another gentle stir before serving, adding more salt, to taste, if necessary. This dish is equally delicious the next day, served cold from the fridge.

Sigara Böreği

Filo Cigar Pastries

We didn't grow up eating these at home, as my mum would always make the Cypriot-style rectangular fried *börek* (fried and baked pastries) with her homemade *yufka* (pastry) instead. However, we did grow up eating *Sigara Böreği* every time we were served hot *meze* at a restaurant in Cyprus or at weddings. They are called *Sigara Böreği* because of their shape. Filled with a herby cheese filling that becomes deliciously oozy once fried, they must be eaten hot. So hot, in fact, that due to my impatience, I can rarely feel the roof of my mouth after eating them. They can be made with *hellim* (halloumi) or *beyaz peynir* (Turkish white cheese), similar to feta – I make mine using a combined mixture of squeaky, squidgy *hellim* and salty, crumbly *beyaz peynir*.

Makes 14

1 large egg
100 g (3½ oz) *beyaz peynir* (Turkish white cheese) or feta
250 g (9 oz) halloumi cheese, finely grated
25 g (1 oz) fresh flat leaf parsley leaves (stalks removed), finely chopped
10 g (¼ oz) fresh mint leaves (stalks removed), finely chopped
½ tsp dried mint
½ tsp *pul biber*
14 triangular-shaped sheets of filo pastry
500 ml (18 fl oz) sunflower or vegetable oil, for frying

Note

If you can't find triangular *üçgen yufka* pastry, then you can use regular filo sheets cut into triangles. However, please note that these filo sheets are a lot thinner, so the texture of the cigars will differ.

Whisk the egg well in a small bowl until light and frothy and leave to one side.

Crumble the *beyaz peynir* or feta into a large bowl with your hands and then break up any larger lumps with the back of a fork. Add the *hellim*, parsley and fresh mint, dried mint and *pul biber* and stir to combine. Add the beaten egg to the mixture and give it another good stir.

Unroll the filo pastry and cover with a damp tea towel, only removing sheets as you need them. Place one of the triangular pieces of filo on a flat surface in front of you, with the long, horizontal edge closest to you, and the point of the triangle furthest away.

Place one heaped tablespoon of the feta filling, in a line along the closest horizontal edge of the filo, leaving 2 cm (¾ inch) on both sides so that you can roll up the pastry without the mixture escaping. Fold over the two shorter sides by a couple of centimetres, then start to roll the closest horizontal edge away from you, as tightly as possible, to encase the filling and create a thin, cigar-shaped pastry. Dab a little cold water on the last point of the pastry to help seal the pastry together. Repeat the process until all the filo and filling has been used.

Pour the oil into a large deep frying pan so that it is about 3 cm (1 inch) deep. The larger the pan, the more oil you will need, and the more *Sigara Böreği* you'll be able to cook in one batch. If you have a food thermometer, heat the oil to around 180°C (350°F). If you don't have one, you can drop in a piece of filo to check that it sizzles – the filo should take its time to turn a lovely golden brown colour as this is how the pastry should cook, rather than burning too quickly (and the filling potentially staying cold). Gently lower 3–4 cigars into the hot oil and cook for 1–2 minutes on each side until golden brown and crispy. Using a large slotted spoon, transfer the cigars straight to a plate lined with kitchen paper to drain off any excess oil. Repeat with the remaining cigars and serve hot.

Tahın

Tahini Dip

Summers spent in Cyprus mean that cooking beautiful, freshly-caught fish and grilling it on the *mangal* (barbecue) is often the highlight of our meals, and no fish barbecue or seafood *meze* is complete without a side of *Tahın*. This nutty, tangy, garlicky tahini dip pairs beautifully with simple barbecued sea bream or bass, and many of the meat and fish barbecue recipes in the book.

Serves 6

200 g (7 oz) tahini
100 ml (3½ fl oz) cold water
100 ml (3½ fl oz) fresh lemon
   juice
¾ tsp sea salt flakes
¼ tsp crushed garlic
¼ tsp paprika (optional)
¼ tsp *pul biber* (optional)
1 tsp extra virgin olive oil
1 tsp finely chopped fresh
   parsley, to garnish

Put the tahini into a bowl and add the cold water. Whisk vigorously with a fork or very small whisk until fully amalgamated; the mixture should have a smooth, creamy consistency. Add the lemon juice and garlic, whisk vigorously again as the lemon juice will initially loosen the mixture and then it will thicken up again. Add the salt, and if using the spices, whisk them in now, too.

Pour the mixture into a serving dish, drizzle over the extra virgin olive oil and garnish with parsley.

The dip will store well in the fridge for 4–5 days.

Haşlanmış Sebze Çeşitler

Cypriot-style Boiled Vegetables

Who knew that a plate of boiled vegetables could be so enticing? Boiled whole, then thickly sliced and dressed generously while they are still warm, Cypriot-style boiled vegetables are simply eaten on their own or typically alongside *gabbar turşusu* (pickled caperberry leaves), black olives, *Melek Nene's Pazılı Kuru Börülce* (Dry Black-eyed Beans with Swiss Chard, page 149) or with oily, smoked fish such as *renga* (kipper), mackerel or tuna.

Serves 4–6

2 large Cyprus potatoes
2 large carrots, peeled
2 courgettes
50 g (1¾) dry black olives
1 onion, thickly sliced
1 tsp dried mint
4 tbsp fresh lemon juice
3 tbsp extra virgin olive oil
1 tsp sea salt flakes
½ tsp coarse black pepper
1 tbsp finely chopped fresh
    parsley leaves

Wash the potatoes and place them in a large pan. Cover the potatoes with cold water, place the pan over a high heat and bring to the boil. Reduce the heat, skim off any foam that rises to the top of the water and simmer the potatoes for 45 minutes–1 hour. Once they are ready, you should be able to easily slide a knife into the thickest part of the potatoes, without them falling apart.

While the potatoes are cooking, put the carrots in another large pan with the courgettes. Fill with cold water so that the vegetables are fully covered, then place the pan over a medium heat and bring to a simmer. Cook for 12–18 minutes (depending on their size) until you can also slide a knife through them with perhaps just a little resistance so that they don't fall apart or turn mushy.

Remove the potatoes, courgettes and carrots from the pans and leave to one side to cool. When the potatoes are cool enough to handle (but are still slightly warm), peel off their skins and thickly slice them. Slice the courgettes and carrots to the same size thickness as the potatoes, and place everything on a plate. Scatter over the dry black olives and onion.

Sprinkle the dried mint over the vegetables. Drizzle over the lemon juice and olive oil and season with the sea salt flakes and coarse black pepper. Garnish with the parsley.

(See image on page 148.)

Easy One-pots
& Slow-cooking

Yahni

Some of the most traditional dishes that, for me, are perhaps most representative of Cypriot cuisine are anything that is cooked *yahni*-style. Always served with rice on the side or bread to dip into, *yahni* is a Turkish word that signifies an oil, onion and tomato-based stew. Although traditionally made with meat, in Cyprus, anything can be cooked *yahni*, as long as it begins with that oil, tomato and onion base. Recipes are slow-cooked, to intensify a depth of flavour that makes *yahni*-style dishes taste even better the next day.

There are two recipes in this section that, for me, epitomise Turkish-Cypriot *yahni* recipes. *Tavuklu Kolokas Yemeği* (Chicken & Taro Root Stew, pages 92–3) is cooked by all Cypriots and will always remind me of Sunday afternoons at my Aunty Emine Hala's house. Emine Hala cooked this stew so frequently that my mum rarely made it at home as we always knew that we'd be graced with it at the dinner table whenever we'd pop in to see her. Taro root can be a little difficult to source, however, you will usually find it in international supermarkets in the springtime.

The second iconic recipe, my favourite and the ultimate Turkish-Cypriot meal for me, is *Molohiya* (Jute Mallow & Lamb Stew, page 76). It is the one dish I could eat any day of the year, as long as it is cooked to my mum's superior recipe, which is always made with lamb and produces a beautifully thick, silky, tomatoey gravy with whole peppercorns and lashings of lemon juice. The steps that form every part of the *molohiya* (jute mallow) ritual, from acquiring the leaves to cooking with them, is woven into unwritten family history. It is a dish that is specific to Turkish-Cypriot cuisine and one, unusually, that is not generally cooked by Greek-Cypriots. *Molohiya* can be cooked in a variety of ways and often gets likened to spinach, which I think is very misleading as it is completely unlike spinach in both texture and flavour. The almond-shaped leaves are more robust than spinach leaves, and in Turkish-Cypriot cuisine they are dried before being used. Their slightly slippery texture when slowly stewed naturally thickens the cooking liquid, resulting in a thick, luscious gravy. Since

Molohiya is a dish that is cooked in a variety of ways across Arabic cuisine, you can usually find the dried leaves in Turkish and Middle Eastern supermarkets.

In Cyprus, the ritual of *molohiya* all begins with the annual communal preparation of the fresh leaves. When we were younger, we would sit and pick the leaves from their stalks while sitting in my aunt Meyrem Teyze's front garden. After countless neighbours had stopped by for chats and infinite cups of Turkish coffee, my aunt would then lay the fresh leaves out on bed sheets to dry in the sun. There would then be (and still is) the excitement of getting the leaves over to our London homes; family members would stuff the dried leaves into pillowcases (which keeps them crisp and dry for the entirety of the year) ready for us to transport in our suitcases back to the UK. Once home, the crux of all our efforts would culminate in the cooking process, the part I enjoyed the most; there was the incomparable aroma as it cooked and the anticipation as my mum would stir the leaves into the braised lamb and tomato gravy. In only a few hours the delicious outcome of the collective ritual that had started weeks, if not months, ago would soon be ready to ladle into bowls and dipped into with freshly made bread. When I now cook it myself, I associate it with memories and mouthfuls that take me back 'home' and straight into my aunt's front garden in *Mağusa* (Famagusta).

There are dishes here, such as the *Deniz Ürünleri Yahnisi* (Mixed Seafood Stew, page 89) and the *Kıymalı Taze Fasulye Yahni* (Green Bean & Minced Beef Stew, page 90) that can be prepared and served quite quickly, but since the flavours of *yahni*-style dishes intensify when made in advance, many of them are best made ahead of time. The dried bean and meat-based dishes take a little longer to cook, so set aside a few lazy hours at the weekend to enjoy the process of cooking and eating these nourishing, wholesome meals – and take further comfort in enjoying the flavourful leftovers the next day.

Molohiya

Jute Mallow & Lamb Stew

I often get asked what my favourite dish is or what my 'last supper' would be. And this is it. There is nothing fancy or aesthetically complex about *Molohiya*, but it is a dish that is doused in memories of visiting my family in Cyprus.

It would always begin with the annual communal preparation of fresh *molohiya* leaves. My memory of this dish is that we would pick the leaves from their stalks whilst sitting in my auntie's front garden, pleasantly interrupted by the countless neighbours stopping by for chats. We would lay the leaves out on bed sheets to dry in the sun. There was then, of course, the excitement of getting the leaves over to our London homes; family members would stuff the dried *molohiya* leaves into pillowcases (which kept them crisp and dry).

Molohiya has an incomparably appetising aroma as it cooks, heightened by a preparation process that is riddled with anticipation. Excitedly, I would watch my mum stir the leaves into the braised lamb and tomato gravy, knowing that in only a few hours the delicious outcome of the collective ritual that started weeks, and even months, ago would soon be ready to ladle into bowls and dipped into with freshly made bread. And that is why the beauty of *Molohiya*, in my opinion, cannot be likened to any other dish or vegetable, and one that I can only associate with memories and mouthfuls that transport me straight back 'home' to my Aunt Teyze's veranda.

Serves 8–10 (with leftovers)

5 tbsp tbsp olive oil
1 kg (2 lb 4 oz) lamb leg or shoulder, cut into 3–4-cm (1–1½-inch) chunks
3 large onions, roughly chopped
6 garlic cloves, finely chopped
200 g (7 oz) dried *molohiya* leaves
2 × 400 g (14 oz) cans chopped or plum tomatoes
6 level tbsp tomato purée
1½ tsp sea salt flakes
1½ tsp ground black pepper
1 tsp whole black peppercorns
100 ml (3½ fl oz) fresh lemon juice
2 litres (3½ pints) water

Add the olive oil to a large pan and place over a high heat. Once the oil is hot, add the lamb and reduce to a medium heat. Brown the lamb for a few minutes until the colour changes completely (the meat won't crisp up as the pan will be overcrowded, but that's fine), then add the onions and garlic and stir well. Reduce the heat to low and let everything simmer with the lid on for around an hour.

Wash the *molohiya* leaves in the sink in lots of cold water, being careful not to crush the leaves. Once washed, place them in a large colander and leave in the sink to drain fully.

After the lamb has been cooking for an hour, add the tomatoes to the pan, breaking them up as you stir them through. Add the tomato purée, salt, pepper and peppercorns to the pan and stir again before adding the lemon juice. Start to add handfuls of the washed *molohiya* leaves to the pan, gently pushing them down into the juices. Stir the leaves well, add the water, increase the heat to bring everything to the boil, then reduce to a medium–low heat and simmer for 2–2½ hours with the lid on, checking every 30 minutes and giving it a gentle stir.

Remove the pan from the heat and let the *molohiya* settle for an hour with the lid on, so that the gravy has a chance to thicken before serving.

Magarına Bulli (Yahni)

Cypriot-style Pasta & Chicken

I adore the name of this dish, *Magarına Bulli*, which in the Turkish-Cypriot dialect simply translates as 'pasta chicken'. The two words combined make such a comforting recipe sound even more beautiful in its rustic simplicity. Upon our many travels to *Kıbrıs* (Cyprus) as children, this would always be the first meal my cousins and I would excitedly ask my aunt Teyze to make us. We would all wait (im)patiently on her beautiful rooftop terrace and watch the sun setting across the *Mağusa* (Famagusta) skyline, eagerly awaiting the finished dish. My own children now do the same when we visit Meyrem Teyze, and I sit and watch my beautiful memories come alive all over again.

The *yahni* refers to the oil, onion and tomato-based sauce that *Magarına Bulli* can be cooked and served with. This really is a gloriously simple, classic Cypriot dish that is made even better with a few extra touches, such as pouring the hot roasted chicken fat over the cooked pasta and spooning over an extra ladleful of the chicken stock to serve. If serving the *yahni* with the *magarına bulli*, then simply cook the *yahni* when you start boiling the pasta.

Serves 4–6

1 chicken stock cube
200 ml (7 fl oz) boiling water
8–10 skin-on, bone-in chicken thighs
3 litres (5¼ pints) cold water
1 tsp sea salt flakes
2 tbsp olive oil
½ tsp coarse black pepper
500 g (1 lb 2 oz) pasta (traditionally a pasta similar to bucatini is used)
200 g (7 oz) halloumi cheese, finely grated
2 tsp dried mint
Juice of ½ lemon (optional)

For the *yahni*

3 tbsp olive oil
1 large onion, very finely chopped
4 ripe tomatoes, grated
1 tbsp tomato purée
1 tbsp Turkish sweet red pepper paste (*tatlı biber salçası*)

Preheat the oven to 220°C/200°C fan/425°F/gas mark 7.

Dissolve the stock cube in the boiling water in a heatproof jug and put to one side.

Place the chicken thighs in a large heavy-based pan and cover with the cold water. Bring to the boil, add the stock and salt and simmer over a low heat. After 30 minutes, remove six of the chicken thighs to an ovenproof dish, add two ladles of the stock to the dish, brush the chicken thighs with the olive oil, season with a little, not all, of the black pepper and place the dish on the bottom shelf of the oven for around 30 minutes until the chicken is golden brown and crispy, basting halfway through. Leave the remaining chicken thighs to boil in the pan for a further 15–20 minutes, then remove from the pan to a plate to cool.

Bring the stock back up to the boil and add the pasta (if using the traditional bucatini-shaped pasta, snap the thin tubes into thirds before adding them to the pan). Cook the pasta for 10–12 minutes. This is when you should also start to cook the *yahni* in a separate pan (see instructions below).

For the *yahni*

While the pasta is cooking, heat the olive oil in a frying pan on a medium–low heat and soften the onion for 10–12 minutes, then stir in the tomatoes, tomato purée and sweet red pepper paste. Allow it to start to bubble and reduce for a minute, then remove from the heat.

Meanwhile, shred the cooled, boiled chicken, removing and discarding the fat, skin and bones and reserve the meat to one side. Remove the baked crispy chicken from the oven and leave to one side.

Put the *hellim*, dried mint and the remaining black pepper in a small bowl and mix together.

When the pasta is cooked, don't drain in a colander. Instead use a large slotted spoon and serve the pasta straight on to a large platter or individual plates that have been sprinkled with a little of the *hellim* and dried mint mixture. Add the reserved shredded boiled chicken to the pasta and pour over all of the delicious chicken-flavoured oils from the dish that was in the oven. Give everything a gentle stir. Pour the *yahni* over the pasta to serve.

Sprinkle the pasta generously with more of the *hellim* and dried mint mixture and a little more black pepper, to taste. You could pour a couple more ladles of the stock over the pasta just before serving, too. Squeeze over the lemon juice, if using, and serve the pasta alongside the roast chicken and a fresh salad.

Check the onions, and when fully softened, add the cumin, paprika and tomato purée and stir well before adding the tomato quarters that you set aside. Allow the tomatoes to soften and bubble for 3—4 minutes, then add the taro root pieces. Stir well so that the vegetable gets coated in the oily spices and tomatoes before returning the chicken and its juices to the pan. Stir well and add the cold water to the pan. Bring everything to the boil, reduce the heat to a low simmer and cook for 35—45 minutes until the taro root is tender (do not overcook as it will start to fall apart) and the sauce has thickened. Add the lemon juice and scatter over the parsley, taste and add a little more seasoning if necessary. Place the lid back on the pan and let the stew sit for 30 minutes before serving, to allow the flavours to intensify.

Quick Cooking for Busy Weeknights

Pratik Yemekler

I don't know if it's because we potentially lead busier lives nowadays, or that because I now have my own family to look after while working, that I appreciate more than ever the need for a hearty catalogue of quick and easy midweek recipes that I can rely on time and time again. I was an energetic child who could never sit still, and my mum would always say to me, '*götünde ispanak tohunu var*' (an old Turkish-Cypriot proverb which translates as, 'you have spinach roots in your bottom', similar to the English saying, 'you've got ants in your pants'). In fact, my mum still says this to me now – and she is no different – we both rarely sit down when working or cooking.

My mum juggled a full-time job as a seamstress while chauffeuring three children back and forth from school and to countless after-school activities, but she never failed to adorn the dinner table with a satisfying family meal every night. She would regularly prepare large trays of slow-cooked oven dishes and one-pot meals that we would eat for two or three days in a row and would simply serve them up with a quick side of *Şehriyeli Pilav* (Vermicelli Rice, page 102) or *Domatesli Bulgur Pilavı* (Tomato Bulgur Wheat Rice, page 103). I also remember eating pasta dishes where the pasta would be cooked in the sauce rather than boiled in water, much like my *Hellimli Domatesli Magarına* (One-pot Halloumi & Tomato Pasta, page 113) to enable the pasta to soak up all the juices and flavours of the ingredients within the pan, just as the rice does in one-pot dishes such as the *Pırasa Yemeği* (Sautéed Leeks, page 100) and Ispanak Yemeği (Spinach, Mince & Rice, page 105).

Then there are quick, practical dishes I remember, that can be served for breakfast, lunch or dinner, and can be prepared in no time at all. Soup is not unheard of at breakfast time in a Cypriot or Turkish household, and hotels in Northern Cyprus and Turkey always have a soup table as you enter the restaurant. My dad would frequently start his Saturday mornings making *Baba's Domatesli Pirinç Çorbası* (Dad's Tomato & Rice Soup, page 110) using rice, canned tomatoes, stock and onions from the store cupboard, and fresh parsley and lemons from the fridge. Just a few humble ingredients, and in a matter of minutes, his soup would be simmering on the hob ready for a late breakfast or lunch.

Store-cupboard ingredients are also essential in enhancing quick, easy meals, and dried herbs and spices like oregano, mint and *pul biber* can really elevate dishes such as scrambled eggs or sautéed vegetables (another Cypriot household favourite). My mum, still to this day, refuses to cook chips any other way than fried in oil on the stove. For a quick meal, she would cut potatoes into cubes, fry them, then add whisked eggs right at the end and quickly scramble them into the potatoes. I have an updated version of this – *Yumurtalı Hellim ve Sebze* (Eggy Halloumi & Sautéed Vegetables) on page 108 – which has become a popular lunch and dinner favourite with my own children.

And there is no denying the versatility of quick-cooking fish, such as cod, salmon and sea bass fillets for fast midweek Cypriot-style suppers. Try the *Domatesli Balık* (Baked White Fish in Tomato Sauce, page 115) or *Kızarmış Levrek, Ayrelli ve Kuru Lima Fasulye* (Pan-fried Sea Bass with Asparagus & Butter Beans, page 120) for a speedy meal. Kids will also adore my *Somonlu Köfte ve Domatesli Arpa Şehriye* (Salmon Fish Balls with Tomato Orzo, page 119).

The recipes in this chapter are a combination of traditional family recipes and my own, quirky adaptations of Cypriot classics to suit modern, busy lifestyles, most of which can be prepared and on the dinner table within 30 minutes. Just make sure your store cupboard is always topped up with the most used and recommended spices and condiments that I have listed at the beginning of the book (see pages 16–17).

Pırasa Yemeği

Sautéed Leeks

This is such a simple plant-based recipe that takes hardly any time to prepare or to cook. *Pırasa* (leeks) are a common ingredient in Turkish and Cypriot dishes, served hot or cold as a *zeytinyağlı* (olive-oil-based) cold *meze* dish. When making this recipe, do try and give yourself that little bit of extra time to really soften and caramelise the finely chopped onions, and the same goes for the leeks and carrots as those caramelised, slightly browned edges really do sweeten and enhance the flavour of vegetable-based dishes like this one.

Serves 2 as a main, or 4 with sides

2 large, ripe plum tomatoes (300 g/10½ oz)
500 g (1 lb 2 oz) leeks
3 tbsp olive oil
1 small onion, finely diced
¼ tsp paprika
¼ tsp ground cumin
300 g (10½ oz) carrots, peeled and sliced
2 garlic cloves, finely grated
1 tbsp tomato purée
1 tbsp Turkish sweet red pepper paste (*tatlı biber salçası*)
40 g (1½ oz) long-grain white rice
¾ tsp salt
¾ tsp coarse black pepper
200 ml (7 fl oz) water
Salt and pepper to taste

Halve the tomatoes, then coarsely grate them, flesh side facing the grater, into a bowl. Discard the skins.

Cut the leeks into 2–3 cm (1 inch) rounds and wash thoroughly to remove any dirt, while trying to keep the layers fully intact.

Heat the olive oil in a large pan over a medium heat and add the onion. Reduce the heat and soften and caramelise the onion for 10–12 minutes, then add the spices and salt and pepper to taste and stir well. Add the carrots and leeks and fry for another 3–5 minutes until the edges of the vegetables start to caramelise. Add the garlic and cook for a minute or two before adding the tomato purée and sweet red pepper paste, carefully stirring to coat the vegetables in the pastes. Add the tomatoes, stir again, reduce the heat, put the lid on the pan and let everything cook for around 8–10 minutes. Stir regularly throughout the cooking time to ensure the bottom of the pan doesn't burn.

Add the rice, stir through the salt and pepper, then pour in the water and let everything simmer with the lid on for another 10–12 minutes until the rice is just cooked. Remove the pan from the heat, keep the lid on for a couple of minutes so that the rice keeps absorbing the juices, and serve with fresh bread and yoghurt.

Şehriyeli Pilav

Vermicelli Rice

Whether you are sitting down to eat a meat or vegetable-based kebab, casserole or stew in a Turkish-Cypriot household, it is very rare not to have a large helping of this rice as a side dish. It is also delicious served on its own with a huge dollop of thick set natural yoghurt (see page 52 on how to strain your own yoghurt).

In Cyprus, *tel şehriye* (fine vermicelli, which is pronounced *şehirge* in the Turkish-Cypriot dialect) is traditionally used as the fried fine pasta base before the rice and stock is added, but in Turkey, *arpa şehriye* (orzo pasta) is more commonly used. I like to make this with easy-cook long-grain white rice as it has a beautiful buttery consistency once cooked in stock (I use a ratio of two and a half parts rice to one part water). This recipe is extremely quick and easy to make, taking no longer than 20 minutes from start to finish, and is perfect any time of year for both midweek dinners and as a wholesome side dish at dinner parties – just allow it some time to settle before serving.

Serves 4–6, as a side dish

250 g (9 oz) easy-cook long-grain white rice
1 chicken or vegetable stock cube
½ tsp salt
625 ml (21 fl oz) boiling water
3 tbsp vegetable oil
4 tbsp crushed vermicelli
20 g (¾ oz) unsalted butter

Pour the rice into a sieve, wash well with cold water until the water runs clear, and leave to drain over a large bowl.

Dissolve the stock cube and salt in the boiling water and leave to one side.

Heat the oil in a medium-sized pan over a medium heat. Add the vermicelli to the pan and stir continuously until it starts to turn a golden brown. Remove the pan from the heat and allow the vermicelli to cool down for a minute or two. The vermicelli will continue to darken a little more once off the heat.

Add the rice to the pan, along with the butter, and stir well so that the rice is coated in the oil, and the vermicelli and rice are evenly dispersed.

Pour the stock into the pan, stir well then return the pan to the hob over a medium–low heat. Bring to the boil, then reduce the heat and allow the rice to simmer for about 10–12 minutes or until the stock has been almost fully absorbed by the rice (bubble holes will start to appear in the rice when it's almost ready).

Remove the pan from the heat, cover with a couple of sheets of kitchen paper and the pan lid, and let the rice sit in the pan for a few minutes. Fluff up with a fork before serving.

(See image on page 77.)

Domatesli Bulgur Pilavı

Tomato Bulgur Wheat Rice

There are some meals that call out for *Şehriyeli Pilav* (Vermicelli Rice, opposite) and there are others that are not complete without a hearty portion of *Domatesli Bulgur Pilavı*. One of the most important elements of this recipe is to ensure that you really soften and caramelise those onions so that they add a lovely sweetness to the grains of bulgur wheat, which are complemented by the sweetness of the *tatlı biber salçası* (Turkish sweet red pepper paste) and contrast with the subtle heat from the *pul biber*. We always cook our bulgur wheat in stock for extra flavour, and it's essential to remove the pan from the heat when there is still some liquid left, and to cover it with kitchen paper and the lid to rest before serving. This ensures a lovely creamy texture and although it's delicious served with *Patates Köftesi* (Cypriot Potato & Mince Fried Meatballs, page 136), *Cacık* (Yoghurt, Mint & Cucumber Dip, page 52) and any salad side dish, I'm quite partial to a bowl of it on its on with a whacking great dollop of thick set natural yoghurt. It stores well in the fridge for a couple of days and can be warmed up again before serving.

Serves 4–6, as a side dish

1 vegetable stock cube
2 tbsp tomato purée
1 tbsp Turkish sweet red pepper paste (*tatlı biber salçası*)
½ tsp *pul biber*
½ tsp salt
600 ml (20 fl oz) boiling water
3 tbsp olive or sunflower oil
1 large onion, finely diced
80 g (2¾ oz) crushed vermicelli
25 g (1 oz) unsalted butter
250 g (9 oz) coarse bulgur wheat

Add the stock cube, tomato purée, sweet red pepper paste, *pul biber* and salt to a heatproof jug, then pour in the boiling water and stir well until everything has fully dissolved. Leave to one side.

Heat two tablespoons of the oil in a medium-sized pan over a medium heat. Add the onion and soften over a low heat for 12–15 minutes until almost translucent and very lightly golden brown. Remove the onion from the pan to a plate, add the remaining one tablespoon of oil to the pan and the crushed vermicelli, stirring continuously for a minute or so until the vermicelli turns a light golden-brown colour. Add the butter to the pan, stir it through the vermicelli, then add the bulgur wheat and cook for another 3–4 minutes to seal the grains (some of them may start to turn white). Return the onion to the pan, stir well for 30 seconds, then remove the pan from the heat and allow it to cool for a couple of minutes (otherwise the stock will violently splutter when it is added).

Return the pan to the hob over a medium–low heat and carefully pour in the stock mixture, stirring gently. Bring back to the boil, then reduce the heat to low, place the lid on the pan and cook for about 8–10 minutes or until the stock has almost fully evaporated (there should be little bubble holes that start to appear in the bulgur wheat). Remove the pan from the heat and cover with a sheet of kitchen paper, then the lid. Leave to rest for 15–20 minutes. Fluff up with a fork before serving.

Ispanak Yemeği

Spinach, Mince & Rice

Meals that include vegetables, meat, grains or pulses all cooked in one pan are typical of traditional Turkish and Cypriot meals. Easy cooking for busy lifestyles, very much suited to the Western way of life, too. There is a clear chronological process for when each ingredient is added to ensure that it is appropriately cooked, never under or over. Often served in a bowl, meals like this *Ispanak Yemeği* are served with yoghurt on the side. When in season, *semizotu* (purslane) is also an excellent and equally nutritious substitute for the spinach.

Serves 4

500 g (1 lb 2 oz) fresh spinach
75 g (2¾ oz) long-grain white
 rice
3 tbsp olive oil
1 tsp salt
1 large onion, finely chopped
2 large garlic cloves, finely
 chopped
500 g (1 lb 2 oz) minced beef
 or lamb
2 tbsp tomato purée
1 tbsp Turkish sweet red pepper
 paste (*tatlı biber salçası*)
½ tsp ground black pepper
400 ml (14 fl oz) water

Wash the spinach really well, then roughly chop. Wash the rice in a sieve until the water runs clear, then leave to drain.

Add the olive oil to a large, deep pan and place over a medium heat. Add the onion and soften for 10–12 minutes (if the onion starts to darken too much, reduce the heat a little). Add the garlic, soften for another minute before adding the minced beef or lamb, breaking it up well in the pan with a wooden spoon. Turn up the heat and cook for 5–6 minutes, then stir in the tomato purée and the sweet red pepper paste and keep cooking for a couple of minutes until it all starts to sizzle. Reduce the heat and add the spinach to the pan, gently pushing it down with the spoon so that the leaves start to wilt. Add the rice to the pan, season with the salt and pepper and pour in the water. Bring the mixture to a simmer, reduce the heat and cook for 8–10 minutes until the rice is tender and the juices have cooked down to a lovely, luscious sauce. Serve with cold, thick set natural yoghurt and a hunk of fresh bread.

Tavuklu Tantuni

Chicken, Tomato, Onion & Parsley Wraps

Tantuni (meat-filled, flour-based wraps) originate from the city of Mersin, a southern Turkish port on the Mediterranean coast. There are of course, many variations of meat-filled, flour-based wraps all around the world, but the nostalgia of growing up with a simple cheat's version of *tantuni* at home (which my mum would often make with minced beef or chicken, served in homemade wraps) has inevitably made this a regularly cooked meal in my own household, too. I frequently make this with chicken, as per the recipe below, simply because it requires less time to cook, but you could use finely chopped quick-frying beef rump or sirloin, or lamb rump.

Serves 4–6

1 kg (2 lb 4 oz) skinless, boneless chicken thighs
2 tbsp olive oil
6 garlic cloves, finely chopped
1 tsp ground cumin
1 tsp paprika
2 tbsp Turkish sweet red pepper paste (*tatlı biber salçası*)
1 tsp salt
½ tsp ground black pepper
100 ml (3½ fl oz) water

To serve

1 large onion, finely sliced
1 tsp sumac
25 g (1 oz) fresh parsley leaves
4 large, ripe plum tomatoes
8 flatbreads, warmed

Cut the chicken into thin strips and then dice the strips as small as possible. Leave to one side.

Heat the olive oil in a large pan over a medium heat, add the garlic and soften for a minute, stirring constantly, then add the chicken pieces and stir well. Brown the chicken for 4–5 minutes, add the spices and sweet red pepper paste, stir well, and let everything start to sizzle before seasoning with the salt and pepper and adding the water. Cook over a high heat for another 4–5 minutes until the juices have reduced down considerably, but not completely.

Place the onion in a bowl, add the sumac, and stir well. Finely chop the parsley and place in separate bowl. Dice the tomato and place in separate bowl.

Take a warm flatbread, place one side down into the pan to absorb the juices, then lay flat and fill with some of the chicken, some onion and sumac mix, a spoonful of tomatoes and a sprinkling of parsley. Roll up to serve.

Yumurtalı Hellim ve Sebze

Eggy Halloumi & Sautéed Vegetables

There was always some kind of vegetable being cooked in olive oil on the stove when I was a kid; potatoes, courgettes, mushrooms, spinach, onions, would be pan-fried on their own, but rarely together as often it would depend on what was in season, or what was in the fridge. In true Meliz style, I've whacked everything together with the addition of my brother-in-law's favourite contribution; unctuous cubes of crispy-on-the-outside-soft-in-the-middle fried *hellim* (halloumi). We all adore this dish, especially my little girl who always asks for it for lunch. Boiling the whole, peeled potatoes omits the need to first fry them heavily in too much oil – just ensure you pat the parboiled potato slices dry before adding them to the olive oil with the courgettes so that they really crisp up while cooking.

**Serves 2 as a main,
4 as a side dish**

250 g (9 oz) small or medium-sized Cyprus or Maris Piper potatoes
125 g (4½ oz) halloumi cheese
1 large courgette
6 large eggs
4 tbsp olive oil
2 spring onions, finely sliced
300 g (10½ oz) chestnut mushrooms, finely sliced
1 tsp dried mint
½ tsp dried oregano
¾ tsp salt
¾ tsp coarse black pepper
200 g (7 oz) baby spinach leaves, roughly chopped
1 tsp freshly squeezed lemon juice
¼ tsp *pul biber*
25 g (1 oz) fresh coriander leaves, chopped
12 dry black olives

Wash the potatoes, leave them whole and add to a large pan of cold water. Bring to the boil and cook for 15 minutes while you prepare the rest of the ingredients.

Pat dry the *hellim* with kitchen paper and cut into 2-cm (1-inch) cubes. Halve the courgette lengthways and finely slice into semicircles. Set to one side.

Whisk the eggs in a bowl and leave to one side.

Drain the cooked potatoes in a colander and allow them to dry and cool for a couple of minutes, then when cool enough to handle, thinly slice.

Add two tablespoons of the olive oil to a large frying pan over a medium heat, and once hot, add the *hellim*, browning the cubes on all sides quickly to avoid burning them. Remove to a plate lined with kitchen paper. Add the remaining two tablespoons of olive oil to the pan, allow to heat up for 30 seconds, then add the sliced potatoes and courgettes. Brown the slices on one side for a couple of minutes, without stirring at first, then flip them over to brown the other side, adding the spring onions and mushrooms to the pan, too. Allow the mushrooms to start browning without stirring them, then add the dried mint and oregano and give everything a stir so that the mushrooms cook on both sides.

Season with the salt and pepper, add the fried *hellim* back into the pan, then add the spinach, stirring well for a couple of minutes to encourage the greens to wilt into the other vegetables. Reduce the heat, pour in the eggs, and as soon as they start to bubble and cook around the edges (after around 30 seconds), give them a gentle toss over into the middle of the pan, and lightly stir a couple of times to scramble them into the *hellim* and vegetables. Serve immediately, squeezing over the lemon juice, a sprinkling of *pul biber* and finally garnish with the fresh coriander and black olives.

Dad's Tomato & Rice Soup

My dad has two signature soups that he would always cook for us. One is a cauliflower soup, which essentially consists of boiled cauliflower florets, rice and lots of lemon juice, but the one I've included here is my favourite, *Baba's Domatesli Pirinç Çorbası* (Dad's Tomato & Rice Soup).

This is not a recipe that has been passed down from my dad's family, but one that my dad concocted using a couple of fresh ingredients from the fridge, and the rest from the store cupboard. It's so simple, both in terms of ingredients and method, and my dad occasionally uses a can of chopped tomatoes in place of the fresh ones I use in my recipe. Rice is a key ingredient in most Cypriot soups and seasoning soups with lemon juice is fundamental to Cypriot cuisine, so do ensure you have some fresh lemon to hand when making this one.

Serves 4

200 g (7 oz) short-grain white rice
6 large tomatoes
50 ml (2 fl oz) olive oil
1 large onion, finely chopped
1 vegetable stock cube
500 ml (18 fl oz) boiling water
1.5 litres (2½ pints) cold water
25 g (1 oz) fresh parsley, finely chopped
½ tsp paprika
½ tsp caster sugar
¾ tsp salt
1 tsp black pepper
2 tbsp fresh lemon juice, plus extra to taste

Wash the rice in a sieve with cold water until the water runs clear. Leave to drain.

Place the tomatoes in a deep heatproof bowl. Pour over boiling water to cover and leave for a minute or two. Remove the tomatoes from the bowl, peel off the skins, discard, and then finely chop the flesh. Leave to one side.

Pour the olive oil into a large pan and place over a medium heat. Add the onion and soften for 10–12 minutes until lightly caramelised.

While the onion is cooking, dissolve the stock cube in the boiling water, then top up with the cold water.

Stir the parsley, paprika and tomatoes into the caramelised onions and let everything sizzle for a minute or two before adding the rice, giving the grains a good stir so that they get fully coated in the tomatoes and onion. Sprinkle in the sugar, then gently pour in the stock and season with the salt and pepper. Allow the soup to simmer over a medium heat for around 10 minutes until the rice is cooked. Add the lemon juice a couple of minutes before you remove the pan from the heat and serve with crusty bread, adding a little more lemon juice to taste.

Hellimli Domatesli Magarına

One-pot Halloumi & Tomato Pasta

This dish does exactly what it says on the tin, a one-pot pasta recipe that begins with a delicious tomatoey base and, in true Cypriot fashion, is finished off with a liberal coating of grated *hellim* (halloumi) and dried mint. Sweet caramelised onions, cinnamon and bay give the dish its essential Cypriot umami – this is a dish that is perfect served on its own, but one that goes well with a fresh and simple portion of *Salata* (Salad, page 54) on the side.

Serves 4–6

3 tbsp olive oil
2 onions, finely chopped
4 garlic cloves, finely grated
½ tsp paprika
1 tsp ground cinnamon
½ tsp sea salt flakes
1 tsp coarse black pepper, plus extra to serve (optional)
6 tsp dried mint, plus extra to serve (optional)
4 tbsp tomato purée
400 g (14 oz) can chopped tomatoes
1 chicken or vegetable stock cube
500 ml (18 fl oz) boiling water
2 bay leaves
300 g (10½ oz) penne pasta
1 tbsp fresh flat leaf parsley, finely chopped
150 g (5½ oz) halloumi cheese, grated, plus extra to serve (optional)
Extra virgin olive oil, to serve

Heat the 3 tablespoons of olive oil in a large non-stick pan over a medium heat and add the onions, softening until caramelised for around 12–15 minutes. Add the garlic and stir for around a minute or two, then add the paprika, cinnamon, salt, half a teaspoon of the black pepper and two teaspoons of the dried mint and stir well. Add the tomato purée and the chopped tomatoes, stir well and reduce the heat down to the lowest simmer and let everything cook for 2–3 minutes while you get the stock ingredients ready. Keep checking the pan and giving it the occasional stir to make sure it doesn't catch on the bottom of the pan.

Add the stock cube to a large measuring jug and dissolve fully in 500 ml (18 fl oz) boiling water. Fill the empty can of chopped tomatoes with cold water, add to the jug, stir, then top up with as much as necessary to bring the stock mixture up to 1 litre (1¾ pints).

Add the bay leaves and the pasta to the pan, stir everything through the mixture, then pour in the stock. Stir the pasta well, bring to the boil, then reduce to a low–medium simmer for around 12–15 minutes.

In a bowl, combine the grated *hellim* with two teaspoons of dried mint and the remaining half teaspoon of black pepper.

Once the pasta has cooked (there should still be some juices in the pan, but the sauce should have reduced down), carefully pour it into a large serving dish, stir through the parsley, the *hellim* and the remaining two teaspoons of dried mint. Drizzle over some extra virgin olive oil to serve and garnish with extra *hellim*, dried mint and black pepper if desired.

Domatesli Balık

Baked White Fish in Tomato Sauce

As I mentioned in the Introduction, my mum's father, Ahmet Dede, was a fisherman, and consequently, we grew up eating a lot of fish at home. Various recipes for fish stews can be found in abundance in Cyprus and across the Mediterranean, and although the ingredients list for my recipe here looks a little lengthy, most of the items are my most-used fresh and store cupboard ingredients. The subtle use of pomegranate molasses adds a tart sweetness to dish, resulting in a luscious sauce that is perfect for dipping fresh bread into or eating alongside *Şehriyeli Pilav* (Vermicelli Rice, page 102) and a fresh salad. Using a fish that cooks quickly, like cod, hake or halibut, will enable you to get this dish from stove to table in under 30 minutes.

Serves 4

4 large ripe tomatoes
1 vegetable stock cube
300 ml (10 fl oz) boiling water
30 g (1 oz) unsalted butter
1 large onion, finely sliced
4 large garlic cloves, finely chopped
1 tsp white wine vinegar
½ tsp *pul biber*
¾ tsp salt
¾ tsp coarse black pepper
1 tbsp tomato purée
1 tbsp Turkish sweet red pepper paste (*tatlı biber salçası*)
1 tbsp pomegranate molasses
4 × 150 g (5½ oz) cod fillets
1 tbsp fresh lemon juice
25 g (1 oz) fresh parsley leaves, finely chopped

Halve the tomatoes and grate them (flesh side facing the grater) into a large bowl, discarding the skins and hard cores. In a heatproof jug, dissolve the stock cube in the boiling water.

Heat the butter in a large pan over a medium heat, and once melted, add the onion and soften for 4–5 minutes, then add the garlic and stir gently for another couple of minutes. Increase the heat and add the white wine vinegar, half of the *pul biber* and most, but not all, of the salt and pepper and give it a stir. Add the tomatoes, tomato purée and the sweet red pepper paste, stirring well and reducing the mixture for 2–3 minutes.

Stir through the pomegranate molasses, then slowly pour in the stock, stirring well. Put the lid on the pan and let the sauce bubble and reduce for 3–4 minutes. Pat the cod fillets dry, season them with the remaining salt, pepper and *pul biber*, then add to the pan, nestling them into the sauce and gently flipping them over so that they are coated on both sides. Reduce the heat and cook the fish, without the lid on, for 4–5 minutes. Squeeze over the lemon juice, put the lid on and remove the pan from the heat. Leave to rest for 2 minutes, then sprinkle over the parsley and serve with fresh crusty bread and a salad on the side.

Karides Sote

Sautéed Prawns

When we visit one of our favourite fish restaurants in *Kıbrıs* (Cyprus), the chef often makes us a complimentary dish of *Karides Güveç* (baked prawn stew); king prawns are sautéed with vegetables, then portioned into small clay pots, covered with *kaşar peyniri* (a smooth, firm, pale yellow cheese made of cow's milk, similar to Gouda or Edam), baked in the oven until the cheese has melted, and served with fresh crusty bread. Omitting the cheese and the oven-baked method results in a very quick and easy midweek meal, but if you find yourself with some extra time on your hands and fancy something a little more indulgent, feel free to add the cheese and pop the pan under the grill for a couple of minutes.

Serves 4

350 g (12 oz) raw tiger or large king prawns, peeled
¾ tsp sea salt flakes
½ tsp cracked black pepper
2 large garlic cloves, finely grated or crushed
25 g (1 oz) unsalted butter, softened
1 large, ripe plum tomato (150 g /5½ oz)
3 tbsp olive oil
1 large onion, chopped into 2½-cm (1-inch) pieces
2 sweet red *kapya* or romano peppers, chopped into 2½-cm (1-inch) pieces
2 long green peppers or Charleston peppers, chopped into 2½-cm (1-inch) pieces
½ tsp smoked paprika
¼ tsp ground cumin
1 tsp dried oregano
1 tbsp Turkish sweet red pepper paste (*tatlı biber salçası*)
1 tsp *pul biber*
1 tsp fresh lemon juice
10 g (¼ oz) finely chopped fresh flat leaf parsley leaves

Devein the prawns, then pat them dry and add to a bowl with a drizzle of olive oil, season with half of the salt and pepper and stir to combine.

Take a separate bowl and add the garlic and softened butter. Mash with a fork until fully combined.

Halve the tomato, then grate into a bowl (cut side facing the grater) and discard the skin and hard core.

Heat one and a half tablespoons of the olive oil in a large pan over a high heat. Add the prawns to the pan and char for a couple of minutes on both sides until their flesh turns lovely and pink. Add the garlic butter to the pan, cooking the prawns in the butter for a minute or so, then remove the mixture to a dish.

Pour the remaining one and a half tablespoons of olive oil into the pan, then add the onion and peppers and cook for 3–4 minutes over a high heat. Add the smoked paprika, cumin and oregano and stir well to allow the spices to release their aromas. Add the sweet red pepper paste and tomato to the vegetables, stir, then allow the mixture to start to bubble and reduce. Return the prawns to the pan, give them a stir to coat in the mixture, then stir through the *pul biber* and lemon juice, garnish with the parsley and serve immediately with rice or fresh bread on the side.

Somonlu Köfte ve Domatesli Arpa Şehriye

Salmon Fish Balls & Tomato Orzo

This recipe combines my mum's recipe for *Domatesli Arpa Şehriye* (Tomato Orzo), which was a regular on-the-table-in-ten-minutes kind of meal when we were younger, with my baked, pescatarian take on traditional *Patates Köftesi* (Cypriot Potato & Mince Fried Meatballs, page 136). Rolling the baked salmon fish balls in the tangy pomegranate molasses, lemon and mint dressing is a method I use when baking any kind of *köfte*, which makes them just as tasty, but inevitably healthier than their fried counterparts. I love to eat this with some steamed green vegetables that can be tossed in the same dressing as the salmon fish balls.

Makes 20 fish balls

2 tbsp olive oil
400 g (14 oz) Maris Piper or Cyprus potatoes, peeled and finely grated
1 onion, finely grated
500 g (1 lb 2 oz) skinless, boneless salmon fillets, roughly chopped into small pieces
30g finely chopped fresh parsley leaves
¼ tsp ground cumin
¼ tsp paprika
½ tsp smoked paprika
¾ tsp salt
¾ tsp coarse black pepper
100 g (3½ oz) fine breadcrumbs
1 egg

For the orzo

1 chicken stock cube
1 tbsp Turkish sweet red pepper paste (*tatlı biber salçası*)
1 tbsp tomato purée
¼ tsp salt
800 ml (1⅓ pints) boiling water
30 g (1 oz) unsalted butter
200 g (7 oz) orzo

For the dressing

1 tbsp pomegranate molasses
1 tbsp fresh lemon juice
1 tsp extra virgin olive oil
1 tsp dried mint
¼ tsp cracked black pepper

Preheat the oven to 200°C/180°C fan/400°F/gas mark 6.

Line a large baking sheet with greaseproof paper and brush with one tablespoon of olive oil.

Prepare the stock for the orzo. In a large heatproof jug, dissolve the stock cube, sweet red pepper paste, tomato purée and salt in the boiling water. Leave to one side.

Put the grated potatoes and onion into a sieve. Squeeze out as much of the liquid as possible. Leave in the sieve to drain a little longer.

Put the salmon pieces into a food processor and pulse a few times until the pieces have been chopped even smaller. Transfer to a large bowl. Squeeze the grated potato and onion one last time, then add to the salmon with the parsley, cumin, paprika, smoked paprika, salt, pepper, breadcrumbs and the egg. Place a large bowl of cold water next to you, and with clean hands, mix together the ingredients. Wet the palms of your hands with the cold water, take a golf-ball-sized portion of the mixture, and shape into a smooth ball. Place on the prepared baking sheet and repeat until you have 20 salmon balls in total.

Place the baking sheet on the middle shelf of the oven and cook for 8 minutes. Remove from the oven, brush each of the fish balls with the remaining one tablespoon of olive oil and put the baking sheet back in the oven for another 8–10 minutes until the fish balls are golden brown.

For the orzo, place a large pan over a medium heat, add the butter and melt. Once sizzling, stir through the orzo, pour in the stock, bring to the boil, then reduce the heat to a simmer for 7–8 minutes.

For the dressing, put the pomegranate molasses, lemon juice, olive oil, dried mint and black pepper in a large dish and stir to combine. Remove the fish balls from the oven and add them straight to the dressing, rolling them around so that they are fully coated.

Serve the dressed fish balls immediately with the tomato orzo.

Kızarmış Levrek, Ayrelli ve Kuru Lima Fasulye

Pan-fried Sea Bass with Asparagus & Butter Beans

I adore fresh asparagus when in season, and seeing it overtake vast masses of Cypriot fields in its wild abundance is a beautiful sight. Asparagus is only eaten seasonally in Cyprus, and I encourage you to do the same wherever you live, as the true beauty of its flavour, bite and vibrancy can only be truly appreciated at its peak (just be aware that seasons differ depending on the country). I have found that the simplicity of fresh, well-seasoned pan-fried sea bass (or bream) fillets pair marvellously with the sweetness of the onion and the lemon juice which are used to flavour the asparagus and butter beans. You could happily make this dish at any time of the year though by replacing the asparagus with green beans.

Serves 4

4 sea bass fillets
¾ tsp sea salt flakes
½ tsp cracked black pepper
300 g (10½ oz) asparagus
2 × 400 g (14 oz) cans butter beans
4 tbsp olive oil
1 large onion, finely diced
½ chicken stock cube
200 ml (7 fl oz) boiling water
3–4 garlic cloves, finely diced
1 tsp dried oregano
2 tbsp fresh lemon juice
Grated zest of 1 large lemon
Small handful of fresh coriander, finely chopped

Using some kitchen paper, pat the sea bass fillets completely dry, and very lightly score the skin in three places. Season both sides with half a teaspoon of the sea salt flakes and a quarter teaspoon of the coarse black pepper and leave to one side.

Wash the asparagus, cut or break off the woody ends, and cut the spears in half or in thirds measuring approximately 8 cm (3 inches).

Drain and wash the butter beans.

Heat two tablespoons of the olive oil in a large frying pan over a medium–high heat. Add the onion to the pan, reduce the heat a little and soften the onion for 10–12 minutes until translucent and caramelised. While the onion is cooking, dissolve the stock cube in the boiling water.

Add the garlic and dried oregano to the onion and stir well for a minute before adding the asparagus and frying for another minute. Add the butter beans to the pan, stir well, then add the remaining salt and pepper, the lemon juice, lemon zest and stock to the pan. Bring to the boil, then reduce the heat and simmer for 3–4 minutes until the stock reduces a little. Remove from the heat.

Heat the remaining two tablespoons of olive oil in another large frying pan over a medium heat.

Place two of the fillets, skin side down, in the hot olive oil and gently, and carefully, push down the fish with the tips of your fingers to ensure the skin is flat to the pan, so that the fillets crisp up, cook evenly and do not curl at the sides. Cook for around 2 minutes on each side (you can check that the underside of each fillet is crispy and golden brown before flipping over). Remove to a warmed plate while you repeat the cooking process with the remaining two fillets.

Stir the coriander through the butter beans and asparagus and serve immediately while the sea bass fillets are still hot.

Traditional Stove-top Dishes, from Meatballs to Dolma

Ocak & Kızartma

This is one of the most traditionally Cypriot chapters in the book. These recipes were cooked regularly while I was growing up, and I have kept them entirely authentic.

When artichokes are in season and both abundantly available and unashamedly sizable, my mum will always make her beautiful *Kıymalı Enginar ve Yaprak Dolması* (Mince & Rice Stuffed Artichokes & Vine Leaves, pages 127–8). As a youngster, I would help her pack the stuffed artichokes into a large pan, nestling the rolled vine leaves beside them and we would simmer them on the stove until the rice was cooked through and had soaked up all the flavours from the rest of the filling ingredients. The beauty of this dish is the ritual that follows once the juicy stuffing has been eaten from the artichokes. Each leaf is plucked, one by one, and the delicious fleshy part at the bottom of the leaf is scraped off between your top and bottom front teeth. The juices unavoidably drip down your hands until only the soft and succulent artichoke heart remains to cut into – the grand finale of the show. My children adore pretty much every kind of *dolma* (stuffed vegetable), but like their mother, this is their favourite, and their faces light up when I bring the pan to the table, as they get ready to start pulling off and devouring those leaves.

If my mum isn't stuffing artichokes or frying her beautiful *Bulgur Köftesi* (Meat-filled Bulgur Wheat Cones, pages 133–5), she is frequently making *yalancı dolma* (meatless stuffed vine leaves). In the summer, we pick and use the leaves straight from the vine, but throughout the rest of the year we use our stash of frozen leaves, which have been preserved, in batches, from the summer's plentiful haul. Even now, whenever I open my mum's freezer (and now mine) I am greeted by a carefully packed shrine in homage to the beautiful vine that grows in the garden, enabling us to eat tender stuffed vine leaves throughout the year.

The filling for *yalancı dolma* can also be stuffed into delicate courgette flowers, another classic Cypriot delicacy. I still fondly remember how every year, as soon as we would arrive at our hotel in Cyprus, my paternal grandmother, Melek Nene would greet us, walking proudly through the hotel lobby with a pan full of *Yalancı Dolma* (Meatless Stuffed Courgette Flowers & Vine Leaves, pages 130–1). We would sit in the hotel room and catch up over her beautifully prepared treats straight out of the pan.

Every single one of the recipes in this chapter ignites so much sentimentality and nostalgia for me, such as my mum's ability to use one chicken to make three meals. She would use the whole bird to create a broth that would form the stock for *Tavuklu Nohutlu Pilav* (Chicken & Chickpea Rice, page 140), then she would shred some of the chicken into the rice, or use it to fill sandwiches for lunch, and would finally roast or fry whatever meat remained. I also loved the pure comfort of a *Kıymalı Garavolli* (One-pot Minced Lamb & Conchiglie Pasta, page 142) that my mum would cover with a blanket of finely grated *hellim* (halloumi cheese) and mint, always leaving the chunks of *hellim* that were too small to grate on the side of the bowl for us to nibble on. My mum would also make *Mercimek Çorbası* (Red Lentil Soup, page 150) at least once a week, as I do now, which my own children affectionately refer to as 'Nene's Soup' (Grandmother's Soup). I love watching them add that extra squeeze of lemon as if it's second nature to them. My mum also has her own fond memories of the recipes, such as *Fatma Nenenin Balık Çorbası* (Fatma Nene's Fish Soup, page 146), a rice and potato soup that holds legendary status – my mum would tell of how when Nene was cooking this soup, news would spread like wildfire and families from neighbouring villages would flock to come and eat it.

They really are such special recipes, the beautiful kind that can be made together as a family, with nothing but the soundtrack of conversation to accompany the process and where the soothing ritual of preparation, cooking and eating become completely intertwined. Taking your time to prepare these precious dishes the traditional way, with care, will always result in food that tastes like it has been made with love at its core. Every single recipe. So many memories. And each time I cook them, I relive those treasured memories over and over again.

Kıymalı Enginar ve Yaprak Dolması

Mince & Rice Stuffed Artichokes & Vine Leaves

Stuffed artichokes are my favourite way to eat *Kıymalı Dolma* (mince and rice stuffed vegetables and vine leaves). *Kıymalı* means 'with mince' and *dolma* means 'filling' or 'stuffing'. Turkish Cypriots use the term *dolma* to describe any leaf or vegetable that has been filled with some kind of rice or grain-based stuffing, such as *yaprak dolması* (stuffed vine leaves). In Turkey, the term *sarma* (wrapping) is used for vine leaf-wrapped *dolma*. Traditionally, for Turkish-Cypriots, artichokes, vine leaves and green peppers are stuffed with a mince and rice-based filling, so feel free to use this filling for any of these vegetables. The stuffing ingredients will remain the same, but the quantities might differ depending on the size of the vegetables and leaves to be stuffed. The *enginar dolması* (stuffed artichokes) require a considerable amount of elbow-grease in terms of their preparation, but very little skill to stuff, and look impressive.

Makes 40 vine leaves and 4 artichokes

100 g (3½ oz) long-grain white rice
6 tbsp extra virgin olive oil
1 large onion, finely chopped
2 large lemons
4 globe artichokes
75 g (2¾ oz) fresh flat leaf parsley leaves, finely chopped
500 g (1 lb 2 oz) minced beef
400 g (14 oz) can chopped tomatoes
5 tbsp tomato purée
1½ tsp fine sea salt
¾ tsp ground black pepper
Approximately 40 vine leaves
200 ml (7 fl oz) boiling water
200 ml (7 fl oz) cold water

Wash the rice in a sieve until the water runs clear, and then let it drain over a bowl.

Add three tablespoons of the olive oil to a pan over a medium heat, add the onion and allow to soften for 10–12 minutes until it starts to caramelise. Remove from the heat and transfer to a large dish to cool down while you prepare the rest of the ingredients.

Gently push down and roll the lemons on a hard work surface (to help release their juices), then cut one of them into quarters.

Cut the stems off the artichokes, then slice 3–4 cm (1–1½ inches) off the tops so that you reveal the open, circular cavity. Using a small paring knife and a spoon, trim off some of the very small leaves around the base and stem, then clean out the insides of the artichokes (including some of the inner leaves, which are often a shade of purple) and completely remove the chokes. Use one quartered lemon per artichoke to rub the inside cavity and the outside leaves with lemon juice to prevent them from turning brown.

Add the parsley to the dish containing the caramelised onions. Cut the remaining lemon in half and squeeze two tablespoons of juice into the same dish, along with the washed rice, one tablespoon of the olive oil, minced beef, chopped tomatoes, four tablespoons of the tomato purée, salt and pepper. Mix everything together with a large spoon, completely breaking up the minced beef as you combine. Half of the mixture will fill the artichokes and the remaining half can be used for the vine leaves.

Recipe continued overleaf

Lay all of the vine leaves in a large dish and cover them in a little boiling water. The water will help you to separate the leaves from the stack without tearing them. Have a large plate ready to roll the *dolma* on, a teaspoon for spooning the mixture, and a large pan to lay the *dolma* in. You will also need a side plate, or two, that fit(s) inside the pan to cover the *dolma* once you have arranged them in the pan. Dissolve the remaining one tablespoon of tomato purée in a heatproof jug with the boiling water, then top up with the cold water and stir well.

Fill each artichoke to the top with the filling, pressing the mixture down with the back of the spoon to really pack it in tightly, and then place them, stem side down, into the pan. Use the remaining filling to fill and roll the vine leaves. Place a heaped teaspoon of the mixture along the widest point of the leaf, leaving just over 1 cm (½ inch) of space at the sides and along the edge closest to you. Fold this closest edge over the filling, fold in the sides, then roll the dolma away from you until you have a tightly-packed cigar-shaped roll (as per the images opposite). Neatly, and snugly, but not too tightly, arrange them next to the artichokes in the pan ensuring that you reserve 4–5 leaves to cover the *dolma* in the pan.

Drizzle the remaining two tablespoons of olive oil over the *dolma* in the pan, then lay the reserved vine leaves over them. Place a side plate, or two, on top of the leaves to lightly weigh down the contents of the pan, leaving a small gap at the sides so that you can pour the tomato purée mixed with water into the pan. Pour in enough liquid so that it comes just over the rim of the plate by 2 cm (¾ inch). Feel free to top up with a little more water if the quantity of liquid is not quite enough, or hold back if it is too much.

Place the pan over a medium heat, bring to the boil, then reduce the heat and simmer on low for around 45–50 minutes until the rice stuffing is cooked through. Remove the pan from the heat, put the lid on, then let it sit for at least 30 minutes before serving.

Note

I often find that jarred and vacuum-packed vine leaves really do not compare to beautiful, homegrown young leaves. However, if you can only source pre-packaged leaves, I would recommend that you wash them thoroughly first and then simmer them in boiling water for 30 minutes before you are ready to roll the *dolma* to tenderise and rid them of the salty brine.

Yalancı Dolma

Meatless Stuffed Courgette Flowers & Vine Leaves

A meat-free *dolma* stuffing is referred to as *yalancı dolma* ('liar' stuffing), the premise being that the stuffing is lying to you by not having any meat in it. I make the stuffing for these beautiful *Yalancı Dolma* using short-grain or pudding rice, which results in a creamier and fuller-textured filling once cooked.

My mum recalls how, in the summer, she and her siblings would set off on an early morning three-mile trek each armed with a large pan, to pick fresh courgette flowers from the family farm. They would make the *dolma* at their aunties' house, then walk back with full, heavy pans stacked high with *Çiçek dolması*, ready to cook as soon as they got home. The most special thing about writing this book is that is has enabled my mum to relive so many of these wonderful memories with me, and this is one I will always think of every time I make this recipe.

Makes approximately 80–100 vine leaves or 40 courgette flowers

250 g (9 oz) short-grain white rice
6 tbsp extra virgin olive oil
2 onions, finely diced
4 tbsp tomato purée
50 g (1¾ oz) fresh flat leaf parsley leaves, finely chopped
400 g (14 oz) can chopped tomatoes
100 ml (3½ fl oz) fresh lemon juice
3 tbsp dried mint
1½ tsp fine sea salt
¾ tsp ground black pepper
80–100 small-medium vine leaves/60–70 larger vine leaves or 40 courgette flowers
200 ml (7 fl oz) boiling water
300 ml (10 fl oz) cold water

Wash the rice in a sieve under cold running water until the water runs clear, then allow to drain fully.

Heat three tablespoons of the olive oil over a low heat and add the onions. Soften for 15–20 minutes until translucent and caramelised. Add three tablespoons of the tomato purée to the onions, gently breaking it down into the oily juices. Stir in the rice, coating the grains fully in the tomato and onion mix, then remove the pan from the heat and transfer the contents to a very large dish.

Add the parsley to the dish with the chopped tomatoes, lemon juice, dried mint, salt and pepper. Stir to combine, then allow to cool. Store in the fridge for an hour to allow the flavours to come together.

While the mixture is cooling in the fridge, prepare the vine leaves as per the method on page 128.

Dissolve the remaining one tablespoon of tomato purée in a heatproof jug with the boiling water, then top up with the cold water and stir well.

Reserve 4–5 vine leaves for later, then use the rest of them to make the *dolma*. Place one vine leaf on a large plate with the widest side of the leaf facing you and the point furthest away. Place a heaped teaspoon of the mixture along the widest point, leaving just over 1 cm (½ inch) of space at the sides and along the edge closest to you. Fold this closest edge over the filling, fold in the sides, then roll the *dolma* away from you until you have a tightly-packed cigar-shaped roll.

Lay the rolled *dolma* (with the pointy end of the leaf facing the underside of the pan to prevent the *dolma* unravelling while cooking) at bottom of the pan and repeat with the remaining leaves and filling, taking care to arrange the *dolma* snugly, but leaving enough space for them to expand while cooking.

If stuffing courgette flowers, carefully open them up and stuff with 3–4 teaspoons of the filling (depending on the size of the flowers) until they are around three-quarters full. Wrap and tuck the the petals in and over the exposed stuffing, to thoroughly conceal what's inside. Lay the stuffed flowers flat at the botttom of the pan, with the tucked petals on the underside to prevent them from opening up while cooking.

Drizzle the remaining three tablespoons of olive oil into the pan, then cover the *dolma* with the 4–5 reserved leaves (if using). Place a side plate, or two, on top of the leaves to lightly weigh down the contents of the pan, leaving a small gap at the sides so that you can pour the tomato purée mixed with water into the pan. Pour in enough liquid so that it comes just over the rim of the plate by 2 cm (¾ inch). Feel free to top up with a little more water if the quantity of liquid is not quite enough, or hold back if it is too much.

Place the pan over a medium heat, bring to the boil, then reduce the heat to a light simmer. Place the lid on and cook for around 20–25 minutes until most of the water has reduced, but so you can still see a small amount bubbling away.

Remove the pan from the heat and allow to cool for a couple of hours before serving.

Bulgur Köftesi
Meat-filled Bulgur Wheat Cones

There are so many variations of what Turkish Cypriots call *Bulgur Köftesi*. These golden nuggets of joy are made of a kneaded bulgur wheat casing and traditionally filled with a minced meat filling, sealed and shaped, then deep-fried. They are heavenly, moreish, utterly delectable and I am uncontrollable around them.

I have spent years watching my mum make these and have now perfected my own recipe. Some people like to add additional ingredients to the dough such as flour, egg and semolina, but we make ours the very old-fashioned way using just extra fine bulgur, boiling hot water and a lot of elbow grease. The first attempt can sometimes end up a little disastrous so I have compiled a comprehensive list of tips and tricks (see page 135) to ensure you get them spot on from the get-go.

The filling is laden with deliciously sweet, softened onions and lots of fresh parsley, and cut lemon wedges are essential for squeezing into the *Bulgur Köftesi* once you bite the crunchy top off.

Makes 25

1 litre (1¾ pints) sunflower or
   rice bran oil
Fresh lemon wedges, to serve

For the bulgur wheat dough
500 g (1 lb 2 oz) extra fine bulgur
   wheat
2 tsp paprika
1½ tsp salt
1 tsp ground black pepper
1 litre (1¾ pints) boiling water

For the filling
4 large onions (500 g/1 lb 2 oz)
3 tbsp olive oil
750 g (1 lb 10 oz) minced beef
   (you can use lamb or chicken
   if you prefer, or make them
   vegan by using finely chopped
   mushrooms)
¾ tsp salt
¾ tsp ground black pepper
100 g (3½ oz) fresh flat leaf
   parsley, finely chopped

Place the bulgur wheat in a large deep dish. Mix in the paprika, salt and pepper, then add the boiling water, one third at a time, stirring constantly with a large spoon until all the water has been absorbed. Flatten the top of the bulgur wheat with the back of the large spoon, cover the dish tightly with plastic film and leave to rest for a minimum of 4 hours.

Make the filling at least an hour in advance, or even the night before you are ready to shape the cones, so that it has time to cool down.

To make the filling, peel and very finely dice the onions (I actually like to use a food processor for this bit, to get the onions as finely chopped as possible). Heat the olive oil in a pan, then add the minced beef and cook over a medium heat for a 5–6 minutes. Once browned, add the salt, pepper and onions, reduce the heat and cook for another 12–15 minutes until the onions soften and caramelise, but don't brown. Remove the pan from the heat, stir through the parsley and pour the filling into a large, shallow heatproof dish to cool.

After 4 hours, take the plastic film off the bulgur wheat and start to knead and squeeze the dough with very clean hands (I wear food prep gloves for this bit as it can get rather messy). Knead for 15–20 minutes until the dough is soft and pliable, which will make it easier to shape without breaking. Fill a small bowl with cold water and wet the palms of your hands a little. Break off pieces of the dough, weighing approximately 60 g (2¼ oz) each, which will ensure that all of the cones are uniform in size and shape.

Recipe continued overleaf

Lightly wet your palms again and roll a piece of the dough into a ball. Dip your right index finger in the water, then make a hole in the dough ball as far down as you can go without making a hole at the bottom. Then wet your right thumb and start opening and flattening the dough by rotating it gently in your palm as you work. Stuff the pouch with three tablespoons of the cooled filling, gently pushing it down and gently sealing it closed without getting any of the mixture on the outside casing of the dough. Use a little water to smooth the dough on the outside, and to create two prominent points at each end. Lay the cone on a baking sheet and repeat the process with the remaining dough and filling, ensuring that you reserve a tiny little ball of dough at the end to test the oil to make sure it is hot enough.

Heat the oil over a high heat in a large, deep non-stick pan. After 5 minutes, use a food thermometer (the oil should be at 190°C/375°F) when you start frying) to check to see if the oil is hot enough, or by carefully popping in the small bulgur dough ball that you saved earlier. If it immediately starts to bubble and sizzle, then the oil is hot enough; if not, remove the ball and wait another couple of minutes.

When the oil comes to temperature, use a slotted spoon to very carefully lower the cones into the oil, one at a time. I fry no more than 3–4 dough cones at once, depending on the size of pan used, as they should not be touching each other at all while they cook, and there should be ample space in the pan for them to brown evenly. As soon as you see them turning a golden-brown colour, give them a gentle nudge with a slotted spoon to make sure they are cooking evenly. Once their golden-brown colour darkens a little, remove with the slotted spoon, and transfer to a plate lined with two sheets of kitchen paper. Repeat in batches until they are all cooked.

Serve with lemon wedges on the side, for squeezing over.

Helpful Tips

Here are some additional top tips for making the recipe work for you:

As this bulgur casing is solely made from bulgur wheat and boiling water, it is imperative to use extra fine bulgur wheat. When the softened extra fine bulgur wheat releases gluten, the much smaller grains come together to create a more pliable dough, making the cones easier to shape.

Make sure your filling is not too wet. Keep cooking the filling until all the moisture has pretty much gone (good-quality minced beef will always release less water when cooked). The filling should be lovely and moist, especially from the softened onions, but not wet. If there is too much liquid in the filling, the moisture will seep through into the bulgur wheat cone and could cause it to go soggy and split in the pan when frying. If necessary, increase the heat and allow the filling to reduce until there is no liquid left in the pan.

Cool the filling right down. Do not fill the dough with hot or warm filling otherwise the heat could cause the bulgur wheat cones to fall apart, and consequently split when cooking.

Make sure the oil is very hot before you carefully fry the *bulgur köftesi*. I always fry a little piece of rolled bulgur wheat first to check that the oil is hot enough (as mentioned in the method).

I always use a deep non-stick pan when frying the cones, as that's what has always worked well for me. The pan needs to be deep enough that the *bulgur köftesi* are fully submerged in oil when cooking, for a thorough, even, golden-brown colour and to prevent the cones from exploding while they fry. Only turn them halfway through when the bulgur wheat has crisped up and changed colour.

Do not overcrowd the pan. Depending on the size of pan or cones, I never put more than 3–4 cones in at any one time. There should be ample space around each and if you're not sure how many to put in, just fry two at a time – it might take a little longer, but you'll be grateful that you did!

N.B. The cones can also be baked, but they do taste much better fried. To bake, brush with a little beaten egg and cook in a preheated oven at 220°C/200°C fan/425°F/gas mark 7 for 25–30 minutes.

Patates Köftesi

Cypriot Potato & Mince Fried Meatballs

No-one makes *patates köftesi* like my mum. Well, no-one other than my mum's mum Fatma Nene, and her mum, Meyrem Nene, who both taught my mum how to make them. While most people throw away the starchy water after grating the potatoes, Meyrem Nene would retain the water, whisk the egg into it and then stir the breadcrumbs in. The soaked breadcrumbs would swell in the liquid and she would add them to the rest of the ingredients and mix together. It is this technique that makes my mum's *patates köftesi* so special and I have always been reluctant to deviate from her family's method and sentiment. I have followed my mum's recipe almost exactly here, apart from the subtle addition of sweet cinnamon and earthy cumin.

Makes 40 meatballs

1 large onion, finely chopped
500 g (1 lb 2 oz) minced beef
500 g (1 lb 2 oz) Cyprus or Maris Piper potatoes
1 large egg
100 g (3½ oz) stale white bread
50 g (1¾ oz) fresh parsley
½ tsp ground cinnamon
¼ tsp ground cumin
1 tsp salt
¾ tsp black pepper
1 litre (1¾ pints) sunflower, vegetable, groundnut or rice bran oil

Note

You can use a food thermometer for this, but if you do not have one, then I would heat the oil over a medium–high heat on the largest hob burner. The oil should not be smoking. When you gently lower the meatballs into the pan, the oil will bubble immediately, but do not be tempted to turn the heat up as they should cook over a steady heat.

Add the onion to a large bowl along with the minced beef.

Peel the potatoes and finely grate them. Squeeze all of the water out of the grated potatoes into a bowl, but do not throw the starchy water away. Add the potatoes to the onion and minced beef mix.

Crack the egg into the bowl of potato water and whisk well. Break the bread into small pieces and blitz in a food processor until fine breadcrumbs form, then add them to the whisked egg mixture. Stir well so that the breadcrumbs soak up the juices.

Add the breadcrumb and egg mixture to the large bowl of minced beef mixture, along with the remaining ingredients and combine everything with your hands until fully amalgamated. Cover the bowl with plastic film and place in the fridge for 30 minutes so that it firms up a little.

Fill a small bowl with cold water and remove the mixture from the fridge. Have a large flat baking sheet ready to place the meatballs on once shaped. Wet your fingers and the palms of your hands with a little cold water and take a small ping-pong-sized ball of the mixture. Roll it around in your hands to form an egg-shaped nugget and place it on the baking sheet. Repeat with the remaining mixture until you have around 40 balls in total.

Heat the oil in a deep pan until it reaches 170°C (340°F). The pan should be deeper than the height of the meatballs so that it can accommodate enough oil to cover them completely while cooking. Carefully lower each meatball one by one into the oil with a slotted spoon until the pan is full, but so there is enough room for the meatballs to move around (they will shrink a little while cooking). Fry each batch for 5–7 minutes until they are a beautifully even golden-brown colour, then remove them from the pan using a slotted spoon and transfer to a large plate lined with a double layer of kitchen paper. Serve with *Şehriyeli Pilav* (Vermicelli Rice, page 102), or with *Melek Nene's Pazılı Kuru Börülce* (Dry Black-eyed Beans, page 149).

Mücendra

Rice & Lentils with Caramelised Onions

Mücendra, or *mercimekli pilav* (lentils and rice) as it is also known in Cyprus, is a descendant of the Arabic *mujaddara* that originates from the Levant. *Mujaddara* is a little more heavily spiced than the Cypriot *mücendra*, but the concept is the same – rice and green lentils are cooked together, with onions, spices and stock and served topped with crispy, caramelised onions. This is a dish that always reminds me of my cousin Ahmet, due to his persistent requests for it as a child.

Serves 4–6

900 ml (1½ pints) boiling water
1 vegetable stock cube
150 g (5½ oz) long-grain white rice
150 g (5½ oz) green lentils
4 tbsp olive oil
4 large onions (400 g/14 oz), finely diced
½ tsp ground cumin
½ tsp ground cinnamon
¾ tsp salt
½ tsp black pepper
¼ tsp *pul biber*

Note

The cooked, lightly spiced grains pair marvellously with the *Altı Saat Yavaş Pişirilmiş Kuzu Eti* (Six-hour Slow-roasted Lamb Shoulder, page 156), or *Türlü* (Roasted Vegetable Stew, page 165), and a fresh Cypriot *Salata* (Salad, page 54).

Put the boiling water and stock cube into a heatproof jug and stir until fully dissolved. Leave to one side.

Add the rice to a sieve and wash under cold running water for 30 seconds until the water runs clear. Place the rice into a large bowl and cover with double the amount of cold water and soak for 10 minutes. Lay the lentils out on a tray and check for any stones and, if found, discard them. Add the lentils to a sieve and wash under cold running water for 30 seconds.

Heat the olive oil in a pan over a medium heat, and once hot add the onions. Cook them slowly for 20–25 minutes (you may need to reduce the heat a little to prevent them from burning) until they have caramelised and are a deep golden-brown colour. While the onions are cooking, drain the rice through a sieve and leave to allow the grains to dry out a little. Remove half of the onions to a plate lined with kitchen paper and leave the other half in the pan.

Add the cumin and cinnamon to the pan and cook with the onions for a further 2–3 minutes, before adding the lentils and cooking for 2 minutes more, ensuring that they are fully coated in the onions and oily spices.

Add half of the stock to the pan, along with the salt and pepper, bring to the boil and simmer over a low heat, with the lid on, until the lentils have absorbed the liquid (around 15–18 minutes).

Add the rice to the pan, stir for a minute or two, then add the remaining stock. Bring it to the boil, and simmer over a very low heat with the lid on for 12–15 minutes until the water has been almost fully absorbed.

Remove the pan from heat, take off the lid and place a large sheet of kitchen paper on the pan so that it hangs over the edges (you may need two sheets). Place the lid back on, then leave the *mücendra* to settle for a few minutes.

Fluff up with a fork before serving, then garnish with the reserved crispy onions, a sprinkling of the *pul biber* flakes, and a dollop of thick set natural yoghurt.

Tavuklu Nohutlu Pilav

Chicken & Chickpea Rice

I do not remember my mum or dad ever buying portioned chicken when we were younger. A whole chicken was always utilised to its full potential. A childhood favourite of mine, this is a meal that is now much-loved by my own children.

Serves 6

250 g (9 oz) long-grain white rice
1.5 kg (3 lb 5 oz) whole chicken
2 bay leaves
1½ tsp fine sea salt
5 tbsp olive oil
45 g (1½ oz) vermicelli
400 g (14 oz) can chickpeas,
   drained and rinsed
Sea salt and pepper to taste

> **Note**
>
> If you are using freshly cooked chickpeas, you will need 250 g (9 oz). See page 53 for instructions on how to prepare dried chickpeas.

Preheat the oven to 220°C/200°C fan/425°F/gas mark 7.

Wash the rice in a sieve under cold running water until the water runs clear and leave to drain fully.

Add the chicken, bay leaves and salt to a large pan and fill with enough cold water to fully cover the chicken. Place the pan over a medium–high heat, bring to the boil and skim off any of the foam that forms on top. Place the lid half on the pan and reduce the heat to a simmer for around 1½ hours until the meat is almost falling off the bone. Remove the whole chicken from the pan and allow to cool a little so that you can handle and carve the meat. Reserve the broth to cook the rice in later.

Line a baking sheet with greaseproof paper and brush with one tablespoon of olive oil. Keeping the skin of the chicken intact as much as possible, carve off the breasts and the legs and lay them on the baking sheet, skin side up. Brush the skin of the chicken portions with another tablespoon of olive oil, season with a little sea salt and cracked black pepper and leave to one side.

Shred the remaining chicken from the carcass and the bones that haven't been placed on the baking sheet and leave to one side.

Heat three tablespoons of olive oil in a large pan over a medium heat and add the vermicelli. Fry for 2–3 minutes until a light golden brown, add the drained rice and chickpeas to the pan and give everything a stir. Remove from the heat and allow to cool down a little.

Place the baking sheet with the chicken pieces in the oven for 15–20 minutes until the skin crisps up.

Measure out 700 ml (1¼ pints) of the reserved, cooled chicken broth. Pour the broth into the pan of rice and add the shredded chicken pieces. Stir to combine, then return the pan to the hob over a medium heat. Bring to the boil, then reduce the heat to medium–low and simmer for 10 minutes with the lid half on until most of the liquid has evaporated. Remove the pan from the heat, take the lid off and place a double layer of kitchen paper or a thin tea towel over the pan, followed by the lid and leave for around 10 minutes.

Remove the chicken pieces from the oven and serve with the rice and plenty of thick set natural yoghurt.

Kıymalı Garavolli

One-pot Minced Lamb & Conchiglie Pasta

Although I grew up watching and assisting my mum in the kitchen making endless numbers of *börek* (fried and baked pastries), there are some beautiful 'shortcut' recipes that we also cooked at home, and this is one of them. Some call this *yalancı mantı* ('liar' dumplings), where dry conchiglie pasta takes the place of freshly made dumplings and traps the cooked minced lamb in and around its perfectly shaped shells. What's even better is that this pasta dish is all cooked in one pan and topped with a dollop of thick garlic yoghurt and a *pul biber* butter, the same flavours that appear in my *Kıymalı Gül Böreği* (Rose-Shaped Filo Meat Pies, pages 169-70) .

Serves 4

1 chicken stock cube
1.2 litres (2 pints) boiling water
3 tbsp olive oil
2 onions, finely chopped
1 tsp ground cumin
1 tsp paprika
1 tsp tomato purée
500 g (1 lb 2 oz) minced lamb
½ tsp salt
½ tsp ground black pepper
300 g (10½ oz) conchiglie pasta
2 bay leaves
Garlic Yoghurt (see Filo Meat Pies with Yoghurt & Chilli Butter recipe, pages 169–70)
Chilli Butter (pages 169–70)
100 g (3½ oz) halloumi cheese, finely grated
1 tsp dried mint

Dissolve the stock cube in the boiling water in a heatproof jug and leave to one side.

Heat the olive oil in a pan over a medium heat and add the onions. Soften for 10–12 minutes until they turn a lovely light golden-brown colour. Add the cumin and paprika to the softened onions, stir well so that the spices release their aromatics, then stir through the tomato purée, ensuring that the onions are fully coated. Add the minced lamb to the pan, breaking it down with the back of a wooden spoon and stirring it through the other ingredients. Increase the heat a little, season with the salt and pepper and brown the meat for 4–5 minutes. Add the pasta to the pan with the bay leaves and stock, stir, bring to the boil, then reduce to a medium simmer for 10–12 minutes. Stir a couple of times as it cooks, being careful not to break apart the pasta shells.

Once the pasta is cooked through (but still al dente) and the liquid has reduced remove the pan from the heat and give it a gentle stir.

Combine the *hellim* and dried mint in a small bowl. Serve the pasta on plates with a sprinkling of the *hellim* and mint mixture, a dollop of the Garlic Yoghurt and a drizzling of the Chilli Butter.

Galamar Tava

Fried Squid Rings

Fried fish suppers transport me back to Saturday nights as a child. My mum would often spend the afternoon cleaning and preparing the fish that we had bought from the market earlier in the day, and I would help her make the salad (my designated kitchen job when I was younger). My mum would either slowly stew small pieces of fresh *kalamar* (which, in the Turkish-Cypriot dialect, is pronounced *galamar*) with garlic, or coat the rings in batter and fry them. My recipe is slightly different to hers, as these rings are double-dipped in spiced flour, with an egg wash in between both coats, which results in a much crunchier, textured coating.

Galamar Tava is great as an appetiser, but also works perfectly as a main meal with Tahini Aioli (see below), or alongside any fresh lemon-juice laden salads and my *Çıtır Çıtır Fırında Patates Kızartması* (Crunchy Baked Chips, page 181). I buy my fresh squid (tubes and tentacles) cleaned, from the fishmongers, but you can use frozen squid tubes (defrosted first) if you prefer. Preparation and cooking takes 30 minutes, and the fried squid is best eaten straightaway, with a good squeeze of lemon juice. If you're serving them with the sides suggested above, prep the salad while the final batch of squid is cooking and bake the chips before you start cutting the squid so that everything is ready to serve at once.

Serves 6

For the squid rings
700 g (1 lb 9 oz) squid, tubes and tentacles
2 large eggs
2 tbsp milk
80 g (2¾ oz) cornflour
100 g (3½ oz) semolina
200 g (7 oz) plain flour
1 tsp coarse black pepper
2 tsp salt
1 tsp dried oregano
1 tsp smoked paprika
½ tsp *pul biber*
750 ml–1 litre (1¼ pints–1¾ pints) vegetable oil

For the tahini aioli
100 ml (3½ fl oz) tahini
50 ml (2 fl oz) cold water
4 tbsp fresh lemon juice
½ tsp finely grated garlic
½ tsp salt
4 tbsp mayonnaise
½ tsp coarse black pepper

Prepare the tahini aioli first. Pour the tahini into a bowl and add the cold water. Whisk vigorously with a fork or very small whisk until fully amalgamated; the mixture should have a smooth, creamy consistency.

Squeeze in the lemon juice and add the garlic, salt, mayonnaise and black pepper, whisking the whole time. Store in the fridge until you are ready to serve the squid rings.

To prepare the squid rings, wash the squid and remove any leftover sinew. Pat dry with kitchen paper and leave in a colander in the sink to drain any excess liquid.

In a large bowl, whisk the eggs and milk together and leave to one side.

Mix all of the dry ingredients and spices together on a large plate and leave to one side.

Remove the drained squid from the colander, pat it dry once more, and on a chopping board, slice the tubes into 2-cm (¾-inch) rings.

Add enough oil to a large, deep pan so it is at least 10 cm (4 inches) deep (the bigger the pan, the more squid you can fry at once without overcrowding the pieces), and place over a high heat. Allow the oil to heat up to 190°C (375°F) using a food thermometer, as you get on with preparing the squid, always keeping an eye on the pan.

Have a large tray ready to lay the prepared squid rings on before frying. Using a fork, lift up a few of the rings at a time, coat them fully in the flour mixture, dusting off any excess, coat in the egg wash (allowing any excess egg to drip off), then dip the rings back into the flour mixture, dusting off any excess again.

Place the coated squid on the tray and quickly repeat the process with all the remaining rings. Once the squid has been coated, the oil will be hot enough to ensure a beautiful crispy coating. Carefully lower a few of the rings into the oil, without overcrowding the pan. The squid will start to colour quite quickly, but do not be tempted to move them until the coating crisps up, which will take a couple of minutes. Flip the rings over for another minute or so, then remove them from the pan on to a large platter lined with a double layer of kitchen paper. Repeat the process until all the squid rings have been cooked.

Serve alongside the tahini aioli and some lemon wedges.

Fatma Nenenin Balık Çorbası

Fatma Nene's Fish Soup

This is one of my most treasured recipes in the book. Not only is it delicious, but it is a recipe that is firmly embedded in our family heritage. My mum recalls how neighbouring families would come to her house to eat Fatma Nene's widely-celebrated *Balık Çorbası* (Fish Soup). My grandmother would cook the fish my grandfather had caught that day, in water, to create a stock. She would then remove the fish, add onions, potatoes and parsley (grown in the garden), beaten eggs (from the hens), lemons (from the trees) and rice to make up the rest of the soup, and once cooked, it would be eaten alongside the fish with an extra, very generous squeeze of lemon juice. And let me tell you, there is nothing quite like the taste of those slightly-green, almost lime-flavoured Cypriot lemons that abundantly hang off the trees – I can only imagine this made the soup even more valued by those that were fortunate enough to eat it, cooked by my Fatma Nene's fair hands.

Serves 4–6

60 g (2¼ oz) long-grain white rice

1 whole sea bream or sea bass (300 g/10½ oz), scaled and gutted

1 bay leaf

2.5 litres (4½ pints), plus 3 tbsp cold water

1 tsp salt

500 g (1 lb 2 oz) Cyprus or Maris Piper potatoes, peeled, washed and finely diced

1 onion, finely diced

2 tbsp fresh lemon juice

1 egg, whisked

25 g (1 oz) finely chopped fresh flat leaf parsley leaves

½ tsp ground black pepper

To serve

Extra virgin olive oil

Lemon wedges

Pinch of cracked black pepper

Fresh crusty bread

Wash the rice in a sieve under cold running water until the water runs clear. Leave to drain in the sieve.

Place the whole fish in a large pan, add the bay leaf, 2.5 litres (4½ pints) of water and the salt, and place over a medium heat. Bring to the boil, then reduce to a simmer for around 15 minutes. Carefully remove the fish and bay leaf from the pan, place it on a large plate or serving dish, and cover the dish with foil.

While the broth is still simmering, add the rice, potatoes and onion to the pan and continue to simmer over a medium heat for another 20 minutes, stirring occasionally to break up the potatoes, which will give the soup a lovely creamy consistency. When cooked, removed the pan from the heat.

Spoon a ladleful of the soup into a small bowl and leave it to cool for around 20 minutes or so. Add one tablespoon of the lemon juice to the cooled soup in the bowl, followed by the remaining three tablespoons of cold water and the beaten egg, whisking constantly until you have a very smooth liquid.

Return the pan to the hob over a medium heat and before it comes back up to a simmer, very slowly pour the beaten egg mixture into the pan, whisking constantly without stopping. Keep whisking while the soup comes back up to a simmer and continue doing the same while adding the parsley, black pepper and remaining tablespoon of lemon juice to the pan. Do not stop whisking until the soup has been simmering for around 3–4 minutes and the colour of the parsley starts to change to a darker, duller tone.

Remove the pan from the heat, drizzle extra virgin olive oil over the whole fish, a pinch of cracked black pepper, a squeeze of lemon juice, and serve the soup with the dressed fish and some fresh crusty bread.

Melek Nene's Pazılı Kuru Börülce

Dry Black-eyed Beans with Swiss Chard

Caramelised onions and garlic fried in olive oil, added to black-eyed beans, cooked with chard and dressed generously in olive oil and lemon take simple, boiled pulses to a regal level. It's a trick that my mum learnt from my dad's mum, Melek Nene, after my parents were married. The cooked onions and garlic add a delicious sweetness and texture to the beans, and it is the perfect dish to serve with *Haşlanmış Sebze Çeşitler* (Cypriot-style Boiled Vegetables, page 69) and some fish, fried, smoked or barbecued. However, some purists will only ever eat this dish alongside *Patates Köftesi* (Cypriot Potato & Mince Fried Meatballs, page 136), another worthy partner for these delicious beans.

Serves 6–8

300 g (10½ oz) dried black-eyed beans
2.5 litres (4½ pints) cold water
1 lemon
200 g (7 oz) Swiss chard (stems removed) or the same quantity of spinach
3 tbsp olive oil
1 large or 2 small onions, finely diced
4 garlic cloves, finely sliced

For the dressing

4 tbsp extra virgin olive oil, plus extra to serve
3 tbsp lemon juice
1 tsp sea salt flakes
1 tsp dried mint

Spread the black-eyed beans on to a clean tray and remove and discard any stones or broken beans.

Wash the beans in a sieve, then add to a large pan with 2.5 litres (4½ pints) cold water and the juice of a whole lemon. Bring the beans to the boil and simmer for around 45 minutes, or slightly longer, checking that they're tender but not overly mushy. You can do this by squeezing one of the cooked beans in between your thumb and forefinger. Once cooked, remove the pan from the heat.

Wash the chard thoroughly to remove any dirt or grit before roughly chopping the leaves.

In a frying pan, heat the olive oil, add the onion and soften over a low heat for 12–15 minutes until translucent. Once softened, increase the heat a little so it starts to caramelise, then add the garlic and cook for another 2 minutes. Add the chard to the pan, reduce the heat and cook until the greens have wilted. Remove the pan from the heat, drain the black-eyed beans, then add them to the cooked chard, stirring well until the beans are fully coated in the greens, onions and garlic. Transfer the mixture to a serving dish.

Drizzle and sprinkle over all of the dressing ingredients, stir well and serve with an extra drizzle of extra virgin olive oil, fresh or canned fish such as tuna or smoked mackerel, chips, bread and a fresh salad.

Mercimek Çorbası

Red Lentil Soup

My children love this soup. It was one of the first things I would make when I started weaning them, exactly as my mum did for us. Their favourite soups are the Cypriot ones, like this *Mercimek Çorbası* which they both affectionately refer to as *çorba* (soup), or Nene's (Grandmother's) soup. This, again, is my mum's recipe and is loaded with caramelised onions which are added, for sweetness and texture, once the soup is cooked. Occasionally, we also add finely diced carrots, celery and potatoes which cook together with the lentils and rice. My kids always ask for extra lemon juice, grilled black olives and some *gabira* (grilled bread) or croutons made from stale *Kıbrıs Çöreği* (Cypriot seeded bread) to eat with their Red Lentil Soup. We've taught them these traditions well, and I couldn't be happier about it.

Serves 6–8

350 g (10½ oz) split red lentils
100 g (3½ oz) long-grain white
  rice
3 litres (5¼ pints) cold water
1 chicken or vegetable stock cube
500 ml (18 fl oz) boiling water
3 tbsp olive oil
2 medium onions, finely diced
4 tbsp fresh lemon juice
1 tsp salt
¾ tsp ground black pepper

To serve
Pul biber
Dried mint
Grilled black olives
Toasted bread
Lemon wedges
Sea salt
Cracked black pepper

In a sieve, wash the red lentils and rice under cold running water until the water runs clear. Add the drained rice and lentils to a large pan and fill with the 3 litres (5 pints) of cold water. Place the pan over a high heat and bring to the boil for 5 minutes, skimming off and discarding the foam that forms on the top. Reduce the heat a little.

Dissolve the stock cube in the boiling water in a heatproof jug. Add the stock to the pan, then stir and simmer over a low heat for around 25–30 minutes until the soup thickens.

While the soup is cooking, add the olive oil to a large frying pan over a medium heat. Add the onions to the hot oil, reduce the heat and soften for 15–20 minutes until translucent. Increase the heat a little so that the onions caramelise and turn a lovely golden-brown colour, then remove from the heat.

Add the lemon juice, salt and black pepper to the soup pan, give everything a gentle stir, cook for a further minute and then remove one-third of the soup and blitz carefully in a food processor. Return the blended soup back to the pan. Stir in half of the caramelised onions, cook for a minute, then remove the pan from the heat.

Serve bowls of the soup with the remaining onions, a sprinkling of *pul biber*, dried mint, grilled black olives, large croutons or toasted bread and an extra squeeze of lemon juice. Season to taste with sea salt and black pepper.

Hearty Dishes from the Oven

Fırın

This chapter includes oven-based recipes that are regularly cooked in my mum's kitchen, as well as some of the most-loved dishes from my blog and Instagram account.

I can't tell you how many times I've been tagged in Instagram posts and stories of my *Altı Saat Yavaş Pişirilmiş Kuzu Eti* (Six-hour Slow-roasted Lamb Shoulder, page 156). I never expected it to be such a popular recipe, and the intense flavour of the lamb is enhanced by its visual allure, garnished with vibrantly pink pomegranate seeds and fresh parsley. It cooks slowly in sweet and tangy juices for hours, absorbing all the flavours. My *Tavuk Döner* (Chicken Doner Kebab, pages 175–6) is also a bit of a showstopper that people seem to like to cook to impress their family and friends with. Skinless and boneless chicken thighs are covered in a yoghurt-based marinade (yoghurt tenderises chicken, in the same way that milk tenderises lamb, especially when barbecuing), then cooked, basted and served with sides and fillings such as lettuce, pickled red cabbage and *Cacık* (Yoghurt, Mint & Cucumber Dip, page 52) served in homemade *Kıbrıs Pidesi* (Cypriot Pitta Bread, pages 246–7).

But perhaps the recipe that stomps on the *Altı Saat Yavaş Pişirilmiş Kuzu Eti* and *Tavuk Döner* is my *Çıtır Çıtır Fırında Patates Kızartması* (Crunchy Baked Chips, page 181). Simple chips. For as long as I can remember, my mum has always oven-roasted potatoes with some kind of coating – be it flour, semolina or cornflour. Inspired by her, my chips are coated in cornflour, tossed with garlic, olive oil, oregano, thyme, salt, pepper and occasionally some additional spices like *pul biber* and smoked paprika, then baked until crispy and golden brown.

My love of potatoes runs deep, so my other favourite recipe is *Golyandrolu Patates* (Coriander Roast Potatoes, page 182). In fact, the *Hellimli Fırında Tavuk* (Roast Chicken Stuffed with Halloumi & Tomatoes, pages 178–9) that the coriander roasties are often served alongside is not one of my grandmother's or mum's recipes, but my Aunty Revza's late mum's, Ülker Abla's recipe. She would always tell me about the recipes she had created, using traditional Cypriot ingredients. One of those recipes is this chicken; I would listen to the intricacies of how she would carefully separate the skin from the breasts of a whole chicken and insert slices of *hellim* (halloumi cheese) and tomato, which had been slathered in a seasoned parsley butter, under the skin.

Some of my favourite showstoppers as an adult are the humble one-tray dishes that are filled with meat and vegetables, like *Küp Kebabı* (Lamb Shanks & Potatoes, page 159) and *Tavuklu Patates Kebabı* (Chicken, Potato & Tomato Roast, page 160). When we were younger my mum would make these one-tray, slow-cooked recipes for ease and quantity. She would bring the huge trays to the table, the sauces and juices still bubbling, which are perfect eaten alongside crusty bread and a fresh salad, black olives and yoghurt.

Although pasta bakes are a common sight on dinner tables all over the world, the key ingredients of *hellim*, mint, parsley, cinnamon and pasta firmly cements *Magarına Fırında* (Cypriot Pasta Bake, pages 162–3) as the champion of global pasta bakes (in my admittedly biased opinion). My mum remembers how on special occasions like *Bayram* (Eid), families who were fortunate enough to have clay ovens in their gardens would invite other families to collectively cook these meals together, a celebration of religion, community and gratitude.

These traditional oven-baked *fırın* dishes really do epitomise a sense of togetherness and family feasting, and the large one-trays are excellent options for casual entertaining. The slow-baked meat and potato dishes require minimal preparation (and washing up) and can be served alongside many of the sides in the Dishes & Salads to Share chapter (pages 44–69). Dishes such as *Magarına Fırında* and *Kremalı Musakka* (Creamy Moussaka, pages 185–6) require a bit more planning (and a few more pots and pans), but along with the *Kol Böreği* (Potato, Spinach & Cheese Filo Pie, pages 167–8) and the *Kıymalı Gül Böreği* (Rose-Shaped Filo Meat Pies, pages 169-70) in this chapter, they can be frozen and then defrosted and reheated at a later date.

Six-Hour Slow-roasted Lamb Shoulder

This is one of my oldest, most popular recipes. I urge you to make it just once, and I can almost guarantee that it won't be the only time you do so. It's not necessarily a Cypriot recipe, but one that has definitely been influenced by the slow-cooked *fırın* cooking methods and fresh flavour combinations such as mint and coriander. In fact, I often make a lot more of the mint and coriander sauce as I could literally eat spoonful after spoonful of it, and it is always such a winner – as delicious drizzled over roast potatoes, as it is over the succulent pieces of lamb.

Serves 6–8

1 chicken stock cube
400 ml (14 fl oz) boiling water
1 garlic bulb
2 tbsp olive oil
2 large onions, thickly sliced
15 g (½ oz) finely chopped fresh mint leaves
3 tbsp extra virgin olive oil
4 tbsp pomegranate molasses
2 tbsp clear honey
1 heaped tsp oregano
1 tsp *pul biber*
1 tsp sea salt flakes
2–2.5 kg (4 lb 8 oz–5 lb 8 oz) shoulder of lamb, bone-in
¾ tsp black pepper
10 g (¼ oz) finely chopped fresh coriander leaves
2 tbsp fresh lemon juice
3 tbsp red wine vinegar
2 tbsp toasted pine nuts
2 tbsp pomegranate seeds

Note

For a full feast serve with *Cacık* (Yoghurt, Mint & Cucumber Dip, page 52) and *Çıtır Çıtır Fırında Patates Kızartması* (Crunchy Baked Chips, page 181) or *Şehriyeli Pilav* (Vermicelli Rice, page 102).

Preheat the oven to 170°C/150°C fan/325°F/gas mark 3.

Dissolve the stock cube in the boiling water in a heatproof jug and leave to one side.

Cut the garlic bulb in half. Drizzle two tablespoons of olive oil in the bottom of a very large, deep roasting tray and add the onions and garlic to the middle of the tray.

Add one-third of the mint leaves to a small bowl, along with one tablespoon of the extra virgin olive oil, half of the pomegranate molasses, one tablespoon of honey, the oregano, *pul biber* and sea salt flakes, and mix together to create a thick green sauce.

Very lightly score the top of the lamb (if there is a lot of excess fat, just trim it off) and sit in the roasting tray on top of the onion and the garlic bulb halves. Pour two tablespoons of the sauce over the lamb (do not let the spoon touch the lamb or contaminate the sauce), and using clean hands, gently rub the sauce all over the lamb so that it embeds itself within the shallow cuts you made across the skin. Pour the stock over the lamb and into the roasting tray (you may need to add a little more water halfway through cooking if necessary), season with the cracked black pepper, cover the tray tightly with foil and place in the oven on the bottom shelf.

Slow-cook the lamb for around 6 hours (or a little more), basting every 2 hours, and always covering the tray tightly with the foil each time you do. Increase the heat to 180°C/160°C fan/350°F/gas mark 4 for the last 30 minutes of cooking time. If you feel like the lamb isn't crisping up as much as you'd like, remove the foil for the last 20 minutes.

Take the herb sauce and add the coriander leaves along with the remaining mint, two tablespoons of extra virgin olive oil, two tablespoons of pomegranate molasses, one tablespoon of honey and all the lemon juice and red wine vinegar.

You will know the lamb is ready when the meat falls off the bone. Serve the lamb on a platter and scatter over toasted pine nuts, pomegranate seeds and the herby green sauce.

Küp Kebabı

Lamb Shanks & Potatoes

Another slow-cooked lamb recipe (because we slow-cook lamb a lot), *Küp Kebabı* is traditionally made using the cheapest, often fattiest cuts of lamb that benefit from being in the oven longer without drying out. There isn't any additional liquid added to this recipe, yet the juices from the tomato and the lamb itself result in the softest, fall-off-the-bone meat. If you pair this lamb with the recommended Cyprus potatoes, I'm sure you'll notice a huge difference in how the potato edges crisp up ever so slightly, and their robust, waxy interior softens enough for a knife to go through like butter, without falling apart.

Serves 4

2 large (400 g/14 oz) onions
4 (400 g/14 oz) ripe tomatoes
1 large green bell pepper or 4 green charleston peppers
olive oil, for brushing
4 large (800 g/1 lb 12 oz) potatoes (Cyprus, Maris Piper or King Edward potatoes are best), peeled
4 large lamb shanks (500 g/1lb 2 oz each)
4 large garlic cloves, peeled
40 g (1½ oz) unsalted butter
4 bay leaves
4 tbsp extra virgin olive oil
2 tsp dried oregano
1 tsp sea salt flakes
1 tsp coarse black pepper

Preheat the oven to 170°C/150°C fan/325°F/gas mark 3.

Peel the onions, leaving the root end and top intact. Halve the onions lengthways and leave to one side. Halve the tomatoes and cut the top off the green bell pepper, scoop out the seeds and cut into quarters.

Cut four large pieces of foil around 60 cm (24 inches) long – wide foil is best, especially if the shanks are large, as the sides of the foil parcel need to come up and be sealed at the top to ensure the juices do not spill out during cooking. Cut four equal-sized pieces of baking paper.

Brush the inside of a sheet of foil with olive oil, then place a piece of baking paper on top, followed by one potato, one lamb shank, one of the onion halves, two tomato halves, one piece of bell pepper and a garlic clove. Equally divide the butter into four and place a piece into the parcel along with a bay leaf, drizzle over one tablespoon of extra virgin olive oil, sprinkle over half a teaspoon of dried oregano, season with a quarter teaspoon of sea salt flakes and finally a quarter teaspoon of coarse black pepper. Wrap the foil into a high tent, ensuring the edges are tightly sealed so that no liquid escapes, but so there is enough room in the foil tent for steam to circulate.

Place in a large deep roasting tray and repeat for the remaining three lamb shanks. Put the tin on the bottom shelf of the oven for 3½ hours.

Remove the tin from the oven, carefully open each of the parcels, baste the shanks and potatoes with the juices in the foil (without tearing the foil or allowing the juices to pour into the tin) and return to the oven for a final 30 minutes until the lamb is falling off the bone and everything has browned a little.

Serve with *Salata* (Salad, page 54), fresh bread and a good dollop of thick set natural yoghurt.

Tavuklu Patates Kebabı

Chicken, Potato & Tomato Roast

Tavuklu Patates Kebabı was a weekly staple dish for us growing up. In fact, my mum still makes it for us now when we all get together; it's such a simple one-tray meal, and it really does go a long way. This recipe and *Küp Kebabı* (Lamb Shanks & Potatoes, page 159) are two meat-based dishes synonymous with slow-cooking in outdoor ovens, which so much of Cypriot cuisine has been traditionally built upon. These recipes can easily be adapted to be cooked in conventional Western ovens, and here I have added my own twist of spices and flavours to my mum's traditional recipe.

Serves 4–6

1 chicken or vegetable stock cube
2 tbsp tomato purée
200 ml (7 fl oz) boiling water
6 tbsp olive oil
4 onions, peeled and quartered
750 g (1 lb 10 oz) Cyprus or
    Maris Piper potatoes, peeled
    and halved
8–10 large high-welfare chicken
    thighs and/or drumsticks
6 garlic cloves, peeled and
    bashed
1 tsp dried oregano
½ tsp paprika
¼ tsp *pul biber*
1 tsp ground cinnamon
½ tsp ground cumin
¾ tsp salt
¾ tsp pepper
2 tbsp chopped fresh parsley
    leaves
400 g (14 oz) can chopped
    tomatoes
400 ml (14 fl oz) cold water
3 bay leaves
1 unwaxed lemon, halved

Preheat the oven to 200°C/180°C fan/400°F/gas mark 6.

Dissolve the stock cube and tomato purée in the boiling water in a heatproof jug and leave to one side.

Drizzle two tablespoons of the olive oil into a deep baking tray, then add the onions, potatoes, chicken and garlic to the tray. Sprinkle over the dried oregano, spices, salt, pepper and parsley. Give everything a gentle stir so that the chicken and vegetables are fully coated in the oily spices.

Pour the chopped tomatoes into the baking tray, then fill up the can with cold water; top up the dissolved stock and tomato purée with enough water from the can to take the total amount of liquid up to 600 ml (20 fl oz), give it a stir and pour this into the baking tray as well. Add the bay leaves and the lemon halves, drizzle over another three tablespoons of the olive oil (save a little for the last 30 minutes of cooking), cover with foil and place the baking tray on the bottom shelf of the oven.

After 35–40 minutes remove the baking tray from the oven, take off the foil, turn the chicken over, baste the potatoes and return to the oven without the foil. After another 25–30 minutes, remove again, turn the chicken over, basting the potatoes in the juices, drizzle everything with the remaining one tablespoon of olive oil and return to the oven for a final 25–30 minutes.

Remove from the oven, allow to rest for 5 minutes, then serve with a liberal pouring of the thick basting juices and onions, accompanied by a fresh salad, and in true Cypriot style, rice and thick set natural yoghurt.

Magarına Fırında

Cypriot Pasta Bake

A pasta bake to top all pasta bakes. The combination of long, substantial tubes of pasta, a slightly sweet and peppery minced beef filling all topped with a thick layer of creamy *hellim* (halloumi) béchamel sauce is the reason why this is my family's most requested meal. Traditionally, the pasta used to make *Magarına Fırında* is called 'Mezzani A' (marketed as such by various Turkish and Greek brands) and is similar to zite; however, bucatini is also used.

Serves 6–8

For the *hellim* bechamel sauce
100 g (3½ oz) unsalted butter
100 g (3½ oz) plain flour
1.2 litres (2 pints) milk
1 bay leaf
½ tsp coarse black pepper
150 g (5¼ oz) halloumi cheese, finely grated
2 tbsp dried mint
4 eggs
1 tsp sesame seeds

For the pasta
2 tsp fine sea salt
500 g (1 lb 2 oz) long tubular pasta
50 g (1¾ oz) halloumi cheese, finely grated
1 tsp dried mint

For the meat filling
3 tbsp olive oil
750 g (1 lb 10 oz) minced beef
1 tsp ground cinnamon
1 tbsp dried mint
3 onions (300 g/10½ oz), finely chopped
1 tsp fine sea salt
1 tsp ground black pepper
50 g (1¾ oz) fresh flat leaf parsley, finely chopped

Prepare the béchamel first as it needs time to cool down before you whisk in the eggs a little later on. Melt the butter in a pan over a medium–low heat, then whisk in the flour to form a roux (thick paste). Once the roux starts to bubble, add the milk a little at a time, throwing in the bay leaf now too and whisking constantly. Keep adding more milk as and when the sauce thickens and bubbles. Once all the milk has been combined and the sauce just starts to come to the boil, remove from the heat. Stir in the *hellim* and dried mint until the cheese melts into the sauce a little and leave to one side until later on.

Fill a large pan with cold water, put the lid on and place it on the hob over a high heat.

Prepare the meat filling next. Heat the olive oil in another large pan over a medium–high heat, and once hot, add the minced beef to the pan, breaking it up with a spoon. Keep browning the minced beef for 5–6 minutes, add the cinnamon and dried mint, giving it all a good stir, then add the onions, reducing the heat and cooking everything for around 10–12 minutes.

By now the water in the large pan should be boiling, so add two tablespoons of sea salt to the boiling water, followed by the pasta and gently push down on the tubes as they soften so that the pasta is fully immersed in the boiling water. Because the tubes are long and thick, they'll probably need cooking for 12–15 minutes, but check them after 12 minutes as you don't want the pasta to be too soft. While the pasta is cooking, return your attention to the meat filling.

Once the onions have softened, season everything with the fine sea salt and ground black pepper, stir through the parsley, cook for another minute, then remove the pan from the heat.

Preheat the oven to 200°C/180°C fan/400°F/gas mark 6.

The pasta should now be cooked, so remove half of the tubes with a large slotted spoon to a deep baking tray or dish (approximately 34 cm × 24 cm/13 inches × 9 inches and around 6 cm/2 inches deep). Mix together the grated *hellim* with one teaspoon of dried mint and add half of it to the pasta, gently stirring through the tubes. Place all of the meat filling on top, followed by the remaining pasta, followed by the remaining half of the *hellim* and dried mint mixture, sprinkled over the top.

Remove the bay leaf from the béchamel. Whisk together the eggs in a bowl until light and fluffy and then slowly pour them into the béchamel, whisking constantly until they are fully amalgamated in the creamy sauce. Pour the béchamel over the top in one even layer, sprinkle over the sesame seeds, and cook in the oven for 35–45 minutes or until golden brown and a little darker in places.

Let it stand for at least 30 minutes to cool down a little and for the layers to firm up before serving.

Türlü

Roasted Vegetable Stew

Türlü literally translates as 'all kinds of', or 'all sorts' and it refers to the assortment of vegetables that are thrown together in this dish. The vegetables are roasted, like an oven-baked ratatouille, with a colourful combination of herbs and sweet, warm spices. It's Turkish in origin and is one of those dishes that can be eaten hot, warm or cold (known as a *zeytinyağlı* – 'with olive oil' – dish in Turkish cuisine). It is simply delicious when served with bread and some thick set natural yogurt or my *Cacık* (Yoghurt, Mint & Cucumber Dip, page 52).

Serves 6–8

1 large aubergine
2 courgettes
1 tsp fine sea salt
2 large onions
2 large sweet red peppers
   (*kapya biber*) or romano
   peppers (200 g/7 oz)
4 large charleston or 2 green
   bell peppers (150 g/5½ oz)
4 large, ripe plum tomatoes
   (500 g/1 lb 2 oz)
4 large garlic cloves, peeled
   and bashed
50 ml (2 fl oz) olive oil
¼ tsp ground cloves
½ tsp ground coriander
½ tsp paprika
1 tsp dried oregano
¾ tsp sea salt flakes
¾ tsp cracked black pepper
1 vegetable stock cube
2 tbsp tomato purée
1 tbsp Turkish sweet red pepper
   (*tatlı biber salçası*)
600 ml (20 fl oz) boiling water
1 tbsp fresh lemon juice
1 tbsp plain flour
½ cinnamon stick
1 large bay leaf
1–2 tbsp extra virgin olive oil

Preheat the oven to 200°C/180°C fan/400°F/gas mark 6.

Cut the aubergine in 3–4-cm (1–1½-inch) chunks. Cut the courgettes into chunks of a similar size. Lay both vegetables out flat on baking sheets or large plates. Sprinkle their flesh evenly with fine sea salt and leave them for around 15 minutes to release their juices. Pat the vegetables dry with some kitchen paper and add them to a large, deep roasting tray.

Peel and cut the onions into chunks roughly the same size as the aubergine and courgette. Cut up the peppers and tomatoes, ensuring they are similar in size to the other vegetables. Add to the large, deep roasting tray containing the aubergines and courgettes. Add the garlic. In a bowl, mix together the olive oil, cloves, coriander, paprika, dried oregano, half of the sea salt flakes and cracked black pepper, then stir this spiced oil into all of the veggies, using clean hands to toss everything together. Ensure that all of the vegetables are coated in the oily spices and redistribute them as flat as possible.

Place the roasting tray into the oven and bake for 30 minutes (stirring gently halfway through) while you prepare the remaining ingredients.

Dissolve the stock cube, tomato purée and sweet red pepper paste in the boiling water in a heatproof jug and leave to one side.

After 30 minutes, remove the roasting tray from the oven, gently stir the vegetables, then drizzle over the lemon juice, sprinkle over the flour, the remaining sea salt flakes and cracked black pepper. Nestle the cinnamon stick and bay leaf into the mixture, and carefully pour over the stock. Increase the oven temperature to 220°C/200°C fan/425°F/gas mark 7 and return the tin to the bottom shelf of the oven for a further 45–50 minutes, gently stirring halfway through the cooking time. Remove the tray from the oven and let the vegetables cool until warm. Drizzle over the extra virgin olive oil just before serving.

Kol Böreği

Potato, Spinach & Cheese Filo Pie

As a child, I knew *börek* as moreish, deep-fried pastries filled with either *hellim* (halloumi), sautéed onions and herbs, minced beef or mushrooms (see *Kızarmış Börek* (Fried Pastries with Mince, Mushroom & Halloumi Fillings) on pages 241–4, *Meyrem Nenenin Ispanakli Börek* (Great-grandmother Meyrem's Spinach Pies, pages 248–50) and *Sütlü Börek* (Custard-filled Filo Syrup Pastries, pages 259–60). I would watch my mum lovingly make them pretty much every weekend for us, or if we had guests coming over.

As we grew older and took more holidays to Turkey or stayed in hotels when visiting our family in Cyprus, I discovered that aside from the *Kıbrıs börekleri* (Cypriot fried pastries) I was brought up on, *börek* came in so many different varieties, often made with pastry called *yufka* (a very thin homemade pastry, similar to filo).

Not all shop-bought filo will do for this recipe – use the best quality filo you can afford and find. Look for packs with large sheets, often marketed in Turkish grocers and international supermarkets as *baklavalık yufka* (baklava filo). I have been disappointed in the past with trying to work with cheaper filo that dries up too quickly and flakes too much when shaping, or sheets that are far too small to work with.

Serves 6–8

3 tbsp olive oil
1 large or 2 small onions, very finely chopped
500 g (1lb 2 oz) Cyprus or Maris Piper potatoes, peeled, washed, coarsely grated, squeezed and drained in a sieve to get rid of excess starchy juices
2 tbsp Turkish sweet red pepper paste (*tatlı biber salçası*)
2 large garlic cloves, crushed
400 g (14 oz) baby leaf spinach or spinach leaves, washed and roughly chopped
200 g (7 oz) Cypriot ricotta (*nor peyniri* or *anari*), *beyaz peynir* (Turkish white cheese) or feta
100g (3½ oz) *kaşar peyniri* or Gouda cheese, coarsely grated

Ingredients continued overleaf

Preheat the oven to 200°C/180°C fan/400°F/gas mark 6.

Heat the oil in a large non-stick pan over a medium heat and soften the onion for 8–10 minutes until completely translucent and slightly caramelised. Add the potatoes and cook for a further 5–6 minutes, stirring continuously until the potato softens – if some of the potato edges crisp up a little, even better.

Add the sweet red pepper paste and garlic, stir well, then add the spinach.

Cook the spinach until the leaves have fully wilted. Transfer to a large dish to cool.

In a separate bowl, crumble in the white cheese, then stir in the grated cheese, parsley, pul biber, lemon zest and dried mint.

Once the spinach and potato mixture has cooled, gently stir in the cheese mixture. Season to taste with the salt and pepper. If using feta, you might need to use slightly less salt as it can be salty depending on the brand. Divide the mixture into six equal portions.

Line a baking sheet with greaseproof paper and leave to one side.

In a small pan, melt the butter. Once melted, carefully skim off the froth that will have formed and discard.

Recipe continued overleaf

4 tbsp, finely chopped fresh flat
    leaf parsley
1 tsp *pul biber*
Grated zest of 1 lemon
1 tsp dried mint
¾ tsp salt
¾ tsp black pepper
12 large sheets of filo pastry
175 g (6 oz) unsalted butter
1 large egg, beaten
1 tbsp sesame seeds

Lay one sheet of filo horizontally on a clean surface, brush it all over with the melted butter, lay another sheet of filo on top, brush with a little more butter, then spread one portion of the filling mixture all along the bottom edge of the filo nearest to you. Roll the pastry away from the edge nearest to you into a log shape, then slowly swirl it round into a spiral (like a snail shell), roughly 10 cm (4 inches) in diameter. Use the warmth of your hands to shape and cup the spiral to prevent it from splitting. Place it in the centre of the lined baking sheet, then repeat the method with the remaining five portions of filo and filling, but instead of rolling into spirals, lift the long filo roll straight on to the baking sheet, connecting it to the end of the previous roll and spiralling it round until you have one huge spiral.

Brush the spiral with the remaining melted butter first, then liberally, all over, with the beaten egg, not forgetting the sides too (the egg will give the pastry its beautiful golden colour and crunchy exterior). Sprinkle with the sesame seeds and bake in the oven, on the bottom shelf, for around 40–50 minutes until beautifully golden brown all over.

Kıymalı Gül Böreği

Rose-Shaped Filo Meat Pies

My Aunt Revza first made me these filo meat pies when I was in my early teens. Whenever we went round for dinner, I would always hope that these crunchy, flaky, buttery, meat-filled pies were on the menu, and I absolutely loved the contrast in texture of the thick garlic yoghurt that was piled on top and then drizzled with butter that had been melted with a little *pul biber*. Some of my fondest food memories are of spending time at Aunt Revza and Uncle Halit's house, playing with my cousins, Jeyda, Eren and Deren, while having what felt like a cookery lesson at the same time! My aunt and uncle have taught me so much about food over the years, and their cooking has had a definite influence over me too.

Please see the introduction on page 167 for how and where to source the best shop-bought filo.

Serves 6

3 tbsp olive oil
750 g (1 lb 10 oz) minced beef
1 tbsp Turkish sweet red pepper paste (*tatlı biber salçası*)
1 tbsp tomato purée
3 large onions, finely chopped
4 large garlic cloves, finely chopped
½ tsp ground cinnamon
½ tsp ground cumin
1 tsp *pul biber*
1 tsp dried mint
1 tsp fine sea salt
½ tsp coarse black pepper
50 g (1¾ oz) fresh flat leaf parsley, finely chopped
125 g (4½ oz) unsalted butter
1 large egg
12 large sheets of filo pastry

For the sauce
1 egg
100 g (3½ oz) thick set natural yoghurt
1 tsp baking powder
1 tbsp olive oil
100 ml (3½ fl oz) sparkling water

Ingredients continued overleaf

Preheat the oven to 200°C/180°C fan/400°F/gas mark 6.

Heat the oil in a large non-stick pan over a medium heat and brown the minced beef for 8–10 minutes, then stir through the sweet red pepper paste and the tomato purée. Add the onions and soften for another 12–15 minutes. The onions don't necessarily need to caramelise but they need to completely soften and soak up the meat juices as they cook. Once softened, add the garlic, cinnamon, cumin, *pul biber*, dried mint, salt and pepper and cook for another couple of minutes so that the garlic and spices become fragrant. Remove the pan from the heat, stir through the fresh parsley and allow the filling to cool completely.

Line two baking sheets with greaseproof paper and leave to one side.

For the sauce, whisk the egg in a bowl and then add the yoghurt. Keep whisking while you add the baking powder and olive oil, and then slowly pour in the sparkling water. You should have a lovely light sauce that you will use to line the filo with.

In a small pan, melt the 125 g (4½ oz) butter that will be used to brush over the top of the filo. Once melted, carefully skim off the froth that will have formed and discard. Whisk the other egg in a bowl and leave to one side.

For the garlic yoghurt, add the grated garlic to a pestle and mortar and bash to a paste. In a bowl, mix the garlic paste into the yoghurt. Season with the salt and taste, adding a little more if necessary. Put the garlic yoghurt in the fridge to chill while you prepare the *börek*.

Recipe continued overleaf

For the garlic yoghurt

1 large garlic clove, finely grated
150 g (5½ oz) thick set natural
 yoghurt
½ tsp sea salt flakes

For the chilli butter

45 g (1½ oz) unsalted butter
1 tbsp extra virgin olive oil
1 tbsp Turkish sweet red pepper
 paste (*tatlı biber salçası*)
1 tsp *pul biber*
1 tsp dried mint

Lay one sheet of filo horizontally on a clean surface, drizzle over a couple of tablespoons of the sauce, lay another sheet of filo on top, brush with a little more butter, then spread one portion of the filling mixture all along the bottom edge of the filo nearest to you. Roll the pastry away from the edge nearest to you into a log shape, then slowly swirl it round into a spiral (like a snail shell). Use the warmth of your hands to shape and cup the spiral to prevent it from splitting. Place it on one of the lined baking sheets, then repeat the method with the remaining five portions of filo and filling and add each spiral to the baking sheet, leaving enough space between the pastries for them to expand a little during cooking.

Brush the spirals with the remaining melted butter, then liberally all over with the beaten egg, not forgetting the sides (the egg will give the pastry its beautiful golden colour and crunchy exterior). Sprinkle with the sesame seeds and bake in the oven, on the bottom shelf, for 35–40 minutes until beautifully golden brown all over. Five minutes before the pastries are ready, prepare the chilli butter.

For the chilli butter, melt the butter in a frying pan over a medium heat, then add the olive oil. When it starts to sizzle, stir through the sweet red pepper paste, *pul biber* and dried mint. Let it just start to bubble, then remove from the heat.

When the *börek* are ready, serve them with the garlic yoghurt on the side and a generous drizzle of the chilli butter.

Fırında Bulgurlu Dolma

Baked Stuffed Vegetables

Aside from cooking on the hob, *dolma* are also traditionally cooked in the outdoor *fırın* (oven). My mum has always used both methods. Even though everything is covered with flat vine leaves and foil before placing in an outdoor *fırın* or a domestic indoor oven, the edges of the vegetables and slightly exposed grains of stuffing caramelise a little. This sweetens the flavour of the vegetables, and gives them a gentle char in places. Please let the *dolma* sit, covered, for at least 30 minutes before serving so that the juices really thicken up and soak back into the stuffing.

Serves 6–8

4 large onions
6 ripe tomatoes
150 g (5½ oz) Swiss chard
50 g (1¾ oz) fresh flat leaf
    parsley
3 tbsp olive oil
1 tsp *pul biber*
¼ tsp paprika
½ tsp ground cinnamon
½ tsp ground cumin
1 tsp salt
1 tsp coarse black pepper
2 tbsp Turkish sweet red pepper
    paste (*tatlı biber salçası*)
3 tbsp tomato purée
250 g (9 oz) bulgur wheat
1 tbsp dried mint
1 tbsp pomegranate molasses
4 tbsp fresh lemon juice
4 tbsp extra virgin olive oil
50 g (1¾ oz) pine nuts
16 vine leaves
1 chicken or vegetable stock cube
400 ml (14 fl oz) boiling water
200 ml (7 fl oz) cold water
30 g (1 oz) unsalted butter
¼ tsp *pul biber*

Preheat the oven to 200°C /180°C fan/400°F/gas mark 6.

Peel the onions and finely chop only one of them. Leave to one side. Cut the bottom off the other three onions and slice horizontally into each onion but only to the core, not all the way through. Place the onions in a pan and cover with cold water. Bring to the boil and simmer over a medium heat for 15 minutes while you prepare the rest of the ingredients.

Cut the tops off four of the tomatoes and put the tops to one side. Scrape out the seeds and some of the flesh with a spoon, leaving the outsides fully intact. Discard the hard cores from the scooped-out flesh, but finely chop the remaining flesh and add to a bowl. Cut the two remaining tomatoes in half, then grate (flesh side against the grater) into the same bowl, discarding the skins.

Cut the stalks off the chard, leaving just a little bit to hold on to, and finely chop the stalks.

Remove the onions from the pan of boiling water with a slotted spoon, leaving the pan over the heat so that the water continues to simmer, and place them on a plate to cool down. One by one, add the chard leaves to the simmering water for 10–20 seconds each until they wilt a little, then remove to a plate. Finely chop the parsley (leaving the stalks and leaves separate from each other).

Heat three tablespoons of the olive oil in a large pan over a low heat and soften the reserved chopped onions for 15–18 minutes. Add the finely chopped chard stalks and parsley stalks to the pan and soften with the onion for 3–4 minutes until soft, silky and lightly browned. Stir through the *pul biber*, paprika, cinnamon and cumin for a couple of minutes until they smell fragrant. Add the grated tomatoes and reserved tomato flesh to the pan with the salt and pepper and let them start to sizzle before adding the sweet red pepper paste and two tablespoons of the tomato purée, stirring well so that everything is combined. Remove the pan from the heat, then stir through the bulgur wheat and dried mint. Transfer everything to a large dish to cool.

Recipe continued overleaf

Once cooled, add the parsley leaves, the pomegranate molasses, lemon juice, three tablespoons of the extra virgin olive oil and the pine nuts. Stir well to combine.

Leave 4–5 vine leaves to one side. Remove a few of the outer layers of the boiled onions, but retain the structure of the onions without breaking them, so that they hold the stuffing mixture securely. Stuff each onion with as much of the bulgur wheat mixture as possible that will still enable you to wrap the onion over itself slightly without the filling spilling out. Place the stuffed onions in a deep baking dish.

Stuff the tomatoes to the top with the bulgur wheat filling and place the reserved 'lids' back on, placing the tomatoes in the dish with the onions.

Take a chard leaf with the widest part closest to you and the stem pointing vertically. Place a line of filling along the widest part, leaving the perimeter around the widest part and at the edges free of the mixture, so that you can tuck in the sides, then roll it away from you to form a log shape. If the chard leaves are too big, then cut them in half before stuffing and rolling. Fill the vine leaves with the remaining filling using the same rolling technique as the chard and line all the rolled leaves up in the dish.

Lay the 4–5 reserved vine leaves flat over the rolled leaves (you do not need to cover the onions or tomatoes) to keep them moist and prevent them from drying out while cooking.

Add the stock cube, boiling water and remaining one tablespoon of tomato purée to a heatproof jug and stir until fully dissolved, topping up with the cold water before carefully pouring it into the dish. Lay a sheet of greaseproof paper that fits snugly over the top of the stuffed vegetables and leaves, followed by a couple of small plates to weigh everything down a little. Cover the dish with foil, then put it on the bottom shelf of the oven for an hour.

Remove the dish from the oven and very carefully remove the foil, the plates and the greasproof paper while wearing oven gloves. Brush the onions and tomatoes with the remaining extra virgin olive oil. Increase the heat to 220°C/200°C fan/425°F/gas mark 7 and put the dish back in the oven for another 20 minutes.

Put the butter in a small pan over a medium heat. Once the butter has melted, add the *pul biber*, then remove the pan from the heat.

Remove the dish from the oven and peel away the vine leaves that were covering the stuffed and rolled leaves. Brush all of the vegetables with a little of the melted butter mixture and put the dish in the oven for a final 10 minutes. Finally, remove the dish from the oven, pour over the remaining melted butter mixture and allow to rest, covered tightly with foil, for 30 minutes before serving. Perfect with a side of thick set natural yoghurt and a fresh salad.

Tavuk Döner

Chicken Doner Kebab

Takeaways were something we never really ate as children, and we certainly never got takeaway kebabs at home as come rain or shine, the *mangal* (barbecue) was lit pretty much every weekend. However, on holiday or a rare family visit to a Turkish restaurant, my dad would always order a Mixed *Döner*. Chicken Doner Kebab has always been his favourite. I have made this so many times at home, and it has definitely been one of my most popular recipes. The longer you can leave the chicken to marinate, the better, so I recommend marinating for 4 hours before you start cooking, to ensure a kebab packed with flavour. Load the chicken into homemade *Kıbrıs Pidesi* (Cypriot Pitta Bread, pages 246–7) and pile on the salad fillings (see recipes in the Dishes & Salads to Share chapter, pages 44–69) for a proper 'fakeaway' treat.

Serves 4–6

1 kg (2 lb 4 oz) skinless, boneless chicken thigh fillets

1 large onion, sliced in half (skin still on)

4 large wooden skewers, soaked in water for 30 minutes prior to cooking

For the marinade

3 tbsp thick set natural yoghurt

2 tbsp pomegranate molasses

2 tbsp Turkish sweet red pepper paste (*tatlı biber salçası*)

2 tbsp olive oil

1 tbsp clear honey

1 tsp dried oregano

½ tsp ground cumin

¼ tsp ground cinnamon

½ tsp *pul biber*

½ tsp paprika

½ tsp onion granules

½ tsp garlic granules

¾ tsp fine sea salt

¼ tsp coarse black pepper

Ingredients continued overleaf

For the marinade, mix all of the ingredients in a large, deep dish that will eventually fit all of the chicken thigh fillets. Add the chicken to the marinade and give a thorough but gentle stir, fully coating the chicken fillets in the marinade. Cover the dish with plastic film and place the marinated chicken in the fridge to chill for a minimum of 4 hours, or even overnight. When the chicken has finished marinating, remove the dish from the fridge 45 minutes before you are ready to start cooking.

Preheat the oven to 200°C/180°C fan/400°F/gas mark 6.

Prepare the potatoes and keep them covered in cold water until the chicken goes into the oven.

Carefully thread each chicken thigh on to the four skewers and push them down as you do, while leaving enough space at the bottom so that you are able to lift up the *döner* with the skewers – all four skewers should go horizontally through each thigh so that they can support the weight of all of the chicken thighs together once they have all been threaded. Don't push the fillets together too tightly, as although they need to be close together to get the desired *döner* effect, the fillets must have room to ensure that they are cooked all the way through.

Lay both halves of the onion cut side down in a deep oven dish that is shorter in length than the skewers so that the skewers can sit on top of the edges of the dish (the *döner* is cooked horizontally, not vertically, but should not lay completely flat in the dish – the onion halves aid in keeping the *döner* propped up). Cook the chicken in the preheated oven for an initial 30–35 minutes.

Remove the dish from the oven, brush the chicken with the juices in the dish, then carefully turn the *döner* over so the other side is facing upwards, and brush with more of the juices. Return the chicken to the oven for a further 25–30 minutes.

Recipe continued overleaf

For the chips

500 g (1 lb 2 oz) Cyprus or Maris
  Piper potatoes, peeled and cut
  into 1–1½-cm (½–¾-inch)
  thick chips
1 litre (1¾ pints) vegetable
  or light olive oil, for frying

For the pickled red cabbage

250 ml (9 fl oz) red wine vinegar
3 tbsp caster sugar
150 ml (9 fl oz) cold water
150 g (5½ oz) red cabbage,
  finely shredded

To make the pickled red cabbage, mix together the vinegar and sugar in a bowl and once dissolved, add the water. Add the cabbage to a large jar or Tupperware box, pour over the pickling liquid, then seal and pop in the fridge for at least a couple of hours before serving.

Meanwhile, prepare the chips. Drain the cut potatoes, pat them completely dry with kitchen paper and pour the oil into a medium-sized, deep non-stick pan. Heat the oil over a medium–high heat. After 5–6 minutes, test the heat by carefully popping in one of the potatoes. If the oil starts to bubble rapidly when the potato hits it, then it is ready. If not, wait a few more minutes or use a food thermometer. Add the potatoes to the pan carefully with a slotted spoon and fry over a medium heat (around 140°C/285°F) for 10–15 minutes or until they look uniformly golden in colour, then increase the heat ever so slightly for the final 2–3 minutes so that they really crisp up.

While the chips are being fried, remove the chicken from the oven, baste, turn over and return to the oven for a final 5–10 minutes. Remove from the oven one last time, baste the chicken again with the juices and allow to rest for 5 minutes before carving (vertically), so that the chicken pieces naturally break up into smaller bite-sized pieces (instead of slices).

By now the chips should have turned a nice golden colour and be crispy on the outside and soft and fluffy in the middle. Carefully remove them with a slotted spoon to a plate lined with kitchen paper to absorb any excess oil.

If there are any juices left in the chicken dish, brush them over the chicken just before serving.

Hellimli Fırında Tavuk

Roast Chicken Stuffed with Halloumi & Tomatoes

Ülker Abla's *hellim*-stuffed roast chicken has been cooked in our household for the past two decades. The *hellim* (halloumi) placed under the chicken's skin seasons the meat and softens, without ever melting and the tomato keeps everything deliciously juicy. I find that spatchcocking the chicken reduces the cooking time, which prevents the skin covering the *hellim* from potentially darkening too much. Ask your butcher to spatchcock a chicken for you or see my note opposite about preparing a spatchcocked chicken yourself. This dish is perfect served with my *Golyandrolu Patates* (Coriander Roast Potatoes, page 182).

Serves 4–6

250 g (9 oz) halloumi cheese
2 large tomatoes, thinly sliced
10 g (¼ oz) finely chopped fresh
    flat leaf parsley leaves
4 cocktail sticks
6 tbsp olive oil
1 large onion, cut in 3–4 cm
    (1–1½-inch) rounds
1 garlic bulb, halved
3 whole sprigs of fresh thyme
75 g (2¾ oz) unsalted butter,
    softened
1 tsp dried oregano
2 kg (4 lb 8 oz) whole chicken
¼ tsp sea salt flakes
¼ tsp coarse black pepper

Preheat the oven to 200°C/180°C fan/400°F/gas mark 6.

Remove the *hellim*, tomatoes and parsley from the fridge at least 30 minutes before using to bring them to room temperature. Soak four cocktail sticks in warm water for at least 30 minutes.

Drizzle a large roasting tray with three tablespoons of the olive oil. Add the onion and garlic bulb halves to the centre of the roasting tray, along with the sprigs of thyme.

Pat the *hellim* dry with kitchen paper, then cut into six thick slices. Mix the parsley and dried oregano into the softened butter in a bowl. Add the *hellim* to the softened butter and carefully coat each slice without breaking up the cheese. Remove the *hellim* to a plate and put to one side. Add the tomato slices to the remaining softened butter mixture and coat fully.

Lay the spatchcocked chicken on a chopping board and gently ease your hand under the skin, starting at the neck and working your way down to a breast, being sure not to tear the skin as you go. Make as much space as possible between the skin and the breast and repeat on the other side. Take three slices of *hellim* and gently slide them under the skin of one of the breasts, followed by half of the tomato slices on top of the cheese. Tuck the skin closest to the neck under the bird, then seal with the cocktail sticks, pushing them as far in as possible at an angle. Repeat this process for the opposite breast of the chicken with the remaining *hellim* and tomatoes, then rub the chicken all over with the remaining three tablespoons of olive oil and season with the salt and black pepper. Please make sure you wash your hands thoroughly afterwards.

Cover the tray with a very large sheet of foil or two sheets joined at the top to make a tent-like covering, ensuring that the foil does not touch or stick to the chicken skin while cooking.

Place the tin in the oven and cook for around 1 hour, then remove the foil and cook for a further 15–20 minutes until the juices run clear and the skin has crisped up.

Allow the chicken to rest for 10 minutes before carving and serving.

Note

To spatchcock the chicken, place it breast side down on a chopping board and using a pair of strong kitchen scissors, or a large, sharp knife, cut through the flesh and bone along both sides of the backbone (if you run your finger along the back of the chicken, you will be able to feel the outline of each side of the bone) from the tail end to the head. Remove the entire backbone, then pull apart each side of the chicken to loosen the ligaments. Turn the chicken over and push down hard on the breast so that the chicken is flattened.

Çıtır Çıtır Fırında Patates Kızartması

Crunchy Baked Chips

Chips. Ah, beautiful chips! I adore potatoes in any shape or form, and I have to say that this probably stems from the fact that we were brought up on Cyprus potatoes that really do make the best fried chips and are perfect when roasted, especially with their delectably crunchy, crispy edges and soft and waxy, yet fluffy interior.

The herby, seasoned cornflour coating mixed with the olive oil creates a light paste that crisps up when the chips are cooking for that perfect bite every time. The measurements and quantities are essential to achieving the crunchy coating, so make sure to use measuring spoons (as in all of my recipes). I've also included a couple of my favourite spices as optional additions to the recipe, which add a nice kick to the crunchy exterior.

These chips work alongside so many of the recipes in this book; for lunch or breakfast with *Menemen* (Spiced Scrambled Eggs, page 34) or *Ispanaklı Yumurta* (Spinach & Eggs, page 30) and as an alternative to the usual breakfast choice of bread; as a side to *Hellimli Fırında Tavuk* (Roast Chicken Stuffed with Halloumi & Tomatoes, pages 178–9) or any of the recipes in the Barbecue Dishes & Accompaniments chapter (pages 192–219). Or how about in true Cypriot beach-side style (and what could be considered an extreme take on the British chip butty), as the star ingredient in *Bidda Badadez* (Wrap and Chips), where the chips are stuffed into a wrap with spiced mince patties, fresh tomatoes, parsley and fried *hellim* (halloumi).

Serves 4

2 tbsp vegetable oil
4 medium-sized (750 g/1 lb 10 oz) Cyprus, Maris Piper or King Edward potatoes
2 tbsp cornflour
2 tbsp olive oil
½ tsp dried oregano
½ tsp dried thyme
½ tsp *pul biber* (optional)
¼ tsp smoked paprika (optional)
¾ tsp sea salt flakes
¾ coarse black pepper
8 garlic cloves

Preheat the oven to 240°C/220°C fan/475°F/gas mark 9.

Once the oven is hot, pour the oil into a large non-stick baking tray and place in the oven so that the oil can heat up while you prepare the potatoes.

Wash the potatoes and fully dry them with some kitchen paper. Cut them into 1½-cm (¾-inch) thick chips, pat dry again, and place in a large bowl. Sprinkle over the cornflour and stir the chips so that they are fully and evenly coated before adding the olive oil, dried herbs and spices, seasoning and garlic. Shake the bowl and stir everything well so that the cornflour and oil fully combine and create a paste-like covering for the chips.

Carefully take the baking tray out of the oven and gently transfer the chips to the hot oil, making sure that they lay completely flat and do not touch each other; this will ensure that the chips crisp up on all sides. Return the baking tray to the oven and bake on the middle shelf for 30–40 minutes, turning once halfway through cooking when the undersides have crisped up.

The chips are ready once they are a lovely, even golden-brown colour on all sides.

Golyandrolu Patates

Coriander Roast Potatoes

My love for potatoes continues with this recipe, where traditional roasties are given
a little lift with lots of fresh lemon, garlic and coriander. Coriander, or *golyandro* as
it is commonly known to all Cypriots, is a key ingredient that distinguishes Cypriot
salads from similar mainland Turkish and Greek recipes, especially when used in
meze and salads. These potatoes are perfect served alongside the *Altı Saat Yavaş
Pişirilmiş Kuzu Eti* (Six-hour Slow-roasted Lamb Shoulder, page 156) and *Hellimli
Fırında Tavuk* (Roast Chicken Stuffed with Halloumi & Tomatoes, pages 178–9).

Serves 4–6

1.5 kg (3 lb 5 oz) Cyprus
   or Maris Piper potatoes
2 tsp fresh lemon juice
1 tbsp plain flour
4 tbsp olive oil
1 tsp sea salt flakes
½ tsp coarse black pepper
1 tsp coriander seeds
¼ tsp garlic, crushed
½ tsp finely grated lemon zest
1 tsp dried oregano
10 g (¼ oz) finely chopped fresh
   coriander leaves

Preheat the oven to 220°C/200°C fan/425°F/gas mark 7.

Peel, wash and cut the potatoes into quarters or chunky wedges, place
them in a large pan and cover with cold water. Place the pan over a high
heat, bring to the boil and then reduce the heat a little and simmer
the potatoes for 6 minutes. Remove the pan from the heat, drain the
potatoes in a colander over a sink until they are rid of all their water.
Wipe out the pan with kitchen paper to ensure it is completely dry,
then return the potatoes to the pan and drizzle over the lemon juice
and sprinkle over the flour. Put the lid on, holding it closed shut, and
give the pan a good shake to rough up the edges of the potatoes.
Carefully transfer the potatoes back to the colander and let them
steam dry for 15–20 minutes.

Pour the olive oil into a large, non-stick baking tray and place it on the
middle shelf of the oven to heat. After around 15 minutes, once the oil
is smoking, remove the tray from the oven and lay it somewhere flat
and heatproof. Carefully transfer the potatoes straight into the hot oil
and gently tilt the baking tray and spoon some of the hot oil over the
top of the potatoes. Ensure that every potato is fully coated with oil,
sprinkle with half of the sea salt and all of the black pepper, then return
the potatoes to the oven. Cook for 20–25 minutes, then remove from
the oven, turn them over and return them to the oven for another
20–25 minutes while you prepare the coating.

Lightly crush the coriander seeds in a pestle and mortar then pour half
of them into a large, deep dish that will be big enough to hold all the
potatoes. Add the crushed garlic, lemon zest and dried oregano and
give everything a good stir.

Remove the tray from the oven, and using a slotted spoon or fish slice,
transfer all of the potatoes to the large dish you placed the coriander
seed mixture into and give the potatoes a really good stir so that they
are fully coated. Then quickly return them to the hot baking tray and
give them a further 5 minutes in the oven before serving. Take the tray
out of the oven, add the fresh coriander and remaining salt to the
tray, gently tossing the potatoes in the herbs and seasoning, then
transfer everything to a serving platter.

Kremalı Musakka

Creamy Moussaka

Turkish *musakka* is traditionally made with just fried aubergines and potatoes, and sometimes courgettes (my mum always bakes the vegetables instead of frying them), then cooked with a tomato-based lamb mince ragù, but without a creamy, cheesy topping. The creamy béchamel-topped *musakka* was a dish we would order when we went out for dinner, as my mum would rarely cook this version, but I have been making this creamy moussaka at home, and for my parents, since moving out 15 years ago. Like my mum, I always bake the vegetables first, as not only is it healthier, but it also means I don't have to clean the hob after a mammoth frying session. In typical Cypriot fashion, this makes a huge trayful of *musakka*, so be prepared to feed a crowd with it, enjoy the leftovers the next day or freeze it for a quick and delicious meal when you're short on time. Simply serve with salad.

Serves 8

For the béchamel
100 g (3½ oz) unsalted butter
100 g (3½ oz) plain flour
1.1 litres (1¾ pints) milk
¼ tsp ground nutmeg
½ tsp sea salt flakes
¼ tsp coarse black pepper
1 bay leaf
150 g (5½ oz) Gruyère cheese, grated
4 eggs
100 g (3½ oz) cherry tomatoes, halved
½ tsp thyme leaves
Coarse black pepper to taste

Ingredients continued overleaf

Preheat oven to 220°C/200°C fan/425°F/gas mark 7.

First make the béchamel so it has time to cool down. Melt the butter in a pan over a medium heat, then whisk in the flour to form a roux (thick paste). Add the milk a little at a time, along with the nutmeg, salt, black pepper and bay leaf, whisking continuously and adding more milk as and when the sauce thickens and bubbles. Once all the milk has been poured in and the sauce just starts to come to a simmer, remove from the heat. Stir in half of the grated cheese ensuring it fully melts, then leave to cool until later.

Grease a very large, deep baking tray with one tablespoon of olive oil. I either use a large, circular *sini* tray (a traditional metal tray) or a 30 cm × 40 cm (12 inch × 16 inch) rectangular dish. Pour in one-third of the passata and the cold water and stir well.

Lay the aubergines and courgettes on to flat trays and sprinkle with the fine sea salt. Leave for 15 minutes so that they release their juices, then pat them dry with kitchen paper.

Place the potatoes in a large bowl and drizzle with two tablespoons of the olive oil, half a teaspoon of the dried oregano, quarter teaspoon of the fresh thyme leaves and black pepper. Mix until the potatoes are fully coated. Lay the potato slices flat at the bottom of the passata-lined baking tray.

Add the courgettes to the bowl you used to oil the potatoes, and drizzle in another two tablespoons of olive oil along with the remaining oregano, thyme and black pepper. Coat the courgette slices well, then add the aubergine to the bowl, along with another tablespoon of olive oil. Stir again and lay the aubergine and courgette slices on top of the potatoes. Place the baking tray on the bottom shelf of the oven and cook for 25–30 minutes while you prepare the ragù.

Recipe continued overleaf

For the base
7 tbsp olive oil
690 g (1 lb 9 oz) jar passata
100 ml (3½ fl oz) cold water
2 aubergines (500 g/1 lb 2 oz),
    sliced into ½-cm (¼-inch)
    rounds
2 large courgettes
    (500 g/1 lb 2 oz), sliced into
    ½-cm (¼-inch) rounds
4 Cyprus (or Maris Piper)
    potatoes (600 g/1 lb 5 oz),
    sliced into ½-cm (¼-inch)
    rounds
1 tsp salt
1 tsp dried oregano
½ tsp fresh thyme leaves
½ tsp coarse black pepper

For the ragù
1 beef stock cube
500 ml (18 fl oz pint) boiling
    water
3 tablespoons olive oil
2 large onions, finely chopped
1 kg (2 lb 4 oz) minced lamb
4 large garlic cloves, finely grated
1 tsp ground cumin
1 tsp paprika
1 bay leaf
1 cinnamon stick
1 tbsp pomegranate molasses
1 tbsp balsamic vinegar
1 tsp salt
¾ tsp ground black pepper

Dissolve the stock cube in a heatproof jug with the boiling water.

Heat up the olive oil in a large pan over a low–medium heat, add the onions and cook for 10–12 minutes until softened and translucent. Add the minced lamb to the pan, breaking it down with the back of a wooden spoon while it browns for 5–6 minutes. Add the garlic, cooking for another minute or two, then stir through the cumin, paprika, bay leaf and cinnamon stick. Pour in the remaining passata and the pomegranate molasses and balsamic vinegar. Season the minced lamb with the salt and black pepper, then pour over the beef stock. Bring everything to the boil, reduce the heat and simmer over a low–medium heat for around 30 minutes until the ragù has thickened.

Remove the vegetables from the oven, turn the courgette and aubergine slices over (without disturbing the potato layer), then brush them with the remaining tablespoon of olive oil, and bake uncovered for another 25–30 minutes.

Whisk the four eggs together in a bowl, then pour them into the cooled cheese sauce and whisk thoroughly to combine.

Remove the baking tray from the oven and transfer the aubergine and courgette slices to a plate. Reduce the oven temperature to 200°C/180°C fan/400°F/gas mark 6. Top the potatoes with the ragù, then layer the aubergine and courgette slices back on top of the ragù. Carefully pour and spread the béchamel on top. Sprinkle over the remaining grated Gruyère, then scatter the cherry tomato halves on the top, cut side up, with the fresh thyme leaves and a sprinkling of black pepper, to taste.

Put the baking tray on the middle shelf of the oven, and bake, uncovered, for 35–40 minutes until golden brown. Allow to cool for at least 30 minutes before serving so that the topping sets.

Etli Güveç

Oven-cooked Beef Stew

When I was nine years old, my dad helped a friend out at work one day, a Turkish gentleman called Kemal. As a gesture of goodwill, Kemal invited us to stay with him and his family in Antalya, Turkey.

This was the first time I had been to Turkey and I will never forget the beauty of the mountainous landscape of Kemer. We swam in one of the stunning waterfall holes and then had lunch by the side of a mountain; we were served a huge tray of *Etli Tava* (an oven-baked dish made with small pieces of lamb and vegetables cooked together), the flavours of which were so familiar to me.

As Cypriots, we often slow-cook meals like this with joints of meat, such as shanks or neck fillet, but traditionally Turkish *Tava* and *Güveç* are made with small pieces of meat. For this recipe I use braising beef, but you could also use the more traditional lamb, or chicken.

The concept of *Tava* is very similar to *Güveç*, the only difference being that the latter is layered into a deep clay pot, with the meat at the bottom, followed by the more robust vegetables, then topped with the tomatoes rather than spread out into a large round metal baking tray. It's the perfect dish for long, lazy weekends due to the slow-cooking methods, but it makes a good, hearty midweek meal too.

Serves 4

2 tbsp tomato purée
2 tbsp Turkish sweet red pepper paste (*tatlı biber salçası*)
1 chicken stock cube
400 ml (14 fl oz) boiling water
4 tbsp extra virgin olive oil
800 g (1 lb 9 oz) beef braising steak, diced
2 large red onions (300 g/10½ oz), thinly sliced
8 garlic cloves, peeled and bashed
2 bay leaves
1 tsp sea salt flakes
¾ tsp coarse black pepper
2 sweet red peppers (*kapya biber*) or 2 romano peppers or 2 small red bell peppers (250 g/9 oz)
2 sweet green peppers or 2 small green bell peppers (250 g/9 oz)

Ingredients continued overleaf

Preheat the oven to 180°C/160°C fan/350°F/gas mark 4.

Dissolve the tomato purée, sweet red pepper paste and stock cube in the boiling water in a heatproof jug and leave to one side.

Drizzle one tablespoon of olive oil in the bottom of a large heavy-based ovenproof pan or deep, lidded ovenproof dish, then evenly layer the meat at the bottom.

Lay the finely sliced pieces of one onion on top of the beef. Put four of the bashed garlic cloves into the pan or dish along with the bay leaves and season with a little of the salt and pepper. Core, deseed and roughly chop all the peppers into 2–3-cm (1–1½-inch) pieces and lay them on top of the onions, then season with a little more salt and black pepper. Peel and wash the potatoes and roughly chop them into 3-cm (1½-inch) chunks, then add them to the pan or dish, along with the lemon slices and the remaining four garlic cloves. Sprinkle over half of the dried mint and oregano. Lay the tomato slices on top of the potatoes, then season with the remaining salt and pepper and dried mint and oregano, finishing off with a good drizzle of the remaining three tablespoons of olive oil.

Recipe continued overleaf

750 g (1 lb 10 oz) Cyprus or
    Maris Piper potatoes
3 slices of fresh lemon
½ tsp dried mint
1 tsp dried oregano
4 tomatoes, halved and sliced

Pour the stock into the pan or dish and cover the top with a sheet of greaseproof paper, followed by a plate that fits inside (to weigh it down a little), and finally the lid. Place the dish on the bottom shelf of the oven for around 2 hours.

After 2 hours, remove the dish from the oven and carefully take off the lid, plate and greaseproof paper. Baste the top of the tomatoes with some of the juices, whilst keeping the layers intact as much as possible. Return to the bottom shelf of the oven, uncovered, for another 30–35 minutes and then increase the oven temperature to 220°C/200°C fan/425°F/gas mark 7 for a final 15–20 minutes, so that the top caramelises.

Remove the pan or dish from the oven, put the lid back on and allow to rest for 30 minutes or so before serving, spooning over the juices as you do.

Fırında Çipura ve Patates

Oven-roasted Sea Bream & Potatoes

I love roasted potatoes and roasting them in stock is a delicious way of seasoning them while they cook, especially when the flavours are enhanced with crispy, baked fish. This is such a simple recipe that requires some lovely, large whole sea bream (but can also be made with sea bass) and is just as fresh in the summer, as it is warming in the winter. I can't help but feel like I'm sitting by the Mediterranean Sea whenever I bring a tray of it to the table.

Serves 4

1 chicken stock cube
500 ml (18 fl oz) boiling water
1 kg (2 lb 4 oz) Cyprus or Maris Piper potatoes, washed, peeled and finely sliced
2 large onions, finely sliced into rounds
6 garlic cloves, finely grated
25 g (1 oz) finely chopped fresh flat leaf parsley leaves
3 sprigs fresh thyme, leaves removed
4 tbsp olive oil
1 tsp sea salt flakes
1 tsp coarse black pepper
1 tsp dried oregano
¼ tsp *pul biber*
2 tbsp fresh lemon juice
2 tsp white wine vinegar
2 large ripe tomatoes, thinly sliced
2 large, whole sea bream (approximately 600 g/ 1 lb 5 oz each), scaled and gutted
1 tsp extra virgin olive oil

Preheat the oven to 220°C/200°C fan/425°F/gas mark 7.

Dissolve the stock cube in the boiling water in a heatproof jug and leave to one side.

Put the potatoes and onions in a large bowl. Add the garlic, one-third of the parsley leaves and the thyme leaves to the potato and onion mix, along with two tablespoons of the olive oil, half a teaspoon of the sea salt, half a teaspoon of the black pepper, three-quarters of the dried oregano, the *pul biber*, lemon juice and white wine vinegar and give everything a really good stir. Transfer to a large roasting tray and pour over the stock. Place the tray on the bottom shelf of the oven and cook for 35–40 minutes.

While the potatoes are cooking, prep the fish. On a clean surface, brush the tomato slices with one tablespoon of the olive oil. Sprinkle the remaining oregano, black pepper, a little of the sea salt flakes, and another third of the chopped parsley over the tomatoes and give the slices a gentle rub to disperse the oil and herbs. Pat the fish completely dry on both sides, cut three deep incisions into each side of the fish, rub the skin with the remaining one tablespoon of olive oil, and season the skin and cavity with the remaining sea salt. Nestle the tomato slices into the cavity of each fish.

Remove the roasting tray from the oven and turn the temperature up to 220°C/200°C fan/425°F/gas mark 7. If the potatoes look dry and like they could do with a little extra liquid, pour another 100 ml (3½ fl oz) or so of water into the tray, then lay the fish on top of the potatoes. Return the tray to the middle shelf of the oven and bake for another 25–30 minutes until the fish is cooked and the potatoes have crisped up.

To serve, drizzle the fish with the extra virgin olive oil and sprinkle over the remaining one-third of parsley. Serve immediately with a fresh salad.

Barbecue Dishes & Accompaniments

Kebap & Köfte

This chapter is all about cooking over the *mangal* (barbecue). A *mangal* is a simple, traditional barbecue on four legs with an open-topped cuboid structure. Evenly spaced grooves run across the longest edges of the *mangal* where the long metal skewers used for *Kuzu Şiş* (Lamb Kebabs, pages 200–1) or grill racks can be rested over the hot coals. To cook something *ızgara* means to 'grill' it.

As a family we have been known to barbecue in the snow, and I know we're not the only ones. Growing up in a culture where until only recently outdoor cooking was traditionally the only way to cook conditions you to fall in love with the whole process without even questioning it. Marinading the meat, making dips and preparing the rice, breads and salads to accompany whatever you have chosen to cook on the *mangal* are all a regular part of a typical Cypriot weekend, family gathering, or even a random Tuesday night in January.

Weekend family barbecues were simple affairs. My mum, aunts and uncles had left their parents in Cyprus to start a new life in London and their way of connecting with 'home' was through these weekly barbecues. The host's house and garden would be a hubbub of excited activity. The kids would all be dancing or running around in the garden, Turkish *Arabesk* music blaring out of the stereo system, the dads congregated around the *mangal*, drinking their first Scotch whisky on the rocks, with the mums catching up in the kitchen while preparing the salads and *meze* dishes. Every *mangal* session would culminate with a *cezve* (pot) of Turkish coffee on the warm coals to end the night. This was our tradition. Our London-Cypriot diaspora tradition. And it was beautiful.

I didn't grow up having my mum's parents nearby, and we had to fly thousands of miles to visit them every year, but our love and connection was of the purest kind. My grandfather, Ahmet Dede, and my grandmother, Fatma Nene, were a miraculous pair, with so much love to give to all of us (during their lifetime, nine children and 23 grandchildren). They suffered indescribable losses that they never recovered from, especially Nene, yet she was always smiling through her beautiful, dark, squinted eyes, giving every single one of us all her heart, in full; always making sure we were all fed before she ever took a single bite.

There was nothing quite like my grandfather's sun-dried *ahtapot* (octopus). It was peppery, smoky, crunchy and chewy and Ahmet Dede would try to catch as many octopuses as he could before we all arrived in order to satisfy everyone's cravings. I would honestly dream about it before going to visit. For me, the smell and taste of my peppercorn and coriander-infused *Izgara Ahtapot* (Grilled Octopus, pages 216–17) cooked on the *mangal* instantly ignites those memories and is consequently one of my most treasured recipes in the book.

When barbecuing meat or fish, the grills always have to be hot before placing anything on them; the fish has to be patted dry, then brushed with olive oil. I always laugh to myself when I cook fish, such as whole bream or bass on the *mangal* as I can instantly hear my mum's voice in my head saying, 'don't touch it' in the gorgeous Cypriot accent that she has never lost, even after 40 years of living in London.

While I urge you to treat the *mangal* as an extension of your indoor kitchen and cook outside whenever you can, I have also included alternative cooking methods for many of the dishes here so that they recipes can still be enjoyed if you don't have an outdoor space. These are the kind of barbecue recipes that can be cooked week after week, and the whole experience of outdoor cooking naturally imbues a feeling of sunny vibes, whatever the weather. Serve the barbecued fish and seafood dishes together with the *Tahın* (Tahini Dip, page 68) and *Kuru Fasulye Salatası* (Cannellini Bean Salad, page 62). The *Kuzu Şiş* (pages 200–1) and *Tavuk Şiş* (Chicken Kebabs, page 199) are delicious served with *Hummus* (Chickpea & Tahini Dip, page 53), *Ezme Salatası* (Chilli Sauce, page 219) and *Summak Salata* (Sumac, Tomato, Onion & Parsley Salad, page 218).

Tavuk Şiş

Chicken Kebabs

I often make these kebabs together with my *Kuzu Şiş* (Lamb Kebabs, pages 200–1). Marinating the chicken like this really does help to infuse the flavours into the meat, while also keeping it tender. I prefer using boneless, skinless chicken thigh fillets (instead of chicken breast) as the dark meat retains so much more moisture than breasts when cooked; however, feel free to use whatever you prefer. Serve in *Kıbrıs Pidesi* (Cypriot Pitta Bread, pages 246–7) or with *Domatesli Bulgur Pilavı* (Tomato Bulgur Wheat Rice, page 103) and *Hummus* (Chickpea & Tahini Dip, page 53).

Serves 4–6

1 kg (2 lb 4 oz) skinless, boneless chicken thigh fillets, cut into 7.5-cm (3-inch) chunks
4–6 long metal skewers

For the marinade
4 tbsp thick set natural yoghurt
1 heaped tbsp Turkish sweet red pepper paste (*tatlı biber salçası*)
1 tbsp finely chopped fresh parsley leaves
1 tbsp olive oil
1 tbsp pomegranate molasses
1 tbsp clear honey
1 tsp salt
1 tsp black pepper
1 tsp *pul biber*
1 tsp paprika

To serve
1 tsp dried oregano
1 tsp fresh lemon juice
1 tsp extra virgin olive oil

For the marinade, mix all of the ingredients together in a large bowl or plastic storage box. Add the chicken pieces, coat in the marinade, and chill for at least 4 hours in the fridge (or overnight if possible).

Thread the chicken pieces on to 4–6 long metal skewers snugly, but not too tightly, to ensure that all the pieces cook evenly.

On the Barbecue

Light your barbecue. Make sure that the coals are mostly white and at a medium–hot, steady heat before cooking.

Cook for around 20–25 minutes or until the dark thigh meat is cooked through yet still tender with lightly charred, crispy edges. Turn the skewers regularly. If there is some marinade left in the bowl or plastic storage box, baste the chicken halfway through the cooking time.

To serve, mix together the dried oregano, lemon juice and extra virgin olive oil in a small bowl and brush over the freshly cooked kebabs.

Under the Grill

If you don't have access to a barbecue, preheat your grill to a medium heat.

Line a baking sheet with foil and lay the skewers across it, trying to balance both ends of the skewers on the raised rim of the baking sheet. Cook the kebabs under the preheated grill for 15–20 minutes (see above), turning every few minutes so they cook evenly. Spoon the delicious juices that have collected in the base of the baking sheet over the kebabs at the end of the cooking time and brush over the dried oregano, lemon and oil mixture before serving (see above).

Kuzu Şiş

Lamb Kebabs

Sometimes, basic really is best and with lamb *şiş* (kebabs) being such a customary feature at all Cypriot barbecues, I felt it was useful to impart some really handy tips (see opposite) to give you super-juicy, addictive lamb kebabs. I like to keep my kebabs simple with just some *kekik* (wild oregano) to flavour the meat, but you could of course experiment by adding some extra spices like paprika or *pul biber*.

If you have the time, please do make some fresh *Kıbrıs Pidesi* (Cypriot Pitta Bread, page 246–7) before preparing your kebabs; they really are the best vessel to serve the lamb *şiş* in. Just before serving the kebabs, warm the pitta bread on the *mangal* (barbecue), then pack the pockets full of freshly made *Salata* (Salad, page 54), *Şehriyeli Pilav* (Vermicelli Rice, page 102), the lamb and some *Cacık* (Yoghurt, Cucumber & Mint Dip, page 52) or *Hummus* (Chickpea & Tahini Dip, page 53).

Serves 4–6

1 kg (2 lb 4 oz) boneless lamb
    shoulder, cut into 3-cm
    (1¼-inch) cubes
2 tbsp olive oil
2 tsp wild oregano
6–8 long metal skewers
1½ tsp fine sea salt, plus extra
    to serve
Fresh lemon juice, to serve

When preparing the lamb, if there is a lot of excess fat on the meat, trim it off (although a little fat is good for flavour). Add the lamb cubes to a large bowl, drizzle over one tablespoon of the olive oil, sprinkle over the wild oregano and give the meat a good mix with your clean hands. Thread the cubes of lamb on to 6–8 long metal skewers snugly, but not too tightly, and drizzle over the remaining one tablespoon of olive oil (see Note opposite for tips on threading the skewers).

On the Barbecue

Light your barbecue. Make sure that the coals are mostly white, and at a medium–hot, steady heat before cooking the kebabs.

Place the skewers over the barbecue (if the shape of your barbecue allows, line the skewers on the edges so that they are directly over the coals rather than on a grill – if using grills over the coals, then make sure they are very hot before placing the kebabs on them). Cook the kebabs for 10–12 minutes, turning every few minutes so they cook evenly and sprinkling over the salt once they start to brown. Adjust the timing depending on how well-done you like your lamb. Once the lamb has browned and charred slightly in places, remove from the grill, sprinkle over a little more sea salt to taste and serve while hot.

Under the Grill

If you don't have access to a barbecue, preheat your grill to a medium heat.

Line a baking sheet with foil and lay the skewers across it, trying to balance both ends of the skewers on the raised rim of the sheet. Cook the kebabs under the preheated grill for 10–12 minutes, turning every few minutes so they cook evenly, sprinkling with the sea salt as you do. Adjust the timing depending on how well-done you like your lamb.

Helpful Tips

Don't overload the skewers with meat, as you want an even cook, and leave a little space at the top and bottom of the skewers, so that the meat is positioned directly over the coals.

Medium–hot coals mean that the coals should be mostly white, but that you can see *some* 'lit' action, without any harsh flames.

Sprinkle salt on the kebabs while they are cooking or after, not before, as salting the meat beforehand can risk the meat becoming tough (you can sprinkle some salt on the barbecue flames if they rage a little from the dripping fat).

Try not to overcook the kebabs – use the best quality meat you can afford, as it will taste beautifully tender. You'll know when the lamb is cooked as each piece should give a little to the touch when squeezed. If you cut your lamb cubes too small, you'll dry them out when cooking, so be sure to cut good 3-cm (1¾-inch) cubes all round when preparing.

If you don't have access to long metal skewers, then you can use wooden skewers that you have soaked in water beforehand (to prevent them from burning on the barbecue or under the grill). Since wooden skewers are smaller than the long metal ones, you may need a few more of them than the recipe states.

Kuzu Pirzola

Lamb Chops

When marinating meat for the *mangal* (barbecue), there are two things that help to tenderise it really well – for chicken, it's yoghurt, and for lamb cutlets or chops, it's milk. The lamb only needs a couple of hours in the marinade for the milk to really work its magic and leave you with the most succulent meat going. Try not to overcook the lamb, and make sure you eat the cutlets hot and fresh off the grill. They are delicious dipped into my *Ezme Salatası* (Chilli Sauce, page 219), or served alongside the *Domatesli Bulgur Pilavı* (Tomato Bulgur Wheat Rice, page 103) and *Cacık* (Yoghurt, Cucumber & Mint Dip, page 52).

Serves 4–6

2 large garlic cloves, crushed
   to a paste
1 tbsp Turkish sweet red pepper
   paste (*tatlı biber salçası*)
1 tbsp olive oil
1 tsp *pul biber*
½ tsp paprika
½ tsp ground cumin
1 tsp dried oregano
100 ml (3½ fl oz) milk
12 lamb cutlets
1 tsp sea salt flakes
½ tsp coarse black pepper

Add the crushed garlic to a large dish. Add the sweet red pepper paste, olive oil, *pul biber*, paprika, cumin, dried oregano and milk and mix everything together to create the marinade. Place the cutlets in between two sheets of plastic film or non-stick baking paper and very lightly bash them with a rolling pin to flatten them a little. Add the cutlets to the dish, coating them on both sides with the marinade. Cover the dish with plastic film and put it in the fridge to chill for 4 hours, turning the cutlets over after 2 hours of chilling time to ensure they fully take on the flavour of the marinade. Remove the cutlets from the fridge 30 minutes before cooking.

On the Barbecue

Light your barbecue. Make sure the coals are very hot, but mostly white, and that the grill is also very hot.

Give the lamb a final swish in the marinade, letting any excess drip off back into the dish and cook the cutlets for 3–5 minutes on each side, until the fat has rendered and is crispy and the cutlets are beautifully browned and lightly charred in places. Feel free to adjust the timing depending on how well-done you like your lamb. Season the cutlets with the salt and pepper as they cook. Serve immediately.

Under the Grill

If you don't have access to a barbecue, preheat your grill to high.

Line a baking sheet with foil, then lay a grill rack on top. Give the lamb a final swish in the marinade, letting any excess drip off back into the dish and lay the cutlets out on the grill rack. Cook under the preheated grill for 3–5 minutes on each side, depending on how well-done you like your lamb. Season with the salt and pepper as they cook and serve immediately.

Izgara Köfte
Grilled Meat Patties

Hot, freshly grilled *köfte* (meat patties) wrapped in *bidda* (flatbreads) or popped into *Kıbrıs Pidesi* (Cypriot Pitta Bread, pages 246–7) with a simple sumac salad and *Kısır* (Fine Bulgur Wheat Salad, page 61) were a weekly occurrence on the *mangal* (barbecue) for us, always prepared and cooked by my mum. However, when I'm feeling nostalgic and want to pay homage to numerous summers spent in Cyprus' beachside cafes, I pop these patties into *bidda*, with freshly made chips, *Hummus* (Chickpea & Tahini Dip, page 53), fresh tomatoes, parsley, grilled *hellim* (halloumi cheese) and make myself an iconic *Bidda Badadez* (which literally translates as 'flatbread and potatoes') wrap.

Makes 12

1 large onion, coarsely grated
50 g (1¾ oz) fresh flat leaf
     parsley, finely chopped
400 g (14 oz) minced lamb
400 g (14 oz) minced beef
3 tbsp Turkish sweet red pepper
     paste (*tatlı biber salçası*)
1 tbsp olive oil
1 tsp ground cumin
1 tsp paprika
½ tsp *pul biber*
2 tsp dried mint
1½ tsp coarse black pepper
1½ tsp sea salt flakes

Place the grated onion in a sieve and squeeze out all the juice before adding to a large bowl. Add all the other ingredients and with clean hands mix well. Divide and shape the mixture into 12 patties and lay them on a baking sheet.

Put the baking sheet in the fridge and chill the patties for an hour, removing them from the fridge 30 minutes before you are ready to cook them.

On the Barbecue

Light your barbecue. Make sure the coals are hot, but mostly white, and that the grill is also very hot.

Cook the patties for 6–8 minutes on each side, turning carefully throughout to ensure even cooking. Try not to turn them over until they have charred and sealed on the underside to prevent them from sticking to the grill. Serve immediately stuffed into flatbreads or pitta breads.

Under the Grill

If you don't have access to a barbecue, preheat your grill to medium–high.

Line a baking sheet with foil, then lay a grill rack on top. Evenly space the patties on the grill rack.

Cook under the preheated grill for 6–8 minutes on each side, turning a couple of times as they cook and serve immediately stuffed into flatbreads or pitta breads.

Izgara Tavuk

Barbecue Chicken Wings & Thighs

The warm and inviting aromas of this dish are a result of the sweetly spiced yoghurt-based marinade I use for all kinds of joints and cuts of chicken – wings, thighs, drumsticks, skinless or boneless. The yoghurt-based marinade helps to gently tenderise the meat, keeping it soft enough to pull apart once cooked. Just before the chicken is cooked, I brush each piece with a delicious glaze which gives the lightly-charred meat an appetizingly decadent sheen and an additional layer of flavour and juiciness. Delicious served with my *Ezme Salatası* (Chilli Sauce, page 219), *Çıtır Çıtır Fırında Patates Kızartması* (Crunchy Baked Chips, page 181) or *Kısır* (Fine Bulgur Wheat Salad, page 61) or *Şehriyeli Pilav* (Vermicelli Rice, page 102) and *Pancar Salatası* (Beetroot Salad, page 50).

Serves 4–6

1 kg (2 lb 4 oz) chicken wings, thighs or drumsticks

For the marinade

2 tbsp thick set natural yoghurt
2 tbsp Turkish sweet red pepper paste (*tatlı biber salçası*)
1 tbsp olive oil
1 tbsp pomegranate molasses
4 garlic cloves, finely grated
2 tsp dried oregano
1 tsp cumin
1 tsp *pul biber*
1 tsp paprika
1 tsp smoked paprika
1 tsp salt
¾ tsp coarse black pepper

For the glaze

1 tbsp olive oil
2 tbsp pomegranate molasses
2 tbsp clear honey

For the marinade, mix everything together in a large dish.

Add the chicken and coat thoroughly in the marinade, cover with plastic film and put in the fridge to chill for a minimum of 4 hours. It's even better if you can leave it overnight.

Remove from the fridge 30 minutes before cooking to bring to room temperature.

On the Barbecue

Light your barbecue, keeping a small space free of any coals. Make sure that the coals are at a moderate, steady heat before cooking, and that the grill is also hot. You need to cook bone-in chicken slowly over direct heat. If you keep a small space on the barbecue that is free of any coals, then you can remove the chicken to this indirect heat if it begins to char too quickly.

Make sure the chicken has absorbed as much of the marinade as possible, but don't leave too much excess on when cooking, otherwise it may result in burnt chicken skin. Cooking times depend on the type of chicken, but as a guide barbecue the chicken wings for 20–25 minutes, drumsticks for 30–35 minutes and if using thighs, cook for 35–45 minutes. Use a meat thermometer to check if you're unsure.

For the glaze, add the olive oil, pomegranate molasses and honey to a small bowl and mix. Five to ten minutes before the end of the cooking time, brush the glaze over both sides of the chicken to give a lovely sweet and sticky coating, then serve immediately while hot.

In the Oven

Preheat your oven to 200°C/180°C fan/400°F/gas mark 6.

Line a baking sheet with foil, then lay a grill rack on top. Evenly space the chicken on the grill rack, spooning any remaining marinade over it before placing the sheet on the middle shelf of the preheated oven. Cook wings for around 35–40 minutes and drumsticks and thighs for 45–50 minutes, turning the heat up to 220°C/200°C fan/425°F/gas mark 7 for the last 5–10 minutes if the skin needs crisping up a little. The juices will run clear once cooked. Remove and brush over the prepared glaze (see opposite), then serve immediately, while hot.

Şeftali Kebap

Lamb Caul Fat Sausages

This is another typically Cypriot recipe, made by wrapping what is essentially a *köfte* (meat patty) mix in lamb caul fat, a delicately thin and lacy internal membrane, to create sausage-shaped patties. Speak to your local butcher about sourcing lamb caul fat for you, as this is not something that is readily found in mainstream supermarkets. When the sausages cook over hot coals, the heat renders the caul fat, sealing it into the *köfte* and creating the most beautiful, charred flavour and deliciously mouth-watering texture. I always keep a stash of these in the freezer and simply defrost (and pat dry) before grilling them on the *mangal* (barbecue). All you need is some *Kıbrıs Pidesi* (Cypriot Pitta Bread, pages 246–7) lightly toasted on the *mangal*, and some freshly made *Salata* (Salad, page 54) to pack into the pitta along with the *Şeftali Kebap* for an exquisite lunch or dinner.

Makes 24–26

500 g (1 lb 2 oz) lamb caul fat
Juice of 1 large lemon

For the filling
500 g (1 lb 2 oz) minced beef
500 g (1 lb 2 oz) minced lamb
2 tsp paprika
2 tsp ground cumin
1½ tsp salt
1 tsp ground black pepper
4 onions (400 g/14 oz), very
    finely diced
100 g (3½ oz) flat leaf parsley,
    finely chopped

An hour before you are ready to prepare your filling mixture, wash the caul fat thoroughly in cold water, wash again and drain in a colander. Place in a bowl with a little water and the lemon juice for 45 minutes– 1 hour (I throw the squeezed lemon into the bowl too).

Place the minced meats in a large bowl and add the paprika, cumin, half a teaspoon of the salt and the black pepper, onions and parsley. Mix the ingredients together until fully amalgamated.

Lay a large piece of the drained caul fat out on a clean chopping board.

Take a small handful, roughly 60 g (2¼ oz) of the mince mixture and, with your hands, mould into a chunky sausage shape. Place the sausage on the corner of the caul fat, roll the fat over the meat, bring in the sides of the fat, roll the fat over a little more so that it goes over on itself, then cut with a sharp knife and seal it around the meat. Repeat with the remaining mixture and caul fat.

If cooking on a barbecue, either place the *şeftali* into a grill basket, or thread each one through two metals skewers which will keep them supported and make them easier to turn when cooking, with 6–8 sausages on a double set of skewers. Repeat the threading process until all the sausages are on skewers.

On the Barbecue

Light your barbecue, keeping a small space free of any coals. Make sure that the coals are mostly white and medium–hot before cooking.

Grill for 15–20 minutes, turning regularly until the fat has been completely rendered into the meat and the sausages are evenly browned. If any flames are ignited from the dripping fat, move the skewers or basket around and off the direct heat. Some salt sprinkled over the coals will calm the flames. For the final 5 minutes of cooking time, sprinkle over the remaining teaspoon of salt.

Serve immediately in warm pitta bread, with the *Summak Salata* (Sumac, Tomato, Onion & Parsley Salad, page 218) and a squeeze of lemon juice.

In the Oven

Preheat your oven to 220°C/200°C fan/425°F/gas mark 7.

Line a baking sheet with foil, then lay a grill rack on top. Evenly space the *şeftali* on the grill rack. Cook on the middle shelf for 20–25 minutes, or a little longer until the fat has been completely rendered into the meat and the sausages are evenly browned. Turn halfway through cooking, or more frequently if necessary. Serve as above.

Balık Şeftali Kebap

Fish Caul Fat Sausages

I first tried *Balık Şeftali Kebap* (Fish Caul Fat Sausages) at Hürdeniz restaurant in Girne harbour and was fascinated by them, as I had only ever eaten the meat ones. These fish kebabs are a great alternative to meat and would work brilliantly as part of a fish *meze* barbecue spread at home too. They are shaped in the same way as the *Şeftali Kebap* (Lamb Caul Fat Sausages, pages 208–9), but I use white fish fillets in place of the lamb, which are gently blitzed in the food processor so that the resulting texture of the fish has a consistency comparable to that of mince. Serve the *Balık Şeftali Kebap* with *Kıbrıs Pidesi* (Cypriot Pitta Bread, pages 246–7), *Bakla Salatası* (Broad Bean Salad, page 57), *Kuru Fasulye Salatası* (Cannellini Bean Salad, page 62), *Tahın* (Tahini Dip, page 68) and *Pancar Salatası* (Beetroot Salad, page 50).

Makes 12

500 g (1 lb 2 oz) lamb caul fat
Juice of 1 large lemon

For the filling
2 red onions (150 g/5½ oz), roughly chopped
50 g (1¾ oz) fresh flat leaf parsley, roughly chopped
500 g (1 lb 2 oz) skinless, boneless cod, haddock or hallbut fillets, roughly chopped
1 large red bell pepper, very finely diced
1 large green bell pepper, very finely diced
1 tbsp Turkish sweet red pepper paste (*tatlı biber salçası*)
1 tsp paprika
½ tsp *pul biber*
1 tsp salt
1 tsp ground black pepper
1 egg

An hour before you are ready to prepare your filling mixture, wash the caul fat thoroughly in cold water, wash again and drain in a colander. Place in a bowl and cover with cold water and the lemon juice for around an hour (I throw the squeezed lemon into the bowl too).

Add the roughly chopped onion and parsley to a food processor, and blitz until finely chopped, then transfer to a sieve and allow any liquid to drain into a bowl while you prepare the rest of the ingredients.

Put the fish pieces into a food processor, pulse the fish a few times until the chunks have been chopped up into much smaller pieces (without it becoming a purée), then transfer to a large bowl. Give the onions and parsley one final squeeze through the sieve, then add them to the peppers, sweet red pepper paste, paprika, *pul biber*, half a teaspoon of the salt and black pepper and stir to combine.

Drain the caul fat as much as you can and lay a large piece of it out on a clean chopping board. Roughly divide the fish filling mixture into 12 portions and, with clean hands, shape into a sausage and place on the corner of the caul fat. Roll the fat over the mixture, bring in the sides of the fat and continue to roll over a little more so that the fat goes over on itself, then cut with a sharp knife and seal it around the fish sausage. Repeat with the remaining mixture and caul fat. If you prefer, you can cut all the 14 cm x 10-cm (5½ inch x 4-inch) pieces of caul fat and roll each one individually, rather than from one large piece of fat.

When all the fish sausages are rolled, thread each one horizontally on two metal skewers (a total of six sausages on each double set of skewers) or arrange them in a grilling basket for ease. If cooking in the oven, there is no need to thread the sausages on to skewers.

On the Barbecue

Light your barbecue. Make sure that the coals are at a medium heat before cooking.

Grill for 15–20 minutes, turning regularly, until the fat has been completely rendered and the sausages are evenly browned. If any flames are ignited from the dripping fat while the kebabs cook, move the skewers or basket around and off the direct heat. Sprinkle the kebabs with the remaining half teaspoon of salt as they cook.

Serve immediately with a squeeze of lemon juice.

In the Oven

Preheat your oven to 220°C/200°C fan/425°F/gas mark 7.

Line a baking sheet with foil, then lay a grill rack on top. Evenly space the *şeftali* on the grill rack. Cook on the middle shelf for 12–15 minutes or until the fat has been completely rendered into the fish and the sausages are evenly browned, turning halfway through cooking, or more frequently if necessary. Serve as above.

Maymun Balık Şiş

Monkfish Kebabs

When I visit Cyprus, I often find myself eating a lot more barbecued fish than meat, as the memories of eating freshly caught seafood by the sea, which are naturally heightened by the aromas, the climate and the very special company of my family are what I long for when I am not there. Monkfish is such a fabulous, meaty fish to barbecue and reminds me of the theatrical hanging fish skewers served at Peri's fish restaurant in Girne. The luxurious spiced butter in my recipe finishes off these kebabs beautifully, giving them a lovely glossy coating. This monkfish dish is best eaten fresh off the *mangal* (barbecue) to really benefit from the juicy, meaty, chargrilled texture of the fish.

Serves 4

750 g (1 lb 10 oz) monkfish tail, cut into 3–4-cm (1–1½-inch) pieces

2 large onions, chopped into 3–4-cm (1–1½-inch) pieces

2 sweet red peppers (*kapya biber*) or romano peppers, chopped into 3–4-cm (1–1½-inch) pieces

2 tbsp olive oil

½ tsp paprika

½ tsp sweet smoked paprika

½ tsp *pul biber*

For the butter sauce

30 g (1 oz) unsalted butter

1 tbsp fresh lemon juice

½ tsp dried oregano

1 tsp finely chopped fresh flat leaf parsley leaves

Zest of 1 lemon

¾ tsp sea salt flakes

¼ tsp cracked black pepper

Put the monkfish, onion and pepper pieces into a large dish or bowl. Mix the olive oil, paprika, sweet smoked paprika and *pul biber* together and spread over the monkfish and vegetable pieces. Cover the dish with plastic film and chill in the fridge for an hour.

Take some metal skewers and thread 5–6 pieces of fish on to each one, with the onion, red and green pepper interspersed between each piece of fish.

Now prepare the butter sauce. Melt the butter in a small pan over a medium heat. Add the lemon juice, dried oregano and parsley, give everything a stir, then remove from the heat. Stir through the lemon zest, sea salt flakes and black pepper.

On the Barbecue

Light your barbecue. Make sure that the coals are at a medium heat before cooking.

Keep the butter sauce hot in the pan next to the barbecue while you grill the monkfish skewers over open hot coals (there is no need to use a grill if your skewers fit across your barbecue). If they don't, then make sure the grill is hot and grease with a little olive oil before placing the kebabs on top to prevent the fish from sticking. Do not be tempted to move the kebabs until the fish has crisped up a little on the underside.

Barbecue the fish for 12–15 minutes, turning the skewers every few minutes for an even cook, and once the pieces are still soft but opaque and cooked through, brush them all over with the butter sauce. Remove from the barbecue and serve immediately with an extra squeeze of lemon juice and a sprinkling of *pul biber*.

Under the Grill

If you don't have access to a barbecue, preheat your grill to a medium heat.

Line a baking sheet with foil and lay the skewers across it, trying to balance both ends of the skewers on the raised rim of the baking sheet. Cook for 12–15 minutes, or until the fish pieces are still soft but opaque and cooked through, turning the skewers every few minutes for an even cook. Once cooked, brush them all over with the butter sauce. Serve immediately (as opposite).

Izgara Jumbo Karides ve Galamar

Grilled Tiger Prawns & Squid

I absolutely adore the tender flesh of beautifully barbecued tiger prawns, my preference being Madagascan tiger prawns (pictured opposite) as they are so much bigger, and this has been one of my most cooked recipes on the *mangal* (barbecue) in the past couple of years. The marinade is warmed through first so that the flavours really get a chance to infuse together, and once cooled, half of it is used to marinade the seafood and the other half is reserved to slather all over the prawns as soon as they come off the *mangal*.

Serves 4–6

12 tiger prawns, raw,
   shell-on (1 kg/2 lb 4 oz)
2 whole squid, tubes and
   tentacles cleaned
   (500 g/1 lb 2 oz)
½ tsp sea salt flakes
½ tsp cracked black pepper,
   plus extra to serve
Sunflower oil, for brushing
   (optional)

For the marinade

3 tbsp extra virgin olive oil
1 tsp smoked paprika
2 tsp *pul biber*
1 tsp crushed garlic
2 tbsp Turkish sweet red pepper
   paste (*tatlı biber salçası*)
4 tbsp pomegranate molasses
1 tsp clear honey
2 tbsp fresh lemon juice,
   plus extra to serve
1 tsp finely chopped fresh
   flat leaf parsley leaves,
   plus extra to serve
1 tsp dried oregano

In a small pan over a low heat, add the olive oil, and once hot, add the smoked paprika, *pul biber* and garlic, and cook for 30 seconds, before adding the sweet red pepper paste. Spread out the sweet red pepper paste with the back of a wooden spoon so that it starts to sizzle, then add the pomegranate molasses, honey and lemon juice and cook until it begins to bubble. Remove from the heat and allow to cool a little.

Prepare the prawns. Do not peel, but gently score along the back of one prawn with a sharp knife, slicing through the shell and a little into the flesh. Remove the vein, discard it, and carefully open up the back of the prawn slightly to half-butterfly it; this will enable the marinade to soak through into the flesh. Repeat this with the remaining prawns. Score the squid tubes slightly in a criss-cross pattern with the sharp knife and keep the tentacles whole.

Take two tablespoons of the marinade and gently rub over the prawns and squid. Season the seafood with the salt and pepper. Add the parsley leaves and oregano to the remaining marinade.

On the Barbecue

Light your barbecue. Make sure that the coals are at a high heat and the grill is very hot as the prawns and squid need fast cooking.

Barbecue the seafood for 3–4 minutes on each side until the prawns turn pink inside and the squid is chargrilled on the outside. Slice the chargrilled squid into rings, and coat everything in the reserved marinade. Serve with an extra squeeze of lemon juice, fresh parsley and cracked black pepper.

On a Griddle Pan

Brush a griddle pan with some sunflower oil and heat on the hob until very hot.

Cook the seafood for 3–4 minutes on each side until the prawns turn pink inside and the squid is chargrilled on the outside. Slice the chargrilled squid into 1-cm (½-inch) rings, and coat everything in the reserved marinade. Serve immediately (as above).

Izgara Ahtapot

Grilled Octopus

This recipe is a tribute to my Ahmet Dede's (my maternal grandfather's) one-in-a-million sun-dried octopus. I braise the octopus in red wine and lots of black peppercorns to try and replicate the intensity of its dehydrated and peppery flavour. This is a recipe that really benefits from being grilled over hot coals, rather than on a griddle pan or under a grill.

Serves 8

1 large octopus (2–3 kg/
   4 lb 8 oz–6 lb 8 oz)
1 whole garlic bulb, halved
250 ml (9 fl oz) red wine
200 ml (7 fl oz) water
2 bay leaves
3 tbsp black peppercorns
1 tbsp red wine vinegar
1 tbsp finely chopped fresh
   coriander
¼ tsp sea salt flakes

For the marinade and dressing

100 ml (3½ fl oz) extra virgin
   olive oil
3 large garlic cloves, crushed or
   finely grated
Zest of 1 lemon
2 tbsp coriander seeds
2 tsp dried oregano
½ tsp coarse black pepper

Cut the head off the octopus with a sharp knife, ensuring that you cut above the eyes. Remove the eyes from the body and push through the hole at the top of the body to remove the beak. Discard the eyes and the beak.

Add the garlic bulb halves to a large pan with the red wine, water, bay leaves, peppercorns and red wine vinegar. Place it over a medium heat and after a few minutes, the mixture will come to a simmer.

Put the end of a wooden spoon through the hole at the top of the body of the octopus and lower the octopus into the pan so that it touches the bottom, without dropping it into the red wine mixture. Lift it back out and you will see that the tentacles have started to curl, then repeat this twice more before taking out the wooden spoon and leaving the octopus in the pan. Place the lid on the pan and simmer over a low–medium heat for 45 minutes–1 hour, until the octopus is tender. You can check to see if the octopus is tender by inserting a knife into the thickest part of the body. If it slides through without resistance, then it's ready. Remove from the heat and transfer the head and body of the octopus to a large dish, draining the excess liquid back into the pan before doing so. Allow to cool to room temperature (the stock is delicious, so once cooled, freeze to use at a later stage).

For the marinade, pour all but 30 ml (1 fl oz) of the extra virgin olive oil into a small bowl. Add the garlic and lemon zest (reserving the lemon to juice later). Break down the coriander seeds a little in a pestle and mortar and add with the dried oregano and black pepper. Give everything a good stir, then pour it into the large dish containing the octopus, coating the octopus on both sides. Cover the dish in plastic film and put it in the fridge to chill for at least 2 hours, or overnight if possible.

Remove the octopus from the fridge 30 minutes before you plan to barbecue it, to allow it to come up to room temperature again.

Light your barbecue. Make sure that the coals are at a high heat and the grill is very hot so that the octopus won't stick to it, which will remove the lovely skin. Lift the octopus straight out of the dish, removing any large chunks of the marinade. Drizzle the octopus with the remaining olive oil, then place it straight on to the barbecue grill.

Do not wash up the dish as you will be placing the octopus back in the marinade once it's cooked.

Grill the octopus head and body for a few minutes on each side so that the skin chars and crisps up fully on both sides – don't be tempted to turn the octopus over until you can see that the underside has chargrilled. Once cooked, remove the octopus from the barbecue and place on a chopping board, slicing the head into thick rings, and carving the body into its eight separate tentacles. Halve the reserved lemon and squeeze two tablespoons of juice into the marinade dish, then add most of the fresh coriander and give everything a good stir. Add the carved-up octopus to the dish and give all the pieces a gentle swish to fully coat them in the marinade. Transfer the pieces to a serving platter, pouring the marinade juices from the dish over the octopus. Garnish with the remaining fresh coriander and a sprinkling of the sea salt flakes to serve.

Summmak Salata

Sumac, Tomato, Onion & Parsley Salad

This fresh and simple salad is sometimes the only salad you need at a (Turkish) Cypriot barbecue, especially if the meat of choice is barbecued lamb. In Cypriot cuisine, sumac is mainly used as a seasoning and topper for *meze* dishes and salads. The citrusy tartness of the sumac really complements grilled meat and fish, especially when it mixes with the slightly sweet, yet tart flavours of the salad dressing. The salad is usually stuffed into a pitta bread with the lamb and a generous dollop of *Cacık* (Yoghurt, Mint & Cucumber Dip, page 52) or *Hummus* (Chickpea & Tahini Dip, page 53).

Serves 4–6

2 large red onions, finely sliced
100 g (3½ oz) fresh flat leaf
    parsley leaves, finely chopped
2 large ripe tomatoes, diced

For the dressing
2 tbsp sumac
3 tbsp pomegranate molasses
3 tbsp extra virgin olive oil
1 tsp sea salt flakes

Add the onions, parsley and tomatoes to a large serving bowl or dish.

Mix all of the dressing ingredients in a small bowl and pour over the salad just before serving. Perfect with any of the grilled barbecued meat and fish recipes in this chapter.

Ezme Salatası

Chilli Sauce

That moreish red and green speckled chilli sauce you see served in Turkish *mangal* (barbecue) restaurants is also frequently made at home at domestic family barbecues too, and this is my very simple and delicious recipe for it. Everything goes straight into a food processor (even though, traditionally, it is all chopped by hand) and is blitzed to your desired consistency – I usually like my sauce to be a little chunky. It keeps well in the fridge for up to five days, and I actually prefer the flavour and texture a couple of days after I have made it. I serve it alongside absolutely everything.

Makes 390-g (14-oz) jar

1–2 red or green chillies
1 large onion, quartered
2 garlic cloves, finely grated
25 g (1 oz) fresh flat leaf parsley
    leaves and stalks, roughly
    chopped
400 g (14 oz) can chopped
    tomatoes
2 tbsp Turkish sweet red pepper
    paste (*tatlı biber salçası*)
1 tsp pomegranate molasses
1 tsp dried mint
2 tsp *pul biber*
2 tbsp extra virgin olive oil
½ tsp sea salt flakes
Pinch of caster sugar

Remove the stalk from one of the chillies, and finely chop the flesh, including the seeds. I always start with one chilli and add another after tasting the sauce if I feel like it needs more of a kick.

Add the chilli and the rest of the ingredients to a food processor and pulse to a consistency of your liking. Taste the mixture and, if necessary, feel free to add some more chilli and an extra pinch of salt.

Store in a sterilised jar (page 26) in the fridge for up to 5 days.

Homemade Breads, Doughs and Pastries

Ekmek & Hamur İşi

When my mum talks about her grandmother, Meyrem Nene, she relives memories of them making flatbreads and fried pastries together, and how my great-grandmother would be called to neighbouring houses to cook fresh batches of *Pirohu* (Cypriot Ricotta-filled Ravioli, pages 236–7) and to bake fresh breads for them out of the goodness of her huge heart, where her humble 'payment' was a plate of the food she had lovingly cooked to take home for herself. So, it is no surprise that after the hours spent in her grandmother's kitchen, my mum is also the most wonderful cook, an inspiration to me, and we have carried on her grandmother's legacy in continuing to make her recipes to this day.

Meyrem Nene was deaf and communicated with my mum through sign language and lip-reading – they had a very special bond. Mum would watch her Nene for hours, helping her take the bread and pastry-filled *sele* (flat Cypriot baskets that were used to transport pastries and breads to communal ovens) to her parents' outdoor clay oven. The oven was offered to other villagers to use and cook their own village loaves and *Kafes Peksemet* (Gate-shaped Breadsticks, pages 251–2).

My mum was around 16 years old when Meyrem Nene passed and her death left a huge hole in my mum's heart and life – one that my mum felt she could only slowly start to heal by learning to perfect the recipes she had spent years watching her grandmother cook.

My mum recalls the first time she tried to roll out her own dough after Meyrem Nene's death, just as she had been taught, but it ended up being a bit of a disaster. My grandmother, Fatma Nene, laughed, took the *oklava* (a long, thin rolling pin) out of my mum's hands and showed her how to roll and turn the pastry at a 45° angle each time she pushed the rolling pin back and forth, which would result in a large circular piece of *yufka* (freshly rolled, thin filo). The same thing happened to me the first time I tried to roll out my own pastry – even though I had watched my mum effortlessly handle her *oklava* for years, doing it myself for the first time required a lot more time and patience than I had anticipated. After various attempts and some determined perseverance over the years, *Meyrem Nenenin Ispanaklı Börek* (Meyrem Nene's Spinach Pies, pages 248–50) now regularly live on in my own kitchen too.

As a young girl, many a school holiday would be spent making pastries with my mum, sister Yeliz and my cousins. My mum would give us small pieces of dough to keep busy and play with, while she artfully honed pastry after pastry, rolling with her *oklava* and shaping and cutting with the edge of a saucer (page 226) exactly as Meyrem Nene would have done.

Thirty years on, I love to fill my own kitchen with the beautiful sweetly spiced fragrances of *mahlep* (a spice made from cherry seeds), cinnamon and cloves. I use these spices to infuse my *Kıbrıs Çöreği* (Cypriot Seeded Bread, pages 224–6), but I also adore the yeasty aromas of lusciously soft, oval-shaped *Kıbrıs Pidesi* (Cypriot Pitta Bread, pages 246–7) and the sticky, flaky, soft textures of *Tahınlı* (Tahini Pastries, pages 231–2) – scents that make me fully appreciate the slow-rise of each ball of pillowy dough, and every roll of the *oklava*.

This chapter is packed full of wholesome, baked recipes to stock your freezer with and to share with your family at breakfast or dinner, or with friends over a cup of tea. They are recipes that can be prepared together, especially with children, and shared – eaten hot or cold, with dips, packed with fillings or sprinkled with something sweet or cheesy. You'll see that there is a Cypriot bread or pastry for every day of the week.

Kıbrıs Çöreği

Cypriot Seeded Bread

I can't tell you how much I love this recipe or how many times I've made this bread over the years –it's a popular recipe on my blog and my Instagram page. We never buy *çörek* (seeded bread) any more because the flavour and texture simply doesn't compare to this one, unless you are fortunate enough to try one from a traditional *fırın* (bakery) in Cyprus.

There are various methods used to make Cypriot seeded bread; I use a spice mix of cinnamon, cloves and mahleb (a spice made from ground cherry stones), but you can also make a spiced black tea, like *Kokulu Çay* (Spiced Cypriot Tea, page 42) and use that as the liquid in place of the water. Traditionally, milk isn't used in the dough, however, I cannot resist the light and fluffy texture it gives the bread when baked, so this is my only non-traditional addition. Allow the bread to cool a little before breaking open. Once the bread goes a little stale, you can thinly slice the segments and toast or grill them or cut them up into chunky cubes and fry them to add to soups as delicious croutons.

Makes 1 loaf

For the dough
225 ml (8 fl oz) lukewarm milk
100 ml (3½ fl oz) lukewarm water
1 tsp caster sugar
7 g (¼ oz) fast-action dried yeast
500 g (1 lb 2 oz) strong white bread flour
¼ tsp ground cinnamon
¼ tsp ground cloves
Pinch of mahleb
1½ tsp salt
1½ tbsp olive oil

For brushing
1 tbsp flour
1 tsp water
1 tsp milk

For coating
4 tbsp sesame seeds
1 tsp nigella seeds
¼ tsp aniseed

In a heatproof jug, mix the milk and water, add the sugar and stir to dissolve. Add the yeast, give it a gentle stir and leave to one side for 5–10 minutes until it's activated. The liquid will rise and turn frothy when ready.

Meanwhile, sift the flour into a large mixing bowl and stir through the cinnamon, cloves, mahleb and salt. Make a well in the centre of the flour and spices.

Stir the olive oil into the activated yeast mixture and pour into the well at the centre of the dry ingredients and start to bring everything together with clean hands to form a dough. Turn the dough out on to a clean surface and start to knead. You shouldn't need any more flour at this point. Keep kneading by hand for 10–12 minutes until a nice smooth dough is formed, tucking the sides under as you finish. Alternatively, place everything into a stand mixer and knead with the dough hook attachment for 10 minutes.

Spread a little oil over the dough, place it back into the bowl and cover the bowl with plastic film and a clean tea towel. Leave the bowl somewhere warm and cosy to prove for at least an hour (but no longer than 1½ hours) until it doubles in size.

Mix all the seeds together on a large tray. The dough will be coated in this seeded mixture once shaped.

Once the dough has risen, take it out of the bowl and gently punch it down for a few seconds.

Recipe continued on page 226

Roll the slightly flattened dough into a long 30-cm (12-inch) smooth, chunky sausage, slightly shaping the ends into curved points, tucking any creases underneath. Using a dough cutter (or a saucer, like my mum has always done) cut horizontally all the way through the dough in eight equal sections to create eight separate segments. Gently push the pieces back together to reform the original sausage shape while maintaining the shapes of those distinct segments. Mix the flour, water and milk in a small bowl to create a smooth paste and brush it all over the dough.

Carefully lift the shaped dough and transfer it to the tray of seeds, coating the bread all over so that no seeds remain in the tray.

Line a deep baking tray with greaseproof paper, place the dough on it and cover with a tea towel. Leave somewhere warm to prove the dough again for another hour.

While the dough is proving, preheat your oven to 230°C/210°C fan/450°F/gas mark 8.

Pour 100 ml (3½ fl oz) water into a glass. Once the dough has finished proving for the second time, place the baking tray on the middle shelf of the oven, and throw the water (not the glass) into the bottom of the oven to create steam. Quickly close the oven door and bake the dough for around 25 minutes until beautifully golden brown. Allow to cool a little before serving.

Note

This will freeze well wrapped in foil. Remove from the freezer a couple of hours before you need it, then preheat your oven to 180°C/160°C fan/350°F/gas mark 4 and put the wrapped loaf on the middle shelf of the oven for 20–25 minutes or until fully warmed through. The crust should harden up again and the middle will be as soft and light as if it has just been freshly baked.

Bulla Ekmek

Halloumi, Olive & Herb Loaf

This is a recipe that I get asked for so often but one that I committed myself to not sharing until I wrote this book; it is essentially the yeasted bread sister of my *Hellimli Zeytinli Kek* (Halloumi & Black Olive Cake, page 40). I remember a friend saying to me that I should save my 'gold', my most treasured recipes, for when I wrote my book and this is definitely one of those recipes.

This recipe results in the softest loaf, ever so slightly crusty on the outside, and loaded with chunks of *hellim* (halloumi cheese), dry black olives, caramelised onion and fresh spring onion, and peppered with green flecks of fresh mint and coriander. It's delicious eaten warm from the oven and dipped into excellent extra virgin olive oil, but it can also be frozen (whole and wrapped in foil), defrosted then reheated in the oven (see Cypriot Seeded Bread, page 226 for a Note on reheating temperatures and method), or sliced and frozen, then toasted and buttered.

There is a taste of Cyprus in every mouthful and I can't help but envisage those beautiful images of large, outdoor *fırın* laden with loaf after loaf, all rising in synchronisation with each other every time I make this recipe.

Makes 2 loaves

For the dough

225 ml (8 fl oz) lukewarm water
100 ml (3½ fl oz) lukewarm milk
½ tsp caster sugar
7 g (¼ oz) fast-action dried yeast
500 g (1 lb 2 oz) strong white bread flour, plus extra for dusting (optional)
1 tsp salt

For the filling

50 g (1¾ oz) fresh coriander leaves, finely chopped
25 g (1 oz) fresh mint leaves, finely chopped
2 spring onions, finely chopped
100 g (3½ oz) pitted dry black olives, roughly chopped
250 g (9 oz) halloumi cheese, cut into 2½-cm (1-inch) cubes
3 tbsp olive oil
1 small onion, finely chopped

In a heatproof jug, mix the water and milk, add the sugar and stir to dissolve. Add the yeast, give it a gentle stir and leave to one side for 5–10 minutes until it's activated. The liquid will rise and turn frothy when ready.

Meanwhile, sift the flour into a large bowl, stir in the salt, then make a well in the centre. Pour the activated yeast mixture into the well. Combine together with your hands to form a dough. Transfer the dough to a clean surface (add a little extra flour for dusting if necessary) and knead for 8–10 minutes until smooth (or knead in a standing mixer using the dough hook attachment). Tuck the dough under to form a nice ball, then place in a large bowl greased with a little olive oil. Cover the bowl with plastic film and leave somewhere warm and cosy to prove for an hour.

While the dough is proving, prepare the filling. Add the coriander, mint, spring onions and olives to a large bowl. Pat the *hellim* cubes dry with kitchen paper and add to the other ingredients.

Heat the olive oil in a frying pan over a medium heat. Once the oil is hot, add the onion and reduce the heat a little so that the onion slowly softens and caramelises. Cook the onion for around 15–20 minutes until translucent and a lovely light golden colour. Add the entire contents of the frying pan, including any remaining oil, to the bowl of filling ingredients and stir everything together.

Preheat the oven to 200°C/180°C fan/400°F/gas mark 6.

Recipe continued on page 229

Once the dough has doubled in size, remove it from the bowl, place it on a clean surface and gently punch it down for a few seconds. Divide the dough equally into two pieces, and put one of the pieces to the side for later. Using your hands, stretch and open out the dough section in front of you so that you have a flat base, around 20 cm (8 inches) square to place the filling into. Put half of the filling into the centre of the dough and fold over the edges so that the filling is encased within it like a parcel. Place the filled dough back into the bowl and, with your hands, squeeze and work the dough so that all the filling ingredients become fully mixed into it. The mixture will be sticky, but the dough and the filling will be fully combined. Lightly flour the surface and turn out the sticky dough on to it. Dust the top of the dough with a little more flour and, using the palm of your hand, shape into a slightly flattened circular loaf measuring around 15–17 cm (6–7 inches) in diameter.

Line a baking sheet with greaseproof paper and place the circular loaf on it. Repeat the whole process with the second piece of dough that you had set to the side.

Place 100 ml (3½ fl oz) water into a glass, and as you place the baking sheet on to the middle shelf of the oven, throw the water (not the glass) into the bottom of the oven and quickly close the door. Bake the bread for 20–25 minutes until beautifully golden brown. Remove from the oven and allow to cool on a wire rack until ready to serve.

Tahınlı

Tahini Pastries

My favourite pastries EVER. No croissant or pain au chocolat could ever compare to the sticky, flaky, flat, yet slightly doughy texture of a beautiful Cypriot *tahınlı*. I think the first time I ate one was from Yaşar Halim patisserie in London. I remember going to the counter with my dad and treasuring my 'gold' in its own brown paper bag all the way home, feeling how warm it still was when we finally got there (because my dad would only buy the freshest ones that were straight out of the oven), and I have had a love affair with them ever since. Like so many of these traditional recipes, there will always be slight variations in texture and shape from one bakery or home cook to another, but for me, the genuine, original and freshly baked texture that I've only really experienced from traditional bakeries in Cyprus is the best. I've tried my hardest to emulate that here with this recipe. Sparkling water is a key ingredient to give the bread that flaky yet light, doughy texture, and if you can get hold of some brown tahini, then use a couple of tablespoons in place of the regular tahini.

Makes 6

For the dough
100 ml (3½ fl oz) warm water
1 tbsp caster sugar
7 g (¼ oz) fast-action dried yeast
250 g (9 oz) strong white bread flour
250 g (9 oz) plain flour
½ tsp salt
1 tsp ground cinnamon
¼ tsp mahleb
200 ml (7 fl oz) sparkling water
2 tbsp olive oil

For the filling
300 g (10½ oz) tahini
100 g (3½ oz) light brown sugar
2 tsp ground cinnamon

For the syrup
4 tbsp clear honey
1 tbsp caster sugar
5 tbsp cold water
½ cinnamon stick

Pour the warm water into a heatproof jug and stir through one tablespoon of sugar until it dissolves. Add the yeast and let it sit for 5–10 minutes until it turns frothy and activates.

While you are waiting for the yeast mixture to activate, add the flour, salt, cinnamon and mahleb to a large bowl and make a well in the centre of the dry ingredients. Pour the activated yeast mixture into the well, followed by the sparkling water and most of the oil (reserving half a teaspoon for later), and use either a standing mixer with the dough hook attachment to knead the dough for 8–10 minutes, or use your hands to knead the mixture on a clean work surface for 10–12 minutes until the dough is smooth and supple. Tuck the sides under the dough to create a smooth ball, rub a little more oil over it, and then place back in the bowl. Cover the bowl with plastic film, then with a tea towel, and leave it somewhere warm and cosy to prove for 20 minutes.

While the dough is proving, prepare the filling. Ensure that you stir the tahini well in its jar or pot, so that the seed oils are mixed through and the thick paste that often gets stuck at the bottom is released. Mix the tahini, light brown sugar and the two teaspoons of cinnamon in a bowl and leave to one side.

After the dough has rested for 20 minutes, remove from the bowl and divide and weigh it into six equal pieces (roughly 140 g/5 oz each). Using the palm of your hand, roll each piece into a smooth ball on a clean work surface, then cover with a tea towel and leave for another 10–15 minutes.

Recipe contined overleaf

Preheat your oven to 190°C/170°C fan/375°F/gas mark 5 and line two baking sheets with greaseproof paper.

Using a rolling pin, roll out the first ball of dough as thinly as you can. It doesn't have to be perfectly shaped, just a rough rectangle with the longest side facing you, but it should be rolled out as thinly as possible without tearing.

Spread 3–4 tablespoons of the tahini mixture all over the dough, as evenly as possibly, using a knife and leaving a 2–3-cm (1–1¼-inch) border all around the edges (to prevent the tahini spilling out on to the surface when you roll and twist the dough). Fold over one-third of the longest side of the dough, then another third until you have a thin rectangular pocket full of the tahini mixture, then start to roll the dough, as if you were rolling a rolling pin so that it gets thinner and longer, until it's around 60-cm (24-inch) long. Take each end of this long piece of dough and twist it by moving your hands in opposite directions. The dough might tear in places and a little of the tahini might seep out, which is absolutely fine and what we actually want. Now turn the long piece of dough into a spiral, taking the end and slotting it through the centre so that the end just pokes through without sticking out. Using the rolling pin, and rolling from the centre outwards, gently flatten the spiral around the edges, leaving the centres just very slightly raised, so that the creases are much less prominent (and will rise together when cooked, but so that the insides will still have that spiral-like texture). The rolled out pastry should have a diameter of around 16 cm (6 inches). Brush the top, and around the creases with a little of the tahini mixture and place the uncooked pastry on the baking sheet.

Quickly repeat the process with the remaining five pieces of dough until you have three uncooked *tahınlı* on each baking sheet and let them all rest for a further 10 minutes before putting the sheets in the oven.

While the pastries are resting, prepare the syrup. Add the honey, sugar, cold water and cinnamon stick to a small pan and place over a medium heat. Bring to a simmer, reduce the heat and let it slowly bubble for 5 minutes until you have a thickened, syrupy liquid. Remove from the heat.

Bake the pastries for 20–22 minutes until beautifully golden brown. Brush each *tahınlı*, all over, with the reduced syrup and place on to a cooling rack over a baking tray (to catch any dripping liquid). Serve warm with a cup of *Kokulu Çay* (Spiced Cypriot Tea, page 42), Turkish coffee, or even a simple cup of milky coffee.

Pilavuna

Cheese & Sultana Pastries

Pilavuna (or *Flaounes*) are beautiful Cypriot cheese-and-sultana-filled pastries, with a very unique flavour combination synonymous with Cyprus. Historically made by Greek-Cypriots to mark the end of their fasting period and the start of their Orthodox Easter, they are also traditionally made by Turkish-Cypriots to mark the end of Ramadan and to signal the start of *Ramazan Bayramı* (Eid-al-Fitr).

The sweet, salty, cheesy, minty mix is just heavenly. I love freezing them and heating them up for breakfast when I fancy something sweet and salty, and the kids love the ritual of making these with me; however, I think they love eating them just that little bit more!

Makes 14

For the filling

250 g (9 oz) halloumi cheese, finely grated
250 g (9 oz) Pecorino, finely grated
50 g (1¾ oz) fresh mint leaves, finely chopped
50 g (1¾ oz) semolina
25 g (1 oz) plain flour
1 tbsp baking powder
1 tbsp caster sugar
125 g (4½ oz) sultanas
¼ tsp ground cinnamon
¼ tsp mahleb
8 large eggs

For the dough

750 g (1 lb 10 oz) plain flour, plus extra for dusting
1 tbsp baking powder
1 tsp fine sea salt
75 g (2¾ oz) unsalted butter
150 ml (5 fl oz) boiling water
1 large egg
2 tbsp thick set natural yoghurt
1 tsp caster sugar
Olive oil, for greasing

Ingredients continued on page 235

To make the filling, put the *hellim* and pecorino cheeses into a large bowl. Add the mint leaves to the bowl along with the semolina, plain flour, baking powder, caster sugar, sultanas, cinnamon and mahleb. Whisk the eight eggs together in another large bowl until frothy and add them to the filling ingredients. Gently stir everything together until fully combined, then cover the bowl with plastic film and chill in the fridge for 4 hours.

Now make the pastry. Sift the flour, baking powder and salt into a large bowl and leave to one side. Melt the butter in a heatproof jug with the boiling water, then top up with another 150 ml (5 fl oz) of cold water. In a large jug, whisk the egg with the yoghurt and sugar and gently pour into the butter. Mix everything together and top up with cold water to bring the entire contents of the jug up to 500 ml (18 fl oz). Make a well in the centre of the flour mixture, and slowly start to pour in the liquid ingredients, using a large spoon to bring everything together. Turn the dough out on to a clean floured surface and knead for a few minutes until smooth.

Spread a little olive oil in the bowl and return the dough, cover with a tea towel and leave for 30 minutes, or at least until the dough has puffed up a little.

Remove the filling mixture from the fridge so that it can come up to room temperature.

On a large baking tray, mix the sesame and nigella seeds, aniseed and boiling water and leave to one side so that the seeds soften and swell a little. Whisk the egg in a bowl and leave to one side.

Line two large baking sheets with greaseproof paper. Preheat the oven to 220°C/200°C fan/425°F/gas mark 7.

Recipe continued on page 235

For coating
100 g (3½ oz) sesame seeds
2 tsp nigella seeds
1 tsp aniseed
90 ml (3 fl oz) boiling water
1 egg

Remove the dough from the bowl and divide it into 14 equal pieces – each piece should weigh approximately 85 g (3 oz). On a clean work surface, roll each piece into a smooth ball using the palm of your hand. Now start to roll out the dough into circular discs, gently pushing down and out with the rolling pin, and rotating at a 45° angle each time you do until you have a disc shape with a 16-cm (6-inch) diameter dusting with a little flour as you go, if necessary. If you have space, roll out all the disks at once, if not, you can roll, coat with seeds, fill and seal each *pilavuna* as you work.

Gently press one of the discs into the seed mixture so that the seeds stick to the dough. Lay the seeded side on the work surface, and place approximately 80 g (2¾ oz) of the filling in the centre. Fold up the sides of the disc in thirds to create a triangular parcel, firmly pressing down the corners of the triangle with a fork, while leaving some of the filling exposed in the centre. Place the parcel on the prepared baking sheet (usually four *pilavuna* will fit on each sheet and have two sheets in the oven on rotation at any one time).

Once you have eight *pilavuna* ready, put the sheets in the oven and bake for 20–25 minutes until golden brown. By the time they're golden, the remaining pastries will be ready for the oven. Place on wire racks to cool.

These freeze well and can be wrapped in foil and heated in the oven or microwaved from frozen.

Pirohu

Cypriot Ricotta-filled Ravioli

These *pirohu* are traditionally made with Cypriot village flour, but I find that a combination of plain and pasta flour gives a very similar consistency to the pasta, once cooked. If you can get hold of the village flour, then simply use the full 500 g (1 lb 2 oz) of it. My great-grandmother Meyrem Nene would make hundreds of these little morsels for her own family and for families who asked her to visit and specifically make some for them. They freeze really well, so if you have a few hours spare and fancy filling up the freezer (laid flat in freezer bags), then I recommend doing so.

Makes 80

For the dough
200 g (7 oz) plain flour, plus extra for dusting
300 g (10½ oz) '00' pasta flour
1 tsp fine sea salt
1 egg
200–250 ml (7–9 fl oz) lukewarm water
2½ tbsp olive oil

For the filling
400 g (14 oz) Cypriot or Italian ricotta cheese
10 g (¼ oz) very finely chopped fresh mint leaves
10 g (¼ oz) very finely chopped fresh flat leaf parsley leaves
¼ tsp coarse black pepper
½ tsp sea salt flakes
1 egg

For the topping
100 g (3½ oz) halloumi cheese, finely grated
1 tsp dried mint
¼ tsp ground black pepper

To make the dough, sift both the flours into a large bowl, and stir through the salt, making a well in the centre.

Whisk the egg in a heatproof jug. Pour enough of the lukewarm water into the jug to bring the liquid level up to 300 ml (10 fl oz), then add two tablespoons of olive oil. Pour into the well, then give everything a good stir with a large spoon before using your hands and turning the dough out on to a clean work surface. Knead the dough for 5–6 minutes until smooth, tuck the sides under to form a ball, then give it a gentle rub of the remaining half tablespoon of olive oil before returning it to the bowl and covering with a tea towel. Leave to rest for 30 minutes.

Meanwhile, prepare the filling. Mash the ricotta with the back of a fork in a flat bowl, then stir through the mint and parsley, along with the seasoning. Taste the mixture and add a little more salt if necessary (but remember, the *pirohu* will be cooked in salted water and served with *hellim*, so don't over-season with salt). Whisk the egg in a small bowl and add it to the ricotta, gently stirring it through the mixture.

Divide the dough into three. Roll each piece into a ball and cover the ones you aren't using with a tea towel. Lightly flour the surface and place one dough ball in front of you. Start to roll out the dough, turning at a 45° angle each time you do, aiming for a large rectangle, around 50 cm × 60cm (20 inches × 24 inches), adding a little dusting of flour when and where necessary. Roll out the dough until it is very thin, but it should still be thick enough to have a little bit of bite to it when cooked.

Now start to prepare the *pirohu* by placing heaped teaspoons of the ricotta filling horizontally along the dough, approximately 8 cm (3 inches) apart, and 8 cm (3 inches) up from the edge closest to you so that you can fold the dough over the filling, releasing any trapped air so that the *pirohu* do not explode while cooking. Using a saucer or pastry cutter, cut around each mound of the filling to create half-moon-shaped parcels, ensuring that they are all as evenly shaped as possible. Crimp the edges of the parcels with a fork, ensuring they are all sealed properly. Repeat until you have used up all the dough and all the filling. If you have any dough left, cut into strips and boil them too to avoid any wastage.

Put the *hellim* in a bowl and stir through the dried mint and black pepper.

Bring a large pan of water to the boil over a high heat and add a good pinch of salt. Add half of the *pirohu* to the pan, without overcrowding them and simmer for 2–3 minutes. Remove them using a large slotted spoon and transfer to a large platter. Cook the remaining *pirohu* in the same way and sprinkle over the *hellim* mixture. Serve immediately.

Sweet Semolina-filled Pastries

There is a shop on the *Mağusa Yolu* (Famagusta Road) called *Tatlım Şamişi ve Lokma Salonu*, a tiny little place, that sells sweet, fried goods, and on our way to and from our hotel to my Meyrem Teyze's house, we would always stop off to pick up my dad and sister's favourite treats; *şamişi*. They are hot, fried pastries made with a combination of plain and self-raising flour which gives the pastry a crispy bubbly texture, complemented by a silky, perfumed filling made from fine semolina and rose water, all dusted with icing sugar once cooked. We make our filling with water (some recipes use milk) so it's an entirely vegan recipe too. Utterly delicious.

Makes 30–36

For the filling
700 ml (1¼ pints) water
150 g (5½ oz) caster sugar
¼ tsp mastic
1 tsp rose water
200 g (7 oz) fine semolina

For the dough
400 g (14 oz) plain flour, plus
    extra for dusting
100 g (3½ oz) self-raising flour
250 ml (9 fl oz) warm water
2 tsp caster sugar
1 tsp red wine vinegar
3½ tbsp olive oil, plus extra
    for greasing

To fry
1 litre (1¾ pints) vegetable,
    sunflower, groundnut,
    rapeseed or rice bran oil

To serve
1 tbsp icing sugar

Firstly, make the filling so that it has enough time to cool down. Add the water and sugar to a pan and stir until it comes to a simmer and the sugar dissolves. Stir in the mastic and rose water and reduce the heat before gradually adding the semolina, stirring constantly for 4–5 minutes until the mixture thickens. Pour everything into a large shallow dish and spread it out completely flat with a palette knife. Lay a sheet of plastic film directly on top of the flattened mixture to prevent a skin from forming and wait for it to cool down while you prepare the pastry dough.

Sift the flour into a large bowl and make a well in the centre. In a heatproof jug, mix the warm water, sugar, vinegar and three tablespoons of olive oil, then pour it into the well and give everything a good stir with a large spoon before using your hands and turning out the dough on to a clean work surface. Knead the dough for 5–6 minutes until smooth, tuck the sides under to form a ball, then give it a gentle rub with the remaining half tablespoon of olive oil before returning the ball to the bowl and covering it with a tea towel. Leave to rest for 30 minutes.

Divide the dough into three equal pieces and roll them into balls, using a little olive oil to smooth them over as you do. Lightly flour your rolling pin and the surface in front of you, place one of the dough balls on the floured surface, and leave the other two to one side, covered with a damp tea towel to prevent them from drying out. Start to roll out the dough, turning at a 45° angle each time you do, aiming for a large rectangular shape, and adding a little dusting of flour when and where necessary. Roll out the dough until it is very thin, around 2 mm, but not so thin that it will tear when filling and sealing. It should be around 50 cm × 60 cm (20 inches × 24 inches) but you don't have to be too precise here, as it's the thickness that matters most. Using a pastry cutter, cut the pastry into equal 12-cm (5-inch) squares. Depending on the size of the rolled-out pastry, you should get between 10–12 squares out of each piece.

Recipe continued overleaf

When the filling has cooled and hardened a little, place a heaped tablespoon of it in the centre of each of the square pieces of pastry, then bring in two opposite corners of the pastry square to the centre, overlapping them slightly, and pinching them together. Lay them down and then repeat with the two opposite corners so that you have a square envelope shape. Using your fingers or a fork, gently press down all the edges together to seal them (without squeezing out the filling). Repeat the process with all of the pastry, and all of the filling until the filling has been used up.

Pour enough vegetable oil into a large, deep frying pan so that it comes up to around 5-cm (2-inches) deep, then heat the oil over a high heat to 190°C (375°F). Test the oil by gently dropping in a small piece of dough. If it sizzles immediately, then the oil is hot enough to cook the şamişi. Using a slotted spoon, carefully lower 3–4 pastries into the hot oil and cook for a couple of minutes on each side (turning them over halfway through). Using a large slotted spoon (or what I prefer to use and my mum has always used, a pitchfork) remove the şamişi from the pan, allowing any excess oil to drip back into the pan, and place them on a large plate lined with a couple of layers of kitchen paper, ensuring that you space them well apart so that any excess oil is absorbed. Repeat until you have cooked all the şamişi, then dust with icing sugar and serve while they are still hot and crispy.

Note

If you have any pastry left, you can simply cut into strips, fry them and dust with icing sugar to avoid any wastage.

Kızarmış Börek

Fried Pastries with Mince, Mushroom & Halloumi Fillings

Try having just one of these, I dare you! It's impossible. Pretty much every weekend, my mum would make a huge bowl of dough and spend most of her time walking around with an *oklava* (rolling pin) in her hand, making *börek* after *börek* for us, and for anyone else who may have just 'popped in'. She would always make them with three separate fillings; *hellim* (halloumi, page 244), *mantar* (mushroom, page 244) and *kıyma* (mince, page 244). After making what looked like 2,000 of them, she'd forget which *börek* were filled with which filling, and so part of the fun for us came with the lottery of never knowing which one you were going to get until you bit into it.

Making *börek* has become my therapy in the kitchen, and I can now see how it has always been my mum's too. I see the escapism she embraces every time she has that *oklava* in her hand, and the stories I have grown up listening to, and will happily listen to again and again, of her watching her great-grandmother Meyrem Nene making *börek* will firmly be etched into my heart and memory as deeply as they are etched into hers.

I have provided the dough recipe below, followed by the three separate filling recipes on page 244.

Makes enough dough for 45–50

500 g (1 lb 2 oz) plain flour, plus extra for dusting
1 tsp fine sea salt
250 ml (9 fl oz) warm water
1 tsp red wine vinegar
3½ tbsp olive oil

To fry

1 litre (1¾ pints) vegetable, sunflower, groundnut, rapeseed or rice bran oil

Sift the flour into a large bowl and stir through the salt, making a well in the centre.

Mix the warm water, vinegar and three tablespoons of olive oil in a heatproof jug and pour into the well, giving everything a good stir with a large spoon before using your hands to turn out the dough on to a clean work surface. Knead the dough for 5–6 minutes until smooth, tuck the sides under to form a ball, then give it a gentle rub of the remaining half tablespoon of olive oil before returning it to the bowl and covering with a tea towel. Leave to rest for 30 minutes. You are now ready to use the dough for the following fried (and pan-fried) *börek* recipes.

Divide the dough into three equal pieces and roll them into balls. Lightly flour the work surface, place one of the dough balls in front of you, and leave the other two to one side, covered with a damp tea towel to prevent them from drying out. Start to roll out the dough, turning at a 45° angle each time you glide over with the rolling pin, shaping it into a large rectangular shape (around 50 cm × 60 cm/ 20 inches × 24 inches) but you don't have to be too precise here, as it's the thickness that matters most), and adding a little dusting of flour when and where necessary. Roll out the dough until it is

Recipe continued overleaf

extremely thin, around 1–2 mm, but sturdy enough that it should not tear when filling and sealing over. It should also have enough flour on it to prevent it from sticking to the surface, but not so much flour that will make it burn while frying.

Now start to prepare the *börek* by placing heaped tablespoons of the chosen filling horizontally along the dough, approximately 8 cm (3 inches) apart, starting 2 cm (1 inch) up from the bottom and stopping halfway up the pastry, so that you can fold the unfilled dough over the other half. Using a thin rolling pin, lift the dough up from the edge furthest away from you on to the rolling pin and lay it directly over the filled section of the pastry. Use the thinnest part of your hands to gently push down in between the filling portions to release any air that could get trapped in the pastry. Using a saucer or pastry cutter, cut around each mound of the filling to create 6 cm × 9 cm (2½ inch × 4 inch) parcels, ensuring that they are all as evenly shaped as possible.

Pour enough oil into a large, deep frying pan so that it comes up to around 5-cm (2-inches) deep, then heat the oil over a high heat to a temperature of 190°C (375°F). Test the oil by gently dropping in a small piece of dough. If it sizzles immediately, then the oil is hot enough to cook the *börek*. Using a slotted spoon, carefully lower 3–4 *börek* into the hot oil and fry for a minute or two on each side (turning halfway through to ensure even cooking). Using the slotted spoon, remove the *börek* from the pan to a large plate lined with a couple of layers of kitchen paper, ensuring that you don't place the *börek* on top of each other, so that they have space to drain of any excess oil. Repeat until you have cooked all the *börek* and serve while hot and crispy.

Note

If you have any pastry left, you can cut it into strips, fry them and dust with icing sugar as a sweet treat and to avoid any wastage.

Kıyma
Mince filling

Makes 45 *börek*

2 tbsp olive oil
750 g (1 lb 10 oz) minced beef
1 tsp salt
1 tsp ground black pepper
2 large onions, very finely diced
100 g (3½ oz) fresh flat leaf
  parsley leaves, very finely
  chopped

Pour the olive oil into a large pan over a medium heat and once hot, add the minced beef, breaking it up with a wooden spoon as it browns. After 5–6 minutes, season with the salt and pepper, and then add the onions to the pan. Reduce the heat so that the onions cook slowly and soften in the meaty juices for 10–12 minutes. Add the parsley, stir well, then remove the pan from the heat so that the parsley retains its colour and freshness.

Pour the mixture straight into a large dish and allow it to fully cool before using to fill the *börek*.

Mantar
Mushroom filling

Makes 22–25 *börek*
(double the quantity to make
45–50 *börek*)

2 tbsp olive oil
2 large onions, very finely diced
600 g (1 lb 5 oz) chestnut
  mushrooms, very finely diced
1 tsp ground black pepper
¼ tsp ground cinnamon
75 g (2¾ oz) fresh flat leaf
  parsley leaves, very finely
  chopped
1 tsp salt

Pour the olive oil into a large pan over a medium heat and once hot, add the onions, reduce the heat a little and soften for 10–12 minutes until translucent. Increase the heat so that the onions start to sizzle, then add the mushrooms to the pan, giving everything a quick stir, then leaving the mushrooms for at least 2–3 minutes before stirring again. The mushrooms need to brown and crisp up as quickly as possible, without releasing too much water. After 2–3 minutes, add the black pepper and cinnamon and give everything a quick stir, then leave again, without stirring, for another 2–3 minutes. Add the parsley and season with the salt, stir well, then remove the pan from the heat so that the parsley retains its colour and freshness.

Pour the mixture straight into a large dish and allow it to fully cool before using to fill the *börek*.

Hellim
Halloumi filling

Makes 22–25 *börek*
(double the quantity to make
45–50 *börek*)

2 tbsp olive oil
1 large onion, very finely chopped
225 g (8 oz) halloumi cheese,
  finely grated
2 tbsp dried mint
½ tsp coarse black pepper
1 large egg
25 g (1 oz) fresh flat leaf parsley
  leaves

Pour the olive oil into a pan over a medium heat, and once hot, add the onion, stir, reduce the heat a little and soften for 12–15 minutes until fully translucent and caramelised.

While the onion is cooking, mix the *hellim*, dried mint and black pepper in a bowl. Whisk the egg in a separate bowl and leave to one side.

Once the onion is cooked, stir through the parsley, then remove from the heat and allow to fully cool. Once cooled, add to the *hellim* mixture, then add the whisked egg to bind everything together. Pour the mixture straight into a large dish and allow it to fully cool before using to fill the *börek*.

Kıbrıs Pidesi

Cypriot Pitta Bread

Another recipe that has been extremely popular on my blog and YouTube channel is for these beautiful soft and puffy, yet delicately thin pitta bread pockets. An essential at any Cypriot barbecue and perfect when filled up with whatever comes off the *mangal* (barbecue). They freeze really well and are so easy to reheat, toast and then fill with grilled *hellim* (halloumi cheese) or even tahini helva, a crumbly spread made from sesame seed paste and sugar syrup, so that it melts within the heat of the toasted bread, perfect for breakfast or a quick snack. They are equally delectable when quickly heated up on the barbecue then packed full of freshly cooked *Kuzu Şiş* (Lamb Kebabs, pages 200–1) and *Izgara Köfte* (Grilled Meat Patties, page 205), and the homemade flavour and texture, like most things, is incomparable to anything that is shop-bought.

Makes 8 pitta breads

225 ml (7 fl oz) lukewarm water
100 ml (3½ fl oz) lukewarm milk
½ tsp sugar
7 g (¼ oz) fast-action dried yeast
500 g (1 lb 2 oz) strong white bread flour, plus extra for dusting
½ tsp salt
2 tbsp olive oil

Put the water and milk in a heatproof jug, stir in the sugar to dissolve, then add the yeast. Leave, covered for 5–10 minutes until it begins to bubble and is activated.

Sift the flour into a large bowl, stir in the salt, then make a well in the centre. Stir the oil into yeast mixture and pour it all into the well in the bowl, bringing everything together with your hands. Transfer the dough to a clean work surface (add a little extra flour for dusting if necessary) and knead for 8–10 minutes until nice and smooth (or knead in a standing mixer using the dough hook attachment). Tuck the dough under to form a nice ball, then place in a large bowl (greased with a little olive oil), cover the bowl with plastic film and leave somewhere warm and cosy to prove for around an hour, until doubled in size.

After an hour, remove the dough from the bowl and weigh it (mine on average weighs roughly 800 g/1¾ lb) every time I make this recipe, so I divide the dough into roughly 100 g (3½ oz) pieces to give me eight equal-sized pieces of dough for the second prove).

Preheat your oven to the hottest setting (mine goes up to 260°C/240°C fan/475°F/gas mark 9) and lay an upturned baking sheet at the bottom of the oven, ready to sit the pitta on.

Once you have divided the dough into eight equal pieces, roll into smooth balls, again tucking the dough under, lay all the dough balls on a tray, cover the tray with plastic film and leave to prove for another 20 minutes.

After 20 minutes, your oven will be super-hot, so very lightly flour your work surface and with a rolling pin, roll out each of the balls into an oval shape – I like mine thin but not too thin, so roll them out to whatever thickness you prefer, ensuring they are a long oval shape (roughly 20 cm × 10 cm/8 inches × 4 inches). If you roll them out too thinly they might get too crisp and could be difficult to stuff your kebab into!

My oven takes two pitta at a time, but they are quick to cook and I wrap the warm pitta in a clean tea towel while I make the others. Lay two of the uncooked pitta on a flat tray or large board and quickly and carefully transfer them to the upturned hot baking tray at the bottom of the oven, closing the oven door immediately. Set a timer for 2½ minutes (they usually take anything from 2–3 minutes to cook and puff up, so keep an eye on them) and once they have puffed up, quickly open the oven door and carefully turn them over for another 30 seconds– 1 minute. Remove from the oven, wrap in the clean tea towel, then repeat the cooking process with the six remaining pitta.

Meyrem Nenenin Ispanaklı Börek

Meyrem Nene's Spinach Pies

Whenever my mum would make *ıspanaklı pilav* (spinach rice) she would always make some dough and use some of the rice to make my great-grandmother's spinach pies. The filling is always heavily seasoned with coarse black pepper (at my dad's request, as his mum, Melek Nene – my paternal grandmother – would add lots of black pepper to her spinach rice) and a hint of lemon. I toyed with the idea of whether I should include this recipe in the book, as it's so specific to my family and not as well-known as other Cypriot recipes. But my personal connection to it meant that I had to put it in here. My mum and her family would eat these pies dipped into fresh sheep's yoghurt, made from their own reared sheep. I love to enjoy them with a cup of black *Kokulu Çay* (Spiced Cypriot Tea, page 42).

Makes 8

For the filling
400 g (14 oz) fresh spinach
50 g (1¾ oz) long-grain white rice
250 ml (9 fl oz), plus 2 tbsp cold water
¾ tsp sea salt flakes
2 tbsp olive oil
1 onion, finely chopped
Zest of 1 lemon
1 tsp coarse black pepper
2 tsp fresh lemon juice

For the dough
250 g (9 oz) plain flour, plus extra for dusting
1 tsp baking powder
½ tsp fine sea salt
150 ml (5 fl oz) warm water
1 tbsp natural yoghurt
2½ tbsp olive oil, plus extra for greasing

Make the filling first so that it has time to cool down.

Wash the spinach thoroughly under cold running water, and then roughly chop the leaves and finely chop the stalks, keeping the leaves and stalks separate from each other.

Wash the rice in a sieve under cold, running water until the water runs clear. Add to a small saucepan with 250 ml (9 fl oz) of the cold water and one quarter of a teaspoon of the sea salt flakes. Place the pan over a medium heat, bring to the boil, then part-cook the rice for 6 minutes. Remove the pan from the heat, carefully drain the rice in a sieve and leave it over the pan until you are ready to use.

Pour the olive oil into a large non-stick pan over a medium heat, and once hot, add the onion. Reduce the heat a little and cook for 8–10 minutes before adding the spinach stalks and softening everything together for another 4–5 minutes. Once the onion has softened and lightly caramelised, add the spinach leaves to the pan and wilt them down for a couple of minutes, before adding the lemon zest and black pepper, stirring everything through to combine. Add the part-cooked rice to the pan, drizzle in the lemon juice, the remaining 2 tablespoons of cold water and the remaining half teaspoon of sea salt flakes. Bring the mixture to a simmer, then reduce to a low heat with the lid on, and cook for another 5–6 minutes, stirring every couple of minutes. Once the rice grains are fully cooked (do not overcook them), remove the pan from the heat, transfer the mixture to a heatproof dish and let it cool down while you make the *börek* pastry.

Sift the flour and baking powder into a large bowl, and stir through the salt, making a well in the centre.

Recipe continued overleaf

Mix the warm water, yoghurt and two tablespoons of olive oil in a measuring jug, pour the mixture into the well, then give everything a good stir with a large spoon before using your clean hands to turn the dough out on to a clean work surface. Knead the dough for 7–8 minutes until smooth, tuck the sides under to form a ball, then give it a gentle rub of the remaining half tablespoon of olive oil before returning it to the bowl and covering with a tea towel. Leave to rest for 30 minutes.

Preheat your oven 220°C/200°C fan/425°F/gas mark 7. Line two baking sheets with greaseproof paper.

Once the dough has rested, divide it into eight equal pieces, roughly 55–60 g (2–2½ oz) each. Grease the palm of one of your hands with a little olive oil, and using that same hand, roll each piece of dough into a smooth ball on the surface. Flour your rolling pin and your surface and roll each piece of dough into a 12-cm (5 inch) disk, turning the dough at a 45° angle each time you roll. Place a large spoonful of the cooled filling into one half of the disc, keeping the edges clear, and brush the circumference of each disk with a little water to aid sealing.

Fold each disc over the filling to create a semi-circle-shaped *börek*, then pinch down to seal the semi-circle edges together. Using your index finger and thumb, twist and slightly fold over the semi-circular edge of the pastry to crimp the edges together. Once all the *börek* have been formed and shaped, place them on the two baking sheets and cook on the middle and bottom shelves of the oven for 15–18 minutes. The *börek* should be very lightly golden brown once cooked. Remove from the oven and allow to cool a little so that the pastry softens. Serve either with a hot cup of *Kokulu Çay* (Spiced Cypriot Tea, page 42) or a dollop of thick set natural yoghurt.

Kafes Peksemet

Gate-shaped Breadsticks

Back when Turkish and international grocers were few and far between in London and online shopping wasn't yet available, a large weekly haul of goods that reminded my parents of home was as essential to keeping their kitchen well-stocked as it was to keeping their hearts full. *Kafes Peksemet* are made in bakeries all over Cyprus and it is their unique shape, and the combination of aniseed, sesame and nigella seeds that makes them so specifically Cypriot. Once of my favourite things to do with *peksemet*, is to dunk it straight into a hot cup of tea. And yes, it's totally a thing. Another very Cypriot thing.

Makes 4

300 ml (10 fl oz) lukewarm water
1 tsp sugar
7 g (¼ oz) fast-action dried yeast
500 g (1 lb 2 oz) plain flour, plus
    extra for dusting
1½ tsp salt

For brushing
1 tbsp flour
1 tsp water
1 tsp milk

For coating
4 tbsp sesame seeds
1 tsp nigella seeds
¼ tsp aniseed

Add the warm water to a jug and dissolve the sugar in the liquid. Add the yeast, give it a gentle stir and leave to one side for 5–10 minutes until it is activated. It will rise and look frothy when it is ready.

Meanwhile, sift the flour into a large mixing bowl and stir through the salt. Make a well in the centre.

Once the yeast has activated in the liquid, gradually pour the mixture into the well and start to bring the wet and dry ingredients together with clean hands. Turn the dough out on to a clean surface and start to knead the dough. You shouldn't need any more flour at this point. Keep kneading by hand for 10–12 minutes until a nice smooth dough is formed, tucking the sides under as you finish. Alternatively, place everything into a standing mixer and knead with the dough hook attachment for 10 minutes.

Sprinkle a little flour over the bottom and sides of the bowl and return the dough to the bowl. Cover the bowl with plastic film, then a clean tea towel and leave it somewhere warm and cosy to prove for an hour until it doubles in size.

Mix all the seeds together on a large tray. The *peksemet* will be coated in this seeded mixture once shaped. Mix the flour, water and milk to a smooth paste in a small bowl and leave to one side.

Preheat oven to 180°C/160°C fan/350°F/gas mark 4. Line two baking sheets with greaseproof paper.

Once the dough has risen, remove from the bowl and gently punch it down for a few seconds.

On a clean work surface, roll the slightly flattened dough into a long chunky sausage and divide it into eight equal pieces (each weighing roughly 100 g/3½ oz). Take one piece and roll it out using your hands until you have a very long piece of dough, roughly 1 m (3 ft) in length and 5-mm (¼-inch) thick. Brush the reserved paste over the dough and

Recipe continued overleaf

transfer to the tray of seeds to coat all over. Place the dough on the baking sheet and form it into a large rectangular frame.

Roll out a second piece of dough to the same length as the first and then cut the piece into four to make the two short pieces that will go horizontally across the shortest edge of the rectangle, and two slightly longer pieces that will run across the longest edges of the rectangle to create a gate-like grid. Brush each of the four pieces of dough with the paste, coat them in the seeds, then lay the two short pieces at equal distances across the rectangular frame widthways, and the two long pieces across the frame lengthways to form a grid or 'gate'. Leave to one side and repeat the process with the next two pieces of dough on the second baking sheet.

Place the two baking sheets in the oven and cook for 40–45 minutes until golden brown. Remove them from the oven and place on a wire rack to cool.

Make two more *peksemet* 'gates' with the four remaining pieces of dough, constructing them on the lined baking sheets, then putting them in the oven to cook for 40–45 minutes, while the first batch of cooked *peksemet* cool down.

After 40–45 minutes, remove from the oven, and transfer to the wire rack to cool. Return the now cooled first batch of *peksemet* to the baking sheets and put them back in the oven for another 25–30 minutes to get really crunchy.

After 25–30 minutes, remove from the oven and transfer to the wire rack to cool fully. Return the now cooled second batch of *peksemet* to the baking sheets and put them back in the oven for another 25–30 minutes.

After 25–30 minutes remove the second batch from the oven and transfer to the wire rack to cool fully.

Serve with hot *Kokulu Çay* (Spiced Cypriot Tea, page 42), *hellim*, olives, tomatoes and cucumber.

Crowd-pleasing Sweets

Kek ve Tatlı

I really don't have a sweet tooth. However, my preference for savoury treats is regularly contradicted by the fact that when I do opt for something sweet, it will usually be the most sugar-laden, syrup-drenched offering on the menu. Again, I can only put this down to sweets like *Sütlü Börek* (Custard-filled Filo Syrup Pastries, pages 259–60), *Tahınlı Pekmezli Baklava* (Tahini & Carob Molasses Baklava, pages 275–6) and *Tel Kadayıf Tatlısı* (Kadayif Pastries, pages 278–9), as drenched in syrup as they are in pure nostalgia for me. When we visit my aunt Meyrem Teyze for one of her beautiful rooftop meals, a glass of cold water and *Karpuz Macunu* (Watermelon Preserve, page 277) followed by *Türk Kahvesi* (Turkish coffee), or a trip to the institutional sweet haven that is *Petek Pastanesi* (Petek's Patisserie) in *Mağusa* (Famagusta), are standard practice. The vivid-hued, tweeting budgerigars that greet you as you enter Petek's are almost as iconic as the abundant line-up of sweet, syrupy treats that entice, as you walk up and down the patisserie, staring into the hypnotic glass cabinets trying to pick 'the one'.

Damla Sakızı (a gum or resin from the mastic tree) is traditionally used to flavour desserts such as *Şamali* (Semolina Syrup Cake, page 266), one of the sweets my mum makes the most at home. It is an extremely easy flourless cake to put together, drenched, of course, in syrup that has been infused with lemon, cinnamon and rosewater. Similar in appearance, yet very different in texture, is *Simit Helvası* (Semolina Helva, page 261), made using semolina, almonds and, yes, you guessed it, a cinnamon-infused syrup. Once cooled, the dessert is uniquely-textured, dense, moist and almost gelatinous – sweet to eat alongside a cup of *çay* (tea). We do, however, use flour to make *İçi Dolu Kurabiye* (Almond-filled Celebration Cookies, pages 268–9) – buttery, short, crumbly cookies filled with roughly chopped almonds that are often served at weddings and special occasions.

Although I will always take a slice or two of *Hellimli Zeytinli Kek* (Halloumi & Black Olive Cake, page 40) in place of any red velvet or lemon drizzle, the only sweet cake that might tempt me to give up my savoury preferences is *Annemin Çikolatalı ve Hindistan Cevizli Kek* (Mum's Chocolate & Coconut Cake, page 273).

I cannot tell you how many trays of this we would make with my mum in the school holidays. The cake was always moist and fluffy, made without any scales or jugs and only her eyes and mugs for measuring. If she didn't have any cocoa or cooking chocolate in the cupboards, then she would improvise with chocolate milk powder. I don't know what it is about Cypriot mums (and I know this sentiment of course extends beyond the Cypriot culture), but they have this innate ability to make whatever they have to hand work perfectly. She would flavour the plain sponge with coconut, and much like when she would make *Sütlü Muhallebi* (Creamed Pudding, page 265) our impatience would get the better of us and we couldn't wait until the cake had cooled to eat it. While the cake was baking in the oven, my mum would prepare our favoured bright yellow custard, made from tinned custard powder, which she would pour over thick slices of the cake, barely out of the oven for 5 minutes.

The syrup-based desserts are all best made in advance, to enable the sweet liquid to seep into the cake or pastry, so allow at least 6 hours to enable this to happen before serving. I recommend using flat-bottomed baking trays, with no ridges or indents, when making the syrup-based desserts so that they syrup has nowhere to go other than into the cake or pastry sitting in it. They keep well, in their trays (so that they keep soaking up the syrup), covered with foil at room temperature for 3–4 days, and are all yummy, indulgent after-dinner desserts. The cookies are quick to make, especially for a baking session with children, and they also keep well stored in a sealed container for a few days. Enjoy them with a cup of tea or coffee.

Sütlü Börek

Custard-filled Filo Syrup Pastries

Beautiful, buttery, flaky, syrupy, semolina custard-filled *Sütlü Börek*, which basically means 'milky pastry'. This is a slightly more indulgent take on my online recipe, and reminds me of special occasions, such as *Bayram* (Eid), where we would visit the Yaşar Halim patisserie, and load up the little white pastry boxes with *Sütlü Börek* and *Tel Kadayıf Tatlısı* (Kadayif Pastries, pages 278–9) to take home to family, both recipes of which were always such firm favourites in my childhood. Much like the savoury, spiral shaped *Kol Böreği* (Potato, Spinach & Cheese Filo Pie, pages 167–8) and *Kıymalı Gül Böreği* (Rose-Shaped Filo Meat Pies, pages 169-70), this is another recipe that is best made using large sheets of really good-quality, shop-bought filo (*baklavalık yufka*).

Makes 16

For the syrup
1 large cinnamon stick
400 ml (14 fl oz) water
350 g (12 oz) caster sugar
3 tbsp clear honey
1½ tbsp rose water
1 tbsp fresh lemon juice

For the custard
750 ml (1¼ pints) whole or
    semi-skimmed milk
2 eggs, whisked
100 ml (3½ fl oz) double cream
75 g (2¾ oz) fine semolina
30 g (1 oz) cornflour
100 g (3½ oz) caster sugar
½ tsp ground cinnamon (optional,
    or just a pinch if you prefer)

For the pastry
200 g (7 oz) unsalted butter,
    melted
16 large sheets of good-quality
    filo pastry

To serve
4 tbsp walnuts, ground (optional)
or
4 tbsp almonds, crushed
    (optional)
or
4 tbsp pistachios, crushed
    (optional)

To make the syrup, add all of the syrup ingredients except the lemon juice to a small pan over a medium heat. Simmer for 10–15 minutes until the syrup has thickened and reduced down by about one quarter. Add the lemon juice and remove from the heat to cool.

To make the custard, add the milk to a medium-sized pan and place over a medium heat. When the milk is warm, add a couple of large spoonfuls of milk to the whisked eggs and whisk the two ingredients together very quickly – this will stop the eggs from scrambling when they are later added to the warm custard. Stir the cream into the egg and milk mixture and leave everything to one side while the pan of milk continues to heat up.

Add the semolina, cornflour, sugar and cinnamon to the warmed milk and whisk continuously until the mixture starts to thicken. Once it starts to bubble, remove from the heat. (It doesn't need to boil and bubble, but it does need to thicken.) Very quickly and vigorously whisk the egg mixture into the custard for a good couple of minutes until creamy and fully blended.

Leave the custard to one side to cool. (I pour mine into a shallow dish so that it cools more quickly and whisk it every couple of minutes to stop a skin forming on top.)

To make the pastry, brush a deep baking tray with a little of the melted butter. (You need a deep baking tray with a completely flat bottom so that the syrup soaks straight into the cooked *Sütlü Börek* and does not disappear into any ridges when poured in.)

Preheat the oven to 190°C/170°C fan/375°C/gas mark 5.

On a clean surface, lay all the layers of filo piled up in front of you (horizontally) and, with a pair of clean scissors, cut the sheets in half, vertically straight down the middle.

Recipe continued overleaf

Take two of the large rectangles of filo and put the remaining layers to one side, covered with a clean damp tea towel to prevent them from drying out.

Brush the first layer of filo with the melted butter, lay the next layer on top, brush with a little more of the butter, then add two heaped tablespoons of the cooled custard mixture to the short edge of the filo closest to you, leaving about 5 cm (2 inches) clear from the edge of the pastry. Fold this short edge of the filo over the filling, then bring in both long sides of the filo over the mixture a little so that they almost meet in the middle, but not quite. Then start folding the shorter edge of the filo away from you to form small rectangular parcels.

Be careful not to fold the parcels up too tightly otherwise they could burst and split open while cooking. Place the assembled *Sütlü Börek* on the deep baking tray. Repeat the process with the remaining sheets of filo and custard.

Once all the *Sütlü Börek* have been assembled, place the baking tray on the middle shelf of the oven for 30–40 minutes until they are golden brown. I usually leave mine in for a full 40 minutes, but keep your eye on them as all oven temperatures vary.

Remove the baking tray from the oven, then immediately pour over the cooled syrup so that it sizzles vigorously. You can also sprinkle either ground walnuts, almonds or pistachios on to each *Sütlü Börek* at this point.

Allow the pastry parcels to cool for at least 4–6 hours on the baking tray before serving, so that the pastry really has time to soak up all those beautiful syrupy flavours. These are just as delicious the next day, or up to three days after (stored in the fridge).

Note

Make them vegan (most filo pastry is vegan anyway). Omit the egg and double cream from the custard (it will still thicken and set, but just add another pinch of semolina to encourage that), use oat or almond milk as a milk alternative, a vegetable-based spread instead of butter and agave syrup instead of clear honey.

Simit Helvası

Semolina Helva

This is an extremely simple dessert to make, which doesn't even require any baking once the semolina mixture is poured into the serving dish. My mum's mum, Fatma Nene, and maternal grandmother, Meyrem Nene, would make this *simit helvası* by using an *oklava* (thin rolling pin) to vigorously stir the mixture. Hot syrup is poured into a pan of nuts and semolina that have been lightly toasted in a little oil or butter; just be careful when you pour the syrup in, as it has a tendency to splutter when it hits the pan.

Makes 24 pieces

200 g (7 oz) whole almonds
1 litre (1¾ pints) cold water
420 g (15 oz) caster sugar
1 tbsp orange blossom water
½ tsp vanilla extract
1 cinnamon stick
3 tbsp sunflower oil
1 tsp ground cinnamon
500 g (1 lb 2 oz) semolina

Note

Serve warm or cold with a cup of tea. These can be stored at room temperature (covered tightly or sealed in a plastic storage box) for up to 5 days.

Place the almonds in a small pan and pour in enough cold water to fully cover them. Place the pan over a medium heat, bring to the boil, then reduce the heat to a simmer for 10 minutes. Remove the pan from the heat, drain the almonds through a sieve and run them under cold water to cool them down. Simply slip off the skins by gently squeezing each almond between your thumb and forefinger. Dry the blanched nuts thoroughly with a clean tea towel and lay them all on another tea towel to dry out thoroughly while you prepare the syrup.

Add 1 litre (1¾ pints) of cold water, the sugar, orange blossom water, vanilla extract and the cinnamon stick to a pan and place over a medium heat, stirring until the sugar dissolves. Reduce to a medium–low heat and simmer for 10–12 minutes, then remove the pan from the heat to cool.

Keep 24 whole blanched almonds to one side, then pulse the remaining almonds in a food processor until they are finely chopped without being reduced to a powder, and stir through the ground cinnamon – there needs to be some texture.

Heat the sunflower oil in a large pan over a medium heat, and once hot, add the semolina and turn the heat right down. This is where you must not take your eyes off the pan and need to stir continuously for 10–12 minutes until the semolina grains change to a very light sandy colour and texture. Once the semolina has changed and is the texture of sand, stir through the finely chopped blanched almonds and keep toasting the semolina and nuts together for another 2–3 minutes.

Stir continuously with a wooden spoon as you add the syrup to the pan, but be very careful as the mixture can really start to splutter when the syrup first hits the pan. Keep stirring until all the syrup has been added and the mixture has thickened. Cook for a further 2 minutes, still stirring, then carefully pour the mixture as evenly as possible into a 20 cm × 25 cm (8 inch × 10 inch) dish or tray. Dip a clean wooden spoon into a cup of cold water and use it to smooth and flatten the top of the mixture. Allow to cool down for a few minutes, then cut it directly in the tray into 24 equal pieces and press the reserved blanched almonds into the centre of each piece.

Nut & Syrup Pastry Swirl

Whenever my mum would make her fried *Börek* (pages 241–4) she would also make her *sini gatmeri*, and it honestly has to be my Number One Cypriot sweet treat. Like every biased offspring, my mum's version is, of course, the best version. The pastry isn't as thin as shop-bought filo or the homemade *yufka* used to make baklava; the denser layers, once rolled, cooked and then covered in syrup, are a little thicker and go slightly sticky and hard on top, and a little softer and squidgier in the centre. The *gatmer* is loaded with nuts and a delicate layer of *kaymak* (clotted cream) that also helps to keep the central layers soft and moist, so that they keep well in the fridge for 3–4 days.

Makes 1 big trayful!

For the syrup
500 ml (18 fl oz) cold water
350 g (12 oz) caster sugar
1 cinnamon stick

For the dough
500 g (1 lb 2 oz) plain flour,
  plus extra for dusting
1 tsp baking powder
1 tsp fine sea salt
300 ml (10 fl oz) warm water
2½ tbsp olive oil
3 tbsp sunflower oil

For the filling
250 g (9 oz) *kaymak* or clotted
  cream
400 g (14 oz) whole almonds,
  chopped
2 tsp ground cinnamon

Make the syrup first so that it has time to cool down. Place the cold water, caster sugar and cinnamon stick in a small pan over a medium heat. Bring to the boil, then reduce the heat and simmer for 10 minutes.

For the dough, sift the flour and baking powder into a large bowl, and stir through the salt, making a well in the centre.

Mix the warm water, and two tablespoons of the olive oil in a heatproof jug, pour into the well, then give a good stir with a large spoon before using your hands to turn out the dough on to a clean work surface. Knead the dough for 7–8 minutes until smooth, tuck the sides under to form a ball, then give it a gentle rub with the remaining half tablespoon of olive oil before returning it to the bowl and covering with a tea towel. Leave to rest for 30 minutes.

Preheat the oven to 200°C/180°C fan/400°F/gas mark 6. Grease a large baking tray (a circular one is traditional, mine is around 40 cm/16 inches in diameter, but a large rectangular one, 34 cm × 24 cm/13 inches × 9 inches is fine) with one tablespoon of the sunflower oil.

Divide the dough into two equal-sized pieces and roll them into balls. Lightly flour the surface in front of you, take one of the dough balls, setting the other to one side, covered with a damp tea towel to prevent it from drying out. Start to roll out the dough, turning at a 45° angle each time you do, aiming for a large rectangular or oval shape (adding a little dusting of flour when and where necessary to prevent the dough from sticking to the surface). Roll out the dough until it is as thin as possible (1 mm/1⁄16 inch), and around 80 cm (2½ ft) at its longest sides and 60 cm (2 ft) at its shortest, with the longest sides facing horizontally.

Spread half of the *kaymak* over the entire rectangle or oval of pastry and sprinkle over half of the almonds and cinnamon, then cut the pastry horizontally and equally in half. Starting from the longest side closest to you, gently roll the pastry up and away from you, and once

Recipe continued overleaf

rolled, gently twist the ends in opposite directions, without tearing. This gentle twisting will give the *gatmer* a more textured finish once cooked. Carefully pick up the roll from each end and place it on the centre of the greased baking tray, swirling it into a spiral from the centre out. Roll up the other piece of filled pastry in exactly the same way as you did the first, and this time, when you place it on the tray, connect it to the end of the first spiral and continue spiralling (and gently twisting) it round the central piece. Continue the entire process with the remaining piece of dough until the baking tray is full of one large spiralled *gatmer* and gently brush it with the remaining two tablespoons of sunflower oil.

Place the baking tray on the bottom shelf of the oven and cook for 35–40 minutes, or until golden on top. Remove from the oven, let the *gatmer* sit for 5 minutes, then spoon ladlefuls of the reserved syrup all over it and allow to cool fully before serving.

Sütlü Muhallebi

Creamed Pudding

'Mum, I fancy something sweet!' was often followed with a response of, 'OK, shall I make some *sütlü muhallebi*?', and our answer was always a collective 'Yes!'. My mum would very quickly whip up the slightly sweet, rose-scented custard that every one of us at home enjoyed hot, and it would be poured straight into glass dessert bowls and liberally sprinkled with chopped almonds and a big pinch of cinnamon. Traditionally however, *sütlü muhallebi* is a set dessert, served either at room temperature or chilled, so feel free to serve whichever way takes your fancy. I have listed the hot and cold serving methods in the recipe.

Serves 6

900 ml (1½ pints) whole milk
70 g (2½ oz) cornflour
120 g (4¼ oz) caster sugar
1 tbsp rose water
½ tsp ground cinnamon
50 g (1¾ oz) whole almonds, finely chopped
50 g (1¾ oz) pistachios, crushed

Pour the milk into a medium-sized pan, sift in the cornflour and add the sugar. Place the pan over a medium heat and whisk continuously for a few minutes until it starts to thicken and turn silky smooth. Add the rose water and half of the ground cinnamon, then as soon as the mixture starts to bubble, evenly pour it into six large ramekins or small dessert bowls.

If serving hot, top the *sütlü muhallebi* with the almonds, pistachios and a sprinkling of the remaining cinnamon.

If serving cold, cover each dish of *sütlü muhallebi* with plastic film as soon as you pour the mixture into the ramekins, allow them to cool to room temperature, then chill in the fridge and top with the nuts and cinnamon when you are ready to serve them.

Şamali

Semolina Syrup Cake

Şamali is a syrupy cake (known as *şam tatlısı* or *şambali* in Turkey) made only with semolina, and no flour. The eggs and baking powder give the cake its wonderful rise and depending on how you like the texture of your cake crumb, a reduced cooking time will result in a softer crust and lighter sponge, whereas an extra 10 minutes or so will give it a thicker, darker crust and a slightly more grainy texture.

One of the key ingredients that gives Cypriot *şamali* its distinct flavour is mastic (*damla sakızı*), so do try and source it if you can as it will make a huge difference to the flavour and texture of the cake.

Makes 21 slices

For the syrup
600 ml (20 fl oz) cold water
400 g (14 oz) caster sugar
1 large cinnamon stick
2 tbsp rose water
1 tbsp fresh lemon juice

For the cake
25 g (1 oz) unsalted butter, softened
6 large eggs
125 g (4½ oz) caster sugar
200 ml (7 fl oz) sunflower or olive oil
Zest of ½ lemon
½ tsp vanilla extract
100 g (3½ oz) thick set natural yoghurt
1 tsp ground cinnamon
400 g (1 lb 2 oz) semolina
1½ tsp baking powder
⅛ tsp ground mastic
21 blanched almonds
2 tbsp pistachios, crushed

Preheat the oven to 200°C/180°C fan/400°F/gas mark 6.

Grease a deep, flat baking tray measuring approximately 22 cm × 34 cm (8½ inches × 13½ inches) with the softened butter.

Make the syrup first so that it has time to cool down fully. Add the water and sugar to a pan with the cinnamon stick and rose water. Bring the syrup to the boil, stirring continuously, then reduce the heat to a gentle simmer for about 10 minutes. Remove the pan from the heat, add the lemon juice and stir. Leave to one side.

In a large bowl, whisk together the eggs and sugar quite vigorously until smooth and fluffy. Add the oil, lemon zest, vanilla and yoghurt and whisk for several minutes more. Add the ground cinnamon, semolina, baking powder and mastic and stir until completely smooth.

Pour the cake batter into the prepared baking tray and dot three almonds across the top of the batter, followed by six more almonds beneath each one so that you have 21 almonds in total (you will use these almonds as markers to cut the cake once cooked). Place the baking tray in the oven and bake for 30–40 minutes on the bottom shelf of the oven until golden brown and slightly risen (a cocktail stick should come out clean). Remove the cake from the oven and leave for around 5 minutes.

Cut the cake directly on the baking tray into around 21 rectangular pieces, using the almonds as a guide, then carefully pour the reserved syrup over the cake. The cake will look like it's drowning in the syrup, but that's fine. Allow it to cool completely, cover with foil and rest at room temperature (preferably overnight) before serving.

Sprinkle with the crushed pistachios before plating up and serve each slice with a scoop of vanilla or *damla sakızı* (mastic) ice cream. Store the *şamali* in the baking tray at room temperature for up to 4 days, ensuring that you seal the cake tightly with foil to keep it moist.

İçi Dolu Kurabiye
Almond-filled Celebration Cookies

These moreish Cypriot delicacies, wrapped in cellophane and secured with ribbon, were handed out to guests at our wedding to take home with them, and growing up, this was one of my favourite reasons (other than the *meze* and the dancing) to go to Cypriot weddings. They are incredibly short and crumbly, and rather large (my mum makes them slightly smaller than the ones I make), as I like mine to be reminiscent of the jumbo wedding cookies I used to savour with a cup of tea the morning after a special celebration. They are buttery, nutty and dusted in a thick layer of icing sugar that, when all stacked up together, makes them look like a delicious snowy mountain scene. Sometimes I mix the nuts into the actual dough, but I love the indulgence of the loaded *içi dolu kurabiye* ('inside full cookie') which are specific to Cyprus and weddings on the island.

Makes 12–14

200 g (7 oz) unsalted butter, softened
125 g (4½ oz) icing sugar
65 ml (2 fl oz) sunflower oil
1 large egg yolk
3 tbsp rose water
½ tsp vanilla extract
¼ tsp ground cinnamon
½ tsp baking powder
385 g (13½ oz) plain flour
50 g (1¾ oz) cornflour
150 g (5½ oz) almonds
200 g (7 oz) icing sugar, to coat

With an electric whisk, beat together the butter and the sugar for 5–6 minutes until pale, light and fluffy. Add all but 1 tablespoon of the sunflower oil, whisk again, then add the egg yolk, whisking for another couple of minutes, followed by two tablespoons of the rose water, the vanilla extract, cinnamon and baking powder. Sift in the flour and cornflour, then bring everything together with your hands to form what will be a very sticky dough. Wash your hands and chill the mixture in the fridge for an hour.

While the dough is chilling, preheat your oven to 190°C/170°C fan/ 375°F/gas mark 5. Line two baking sheets with greaseproof paper and put the almonds on one of the sheets. Once the oven is hot, roast the almonds for 6–8 minutes, then remove from the oven and transfer them to a plate to cool. Pulse the roasted almonds in a food processor for a few seconds until roughly chopped, but still mostly in large chunks, then pop them back into the dish and stir through the remaining one tablespoon of rose water and one tablespoon of sunflower oil until the almonds are fully coated.

Remove the prepared dough from the fridge and fill up a small bowl with cold water. Wet the palms and inside of your hands with the water, and break off a piece of the dough, around 60 g (2¼ oz), roll into a ball, then poke a hole through it with your thumb and gently ease open the dough, much like the method for *Bulgur Köftesi* (Meat-filled Bulgur Wheat Cones, see images on pages 134–5). Place around two heaped teaspoons of the ground almonds in the cavity you made with your thumb, then bring up the sides of the dough to start sealing the cookies, wetting your hands if the mixture gets too sticky, ensuring the chopped almonds are not poking out at all. Shape into a slightly flattened oval, making it slightly pointed at the ends, then place the finished cookie on one of the baking sheets. Using a fork, very slightly score a fork-shaped ridge across the top of the *kurabiye*, from one of the pointed ends to the other; these ridges will enable the *kurabiye* to hold on to more of the icing sugar coating once cooked. Repeat this shaping and filling process with the remaining dough, filling both baking sheets with the *kurabiye*.

Place the *kurabiye* into the preheated oven for 18–20 minutes until they turn very lightly golden. They will still be soft when you remove the trays, so allow them to cool slightly on the baking sheets before transferring them to the icing sugar coating.

Fill a large, deep dish with the icing sugar and while the *kurabiye* are still slightly warm, place them, one by one, into the icing sugar and coat liberally with the sweet powder. Transfer to a large platter to serve or wrap them up to hand out as gifts.

Fırında Sütlaç

Baked Rice Pudding

If my son ever requests a dessert or gets the opportunity to select one from the menu on a visit to a Turkish restaurant, you can bet your money on the fact that he'll go straight for the *Fırında Sütlaç*. It is a slightly more indulgent version of the *Sütlaç* (Milky Rice, page 43) my mum would make us for breakfast when we were kids and, even though it is traditionally served cold, we love ours warm and fresh out of the oven while the cream still retains that luxurious consistency and the scent of cinnamon and orange blossom water continues to subtly drift through the kitchen.

Serves 6

100 g (3½ oz) short-grain
   pudding rice
250 ml (9 fl oz) cold water
1 litre (1¾ pints) whole milk
75 g (2¾ oz) icing sugar
1 cinnamon stick
¼ tsp ground cinnamon
½ vanilla pod
35 g (1¼ oz) cornflour
50 g (1¾ oz) almonds or
   hazelnuts
1 tsp orange blossom water
100 ml (3½ fl oz) double cream

Preheat the oven to 230°C/210°C fan/450°F/gas mark 8.

Add the rice to a pan with the cold water, bring to the boil and cook for 7–8 minutes until tender, but still with a bite. Drain the rice in a sieve and leave to one side.

Add 900 ml (1½ pints) of the milk, the icing sugar, cinnamon stick, ground cinnamon and the seeds from the vanilla pod to a medium-sized pan. In a separate bowl, mix the cornflour and remaining 100 ml (3½ fl oz) of milk and leave to one side.

Place the nuts on a baking sheet and roast on the middle shelf of the oven for 7–8 minutes, checking regularly to make sure they don't burn. Remove from the oven and set to one side.

Place the pan of spiced and sweetened milk over a medium heat, stirring constantly with a wooden spoon until it starts to come to a simmer. Add the cornflour paste and orange blossom water to the pan and swap the spoon for a whisk to continuously whisk the mixture while the custard thickens. Add the double cream, still whisking, then add the cooked rice to the pan and stir well with the wooden spoon until all the rice grains are coated in the milky mixture.

Ladle the rice pudding into small ovenproof dessert dishes, ensuring that the rice and milk are evenly dispersed between the dishes, giving them a little stir. Place the dishes into a deep baking tray and pour 400 ml (14 fl oz) cold water into the baking tray, around the dishes. Carefully place the baking tray on to the top shelf of the oven. Bake for 25–30 minutes, or until the *sütlaç* browns and forms a thick skin on top. Remove from the oven. Allow to cool, then serve warm or cold. Roughly chop the roasted nuts and sprinkle them over the *sütlaç* just before serving.

Annemin Çikolatalı ve Hindistan Cevizli Kek

Mum's Chocolate & Coconut Cake

These sponge cakes are affectionally referred to as *Anne Keki* (Mums' Cakes) because they are usually the off-the-cuff-and-use-a-mug-and-a-bit-of-guess-work cakes that our mums would quickly whip up using whatever ingredients they had at home and a mug to measure it all out with, and would usually be baked in a large *tepsi* or *sini* (a traditional circular baking tray) or bundt tin.

Cakes that have been baked with olive oil are not only healthier than butter-based cakes, but they have a beautifully moist texture and an ever so slightly richer depth of flavour, without overpowering the other key ingredients. So, get the hot custard ready and pour it all over this deliciously nostalgic chocolate and coconut olive-oil based cake; it doesn't have to be a fancy custard (as I explained in the introduction to this chapter, my family are unashamedly partial to making a thick yellow custard using good old custard powder) but it absolutely has to be hot, and served alongside a hot drink too.

I am sure a version of this cake still exists in many Cypriot and Turkish households.

Serves 8–10

250 ml (9 fl oz) olive oil
350 g (12 oz) self-raising flour, plus extra for dusting
100 g (3½ oz) dark chocolate
250 g (9 oz) caster sugar
5 eggs
1 tsp vanilla paste
50 ml (2 fl oz) milk
1 tsp baking powder
½ tsp salt
75 g (2¾ oz) desiccated coconut

Preheat the oven to 190°C/170°C fan/375°F/gas mark 5.

Grease the inside of a bundt cake tin (26 cm/10½ inches in diameter) with a little of the olive oil, then dust it very lightly with flour, tapping and shaking the tin to evenly disperse the flour.

Break up the chocolate and place it in a large heatproof bowl over a pan of simmering water, stirring until it melts.

In a large bowl, use an electric whisk to whisk together the sugar, eggs and vanilla paste for 3–4 minutes until light and fluffy. Slowly pour in the olive oil, a little at a time, continuously whisking until fully incorporated. Slowly pour in the milk, still whisking, then sift in the flour and the baking powder, one-third at a time, folding with a wooden spoon to keep it light and fluffy and making sure there are no lumps.

Add half of the mixture to the melted chocolate and stir gently to combine. Stir the desiccated coconut into the other half of the mixture.

Place a large spoonful of each mixture into your cake tin, alternating between each mixture until it has all been placed in the tin. Using a large skewer or a knife, swirl the two batters into each other a little, creating a marble effect, without overmixing.

Place the cake tin in the preheated oven and bake for 30–35 minutes (a cocktail stick stuck into the cake should come out clean when the cake is ready). Allow to cool, then turn out on to a plate to serve.

Tahınlı Pekmezli Baklava

Tahini & Carob Molasses Baklava

Having told you about the heavenly combination of tahini and carob in the Breakfast chapter, it only felt right to include another recipe showcasing these two ingredients together again. I have taken a classic baklava recipe and indulgently separated the buttery layers with tahini and carob molasses running through them.

My mum and husband Joel are both huge baklava fans, especially when we're in a Turkish restaurant or on holiday in Turkey and Cyprus. Our family's favourite baklava is by Antepliler, a restaurant who make traditional Gaziantep-style baklava, a city famed for its pistachios – there are two branches of Antepliler in London where you can buy it from. Two of the signature traits to their baklava is to stir a homemade cream (*kaymak*) into the nuts (traditionally pistachios) before spreading this mix over the buttered filo sheets. This keeps some moisture locked into the nuts (to prevent them from burning) and also makes them a little more porous, enabling them to soak up the flavours of the cooled syrup. The second one is to use clarified butter, a tip that I also picked up from my talented friend and chef, Melek Erdal, who makes the most wonderful baklava. Clarified butter is butter that has had the milk solids removed, and is consequently clear (clarified) in appearance and consistency, like ghee.

This recipe makes a deliciously nutty baklava, made a little bit better (and ever so slightly more extravagant) with a generous scoop of ice cream – preferably *damla sakızlı dondurma* (mastic ice cream) – to serve alongside it.

Makes 40

For the syrup
300 g (10½ oz) caster sugar
3 tbsp clear honey
400 ml (14 fl oz) water
1 cinnamon stick
1 tsp orange blossom water

For the *kaymak* (cream)
100 ml (3½ fl oz) milk
1¼ tsp caster sugar
1¼ tsp fine semolina

For the baklava
500 g (1 lb 2 oz) walnuts
2 tsp ground cinnamon
100 g (3½ oz) tahini
30 ml (1 fl oz) carob molasses
250 g (9 oz) unsalted butter
16 large sheets of filo pastry
30 g (1 oz) crushed pistachios

Preheat the oven to 200°C/180°C fan/400°F/gas mark 6.

Add the sugar, honey, water, cinnamon stick and orange blossom water to a small pan and place over a medium heat, stirring until the sugar starts to dissolve. Bring the mixture to the boil, reduce the heat and simmer for 12–15 minutes until the syrup has thickened and reduced by around a quarter. Remove the pan from the heat and leave to one side to cool completely.

To make the *kaymak*, heat the milk and sugar in a small pan over a medium heat and once hot, add the semolina and keep stirring the mixture until it thickens and starts to bubble. Remove the pan from the heat, cover with the lid, and leave to one side to cool.

Pulse the walnuts for a few seconds in a food processor to coarsely grind them into small pieces, without turning them to powder. Mix the ground cinnamon with the walnuts and leave to one side.

In a small bowl, mix the tahini and carob molasses until dark in colour and creamy in texture and leave to one side.

Recipe contined overleaf

Melt the butter in a pan over a medium heat and when it starts to bubble, use a spoon to skim off the froth from the surface and discard. Pour the butter into a jug carefully, decanting the clear fat to use in the recipe and keeping the milky solids in the pan.

Stir the ground walnuts into the *kaymak* pan until fully combined. Then pour the tahini and carob molasses mixture into the same pan and stir them through the nutty cream mixture until fully combined again.

Lightly grease a 25 cm × 35 cm (10 inch × 13 inch) deep, flat baking tray with some of the clarified butter from the jug.

Lay one of the sheets of filo in front of you, with the longest side facing you, then using a pair of scissors, cut the sheet in half straight down the middle, vertically. Repeat for all of the remaining sheets and cover with a damp tea towel to prevent them from drying out. You will now have 32 sheets of filo to make the baklava with.

Lay one sheet of filo in the bottom of the baking tray and brush liberally with some of the clarified butter. Lay another sheet of filo directly on top so that it sticks to the bottom sheet, then brush liberally with butter again. Repeat this process until you have layered 20 sheets together. Carefully pour the walnut, tahini and carob mixture all into the baking tray and evenly spread it over the stacked filo sheets. Using the back of a wooden spoon, gently push down on the nuts to pack them in tightly.

Now start to layer up the remaining 12 sheets of filo exactly as you did the first time round, and slowly and evenly pour any remaining butter over the top of the final sheet. With the shortest side of the tray facing you, cut four equally-spaced lines vertically, all the way through the baklava from the top to the bottom of the baking sheet, so that you have five vertical baklava strips. Do the same horizontally, but this time cut seven lines so that you create 40 small, rectangular pieces of baklava.

Place the baking tray on the bottom shelf of the oven and after 25–30 minutes, reduce the heat to 180°C/160°C fan/350°F/gas mark 4 for another 25–30 minutes.

Remove the baklava from the oven, leave it for a couple of minutes, then pour the cold syrup over the crunchy baked filo, ladleful by ladleful. Sprinkle the pistachios over each piece as soon as you have poured over the syrup, then allow the baklava to cool fully before serving, preferably overnight. Store at room temperature, covered in foil.

Karpuz Macunu

Watermelon Preserve

What do you during a hot summer's day or evening in Cyprus, when you are not
at the beach or around the *mangal* (barbecue)? Well, you walk the humid streets
of the local neighbourhood or village, stopping off at neighbours' houses for *macun*
(sweet, preserved fruits), a refreshing glass of ice-cold water and Turkish coffee.
Preserving fruits and peels that would otherwise be thrown away is a delicacy in
Cyprus, and most households store jars of them, ready to hand out to the next guest
that unexpectedly arrives through the front, or back door (which is always left open).

Makes 40

½ large Cypriot/Mediterranean/
   Middle Eastern watermelon,
   peel and white rind only
2 tsp baking soda
500 ml (18 fl oz) cold water
500 g (1 lb 2 oz) caster sugar
1 tsp whole cloves
1 tbsp fresh lemon juice

Firstly prepare the watermelon pieces. Cut the watermelon peel into
3–4-cm (1–1½-inch) thick strips, then divide each strip into roughly
3 cm × 4 cm (1 inch × 1½ inch) rectangular or diamond shaped pieces.
Using a sharp paring knife, completely slice off the green peel without
removing too much of the white rind. It is the rind that we will be
using for the *macun*. Keep repeating this until you have 40 pieces
of prepared white rind.

Fill up a large pan three-quarters of the way with cold water and stir
in the baking soda until it fully dissolves. Add the prepared pieces of
watermelon rind to the soda water, cover the pan with a lid and leave
for a minimum of 6 hours, or overnight.

Drain the soaked watermelon rind and wash the pieces under cold
running water. Rinse out the pan, then return the watermelon rind
pieces and top up with enough cold water so that the pan is again
three-quarters full. Place the pan over a medium heat, and as soon as
the water starts to boil, remove the pan and carefully drain and wash
the watermelon rind pieces in a sieve under cold running water again.
Return the rind back to the pan, cover with the same amount of cold
water again, bring to the boil, drain immediately and wash the pieces
in the colander under cold running water one more time. Let the
watermelon pieces cool down completely in the colander while you
prepare the syrup for the *macun*.

Add the 500 ml (18 fl oz) cold water and sugar to the same (clean)
pan along with the whole cloves. Place the pan over a medium heat,
stirring the liquid continuously to encourage the sugar to dissolve.
When the syrup comes to a simmer, reduce the heat a little and
cook for another 5 minutes before carefully adding each piece of the
watermelon rind to the syrup. Simmer the watermelon rind in the syrup
for 45–50 minutes, add the lemon juice in 5 minutes before you turn
off the heat, then immediately transfer the pieces to sterilised jars
(page 26), ensuring that they are fully covered in the syrup. Close
the jars tightly with the lids, then allow to cool before placing them
in a cool, dark cupboard or the fridge. They can be stored for up to
a year, as long as the pieces are always covered in the syrup.

Tel Kadayıf Tatlısı

Kadayif Pastries

Back in the day, *Sütlü Börek* (Custard-filled Filo Syrup Pastries, pages 259–60) and *Tel Kadayıf* were the two desserts we regularly picked up from Yaşar Halim patisserie. However, my mum would also make her delicious version of *kadayıf* for us too. *Tel Kadayıf* (*tel* translating as 'wire') is a very finely shredded filo, consisting of thin wiry strands of pastry that can be pulled apart and pushed together, depending on what kind of texture your recipe requires. My mum recalls how her maternal grandmother Meyrem Nene would effortlessly make her own *tel kadayıf*, forming each wiry strand like a machine.

My mum makes the syrup for her recipe with a much higher water to sugar content than some of the other sweet treats in this chapter, which really softens the *tel kadayıf* at the base of the baking dish, contrasting with the slightly more sticky and crunchy top part. I have used my mum's trick in this recipe too.

Makes 20

For the syrup
350 g (12 oz) caster sugar
3 tbsp clear honey
600 ml (20 fl oz) cold water
1 cinnamon stick
6 whole cloves
2 tsp rose water
1 tbsp fresh lemon juice

For the kadayif
150 g (5½ oz) walnuts
¼ tsp ground cinnamon
250 g (9 oz) unsalted butter
1 × 500-g (1 lb 2 oz) pack *kadayıf* pastry
50 g (1¾ oz) shelled and finely chopped pistachios

Add the sugar, honey, water, cinnamon stick, cloves and rose water to a small pan and place over a medium heat, stirring a little until the sugar starts to dissolve. Bring the mixture to the boil, reduce the heat and simmer for around 10 minutes until the syrup has thickened and reduced by about one-third. Add the lemon juice, stir well, then remove the pan from the heat and leave to one side to cool completely.

Preheat the oven to 200°C/180°C fan/400°F/gas mark 6.

Pulse the walnuts in a food processor until they are coarsely chopped. Mix the ground cinnamon in with the chopped walnuts.

Melt the butter in a small pan and use a little of it to grease a 25 cm × 30 cm (10 inch × 12 inch) deep baking tray.

Place the *kadayıf* pastry into another large deep dish or baking tray, and using your hands, start to pull apart and shred the long strands into smaller pieces. Pour the melted butter over the shredded *kadayıf* and, using your hands, mix well to ensure every strand is fully coated in the butter.

Using a small espresso or Turkish coffee cup (mine are roughly 5-cm/ 2-inches high with a 6-cm/2½-inch diameter), pack one tablespoon of the *kadayıf* into the bottom of the cup, pushing the strands down with the back of a teaspoon or your fingers so that they are packed tightly. Place one tablespoon of the chopped walnuts on top of the packed *kadayıf*. Place another heaped tablespoon of the *kadayıf* over the top of the walnuts, pushing down again with the teaspoon to pack the strands tightly. Turn the cup over into one of the corners of the greased baking tray so that the moulded shape of the *kadayıf* eases out of the cup without breaking up. Repeat this process with the remaining pastry and walnuts, until you have 20 moulded *tel kadayıf* domes lined up on the baking tray.

Place the baking tray on the middle shelf of the oven and bake for 25–30 minutes, or until golden brown all over. Remove the tray from the oven, leave to stand for 5 minutes. Use a ladle to pour the cooled syrup all over the *tel kadayıf* domes.

Allow the *kadayıf* to cool for at least 4 hours before serving, to enable the pastry to fully soak up the syrup. Sprinkle the chopped pistachios over each of the domes and serve with ice cream or *kaymak*.

Store at room temperature (covered tightly with foil) for up to 4 days.

Index

Acknowledgements

Anneciğim (my mama), thank you for always letting me be a part of your kitchen, for always having your "door open" so that friends and family could come over, and for keeping our traditions alive by feeding us the food that has shaped our beautiful island and its people. I also want to thank you for your *göz karar* (eye judgement) methods, and for never giving me a single measurement in grams or millilitres; this is what drove me to get all these beautiful recipes written down. I'm sorry I would wreck your kitchen on the daily and leave you with piles of washing up (which I continued to do whilst writing this book), but it was never done in vain, and here we now are. Baba (Dad), thank you for teaching us to be humble, to appreciate everything we have, for your love of the simple life, your delicious yet unassuming soup concoctions and for always making sure I put that extra teaspoon of black pepper in everything. Yeliz and Taylan, for giving me the space I needed in mum and dad's kitchen by never learning cook when you were younger (haha), and for now being two of my biggest supporters – I love you all.

To my wonderful, greatly-loved late grandparents Fatma Nene, Ahmet Dede, Ali Dede, (great grandmother) Meyrem Nene, my surviving Melek Nene, and all my aunts and uncles, especially Selçuk Dayı, Meyrem Teyze, Aysan Teyze, and my late Izzet Dayı; thank you for all the memories, the celebrations, for teaching me about our family history and our food traditions, without even realising you were doing it. Our beloved Ömer Dayı and Terazi angels, you are always in our hearts. Emine Hala, thank you for your *Kolokas* recipe and for making every Christmas of our childhood so special – the combination of roast turkey, *hummus, salata, nohutlu pilav* and Cyprus roast potatoes have left me with the best Christmas Day memories. Revza Abla and Halit Abi, thank you for subtly inspiring my love of cooking from a young age, introducing me to the Turkish recipes, ingredients and methods you acquired throughout your youth, connections and travels.

Elyse, for all the photography advice, for lending me things that I had no idea how to use but can now proudly say I do; love you, my "Turkish Delight." Dan, for capturing the essence of those beautiful family and prep shots with Hannah. Daisy, thank you for introducing me to Juliet, as without you this book may never have happened. Juliet, for your belief in me and *Terazi* from the outset, my recipes, my story, and for always making sure my voice can be heard through my words. You are my professional voice of reason. Laura, I can't thank you enough for taking a punt on me and welcoming me to Ebury; I have missed you these past few months but you certainly left me in very capable hands. Sam, you are so much more than an editor; you have listened, conversed, laughed, been frank, taken the time to research and look into every concern I have raised, pushed me, pulled me back, calmed me, raised me up and have even cooked some of my recipes. You are an absolute gem and I am so grateful that I had you here to guide me through all of this. Thank you for taking so much time to get to know my family too. Vicky and Laura M, for going through everything with a fine toothcomb; you may now even be able to add "fluent in the Turkish Cypriot dialect" to your CV! Clare, for bringing my photography and recipes to life with your beautiful, vibrant designs. Sam H, LouLou and Lucy, thank you for holding things together during the final "push" week. My ideas, my visions, have all been fulfilled and I am over the moon and so grateful to the stellar team at Ebury for creating something so special.

And finally, my number ones. My babies, R & A; your love of being in the kitchen with me, cooking (and eating), is honestly what keeps me going. I really hope you continue to cook these recipes in your own kitchens one day and I will be asking for *Badadez Köftesi* and *Magarına Fırında* when you do. Joel, you make me feel like there is nothing I can't do; every time I get scared and want to give up, you give me that lift, that pep talk, that hug, that kick up the backside I need to keep going. You are my biggest supporter, the best, yet slightly over-worked, washer-upper (sorry), and the most honest feedback-giver of all. We've encountered a pandemic, home schooling (twice!), a house-move, relocation and renovation all whilst writing this cookbook, but we got there. I love you so much Xx

7

Ebury Press an imprint of Ebury Publishing,
20 Vauxhall Bridge Road,
London SW1V 2SA

Ebury Press is part of the Penguin Random House group of companies
whose addresses can be found at global.penguinrandomhouse.com

Penguin
Random House
UK

First published by Ebury Press in 2022

www.penguin.co.uk

A CIP catalogue record for this book is available from the British Library

ISBN 9781529109504

Photography: Meliz Berg and Dan Jones

Colour reproduction: Altaimage Ltd, London

Printed and bound in in Italy by LEGO SpA

The authorised representative in the EEA is Penguin Random House Ireland,
Morrison Chambers, 32 Nassau Street, Dublin DO2 YH68.

Penguin Random House is committed to a sustainable future for our business,
our readers and our planet. This book is made from Forest Stewardship
Council® certified paper.